IDENTITY AND AFFECT

Anthropology, Culture and Society

Series Editors:
Dr Richard A. Wilson, University of Sussex
Professor Thomas Hylland Eriksen, University of Oslo

IDENTITY AND AFFECT
EXPERIENCES OF IDENTITY IN
A GLOBALISING WORLD

EDITED BY
JOHN R. CAMPBELL AND ALAN REW

Pluto Press
LONDON • STERLING, VIRGINIA

First published 1999 by Pluto Press
345 Archway Road, London N6 5AA
and 22883 Quicksilver Drive,
Sterling, VA 20166–2012, USA

British Library Cataloguing in Publication Data
A catalogue record for this book is available from
the British Library

ISBN 0 7453 1428 7 hbk

Library of Congress Cataloging in Publication Data
Identity and affect : experiences of identity in a globalising world /
edited by John R. Campbell and Alan Rew.
    p.   cm. — (Anthropology, culture, and society)
Includes bibliographical references.
ISBN 0–7453–1428–7 (hbk)
    1. Ethnicity. 2. Group identity. 3. Acculturation. 4. Social
change. I. Campbell, John R., 1951–   . II. Rew, Alan, 1941–   .
III. Series.
GN495.6.I336   1999
305.8—dc21   98–42633
                                                  CIP

Designed and produced for Pluto Press by
Chase Production Services, Chadlington, OX7 3LN
Typeset from disk by Stanford DTP Services, Northampton
Printed in the EC by TJ International, Padstow

CONTENTS

Part III   'Being ...'

NOTES ON CONTRIBUTORS

John R. Campbell is a lecturer in anthropology at the University of Wales, Swansea. He has conducted fieldwork in Ghana, Tanzania and Ethiopia, and has been involved in development work in Ethiopia, Tanzania, Kenya and Botswana. His work has focused on urban and rural development, ethnicity and identity, NGOs, and on nationalism and development in the Horn and in East Africa.

Anne-Marie Fortier is a postdoctoral research fellow at the Centre for Research on Citizenship and Social Transformation at Concordia University, Montreal; she will shortly be joining the Department of Sociology at the University of Lancaster. Her areas of study include identity, gender, sexuality, race and ethnicity. Her forthcoming book *Italians Never Die, They Just Pasta Away? Indeterminacy, Continuity and the Location of Culture*, examines the formation of an Italian emigré culture in Britain, with a special emphasis on the construction of gendered, generational and ethnic subjects.

Ralph Grillo is Professor of Social Anthropology in the School of African and Asian Studies, University of Sussex. Formerly the Dean of the School, he is presently the Director of the Graduate Research Centre for Comparative Study of Culture, Development and the Environment. His publications include *African Railwaymen* (1973), *Ideologies and Institutions in Urban France* (1985), *Dominant Languages* (1989) and *Pluralism and the Politics of Difference: Ethnicity, State and Culture in Comparative Perspective* (Berg, 1988).

Leonard Mars is a lecturer in social anthropology at the University of Wales, Swansea. In addition to *The Village and the State* (1980), he has published in *Comparative Studies in Society in History, Jewish Social Studies, Food and Foodways* and elsewhere. He is currently engaged in

ESRC-funded research on the reconstruction of ethnic and religious identity in post-communist Hungary.

David Mosse is at the Anthropology Department of the School of Oriental and African Studies, University of London. He has lived and worked in India since 1978. His research interests in south India focus on popular religion and vernacular Christianity, *dalit* movements, environmental history and indigenous irrigation. He worked as Oxfam Country Representative in Bangalore (1987–91) and as a long-term social development consultant with a participatory natural resources project in tribal western India (1990–98). He now combines active engagement in rural development with teaching and research on the anthropology of development.

Alan Rew is Professor of Development Policy and Planning in the University of Wales and Director of the Centre for Development Studies at Swansea. He is an anthropologist whose main area of writing and teaching concerns the interface between development practice and social institutions. He has extensive academic and planning experience in the Pacific, and is currently investigating, and advising on, the impact of poverty reduction initiatives in Orissa and in Kenya.

R.L. Stirrat teaches in the School of African and Asian Studies at the University of Sussex. His main research interests are concerned with religion and the anthropology of development, primarily in Sri Lanka.

Philip Quarles van Ufford teaches anthropology and development sociology at the Free University of Amsterdam. He has a special interest in the analysis of development policy and has published many papers on NGOs, rural development, chaos theory, the ideology of the market, development morality and religion and development. His main areas of study are in Southeast Asia.

Michael W. Young teaches anthropology in the Research School of Pacific and Asian Studies, the Australian National University. He has been carrying out fieldwork in Kalauna in the Massim area of eastern Papua New Guinea since the late 1960s about which he has written extensively. Recently, and at the request of the family, he has been working on an official biography of Bronislaw Malinowski.

PREFACE

The chapters in this book focus on the experience of identity as a key problem in social organisation. Most commentators on global and local social change can readily acknowledge that 'identity' will be fundamental to their social analysis; yet most also find it a perplexing and contradictory concept when trying to capture the force and experience of self-consciousness and collective awareness. 'Identity' is regularly thought of as intimate in its meaning and referents; yet is also often macro-political in its texture, context and effects. The pathways to and from social identity suggest divergent causal sequences – use is made of the affectual element in intimate bonds in order to source the meaning of binding political ethnicity; reference is made to national political and economic fault lines to explain enforced choices in the primary social roles of gender, employment, caste, religion and citizen.

These perplexities led us to explore social identity further, through the present volume and through the formulation of two central questions: How do the intensely felt emotions aroused within individuals by their participation in the intimate cultures of family and locality feed into the experience of shared *social* identity at local, regional and national levels; and how are the trials, processes and experiences of individual life-projects and identity structured and fragmented under radically different global conditions? Alternation between the intimate and political economic aspects of identity has been central to the discussions in and around the development of the chapters in this book. These were also questions which emerged in explicit form in the workshop held at the University of Wales Swansea in June 1996 to consider the first drafts.

In addressing these questions in the chapters in this book, and at the workshop, we have been more than usually aware that the volume is a joint one. The collaborators came to the discussions with a wide range of theoretical and ethnographic problems about identity: the use of psychoanalytic theory in the anthropology of identity; the historical evolution of ethnic and national identities which either divide or unite contemporary nation-states; the changing character of work and employment as a source of primary identity; the salience of identity and affect in South Asia, Melanesia, East Africa and contemporary Britain. The workshop discussions and the large volume of preceding and subsequent joint thinking confirmed our view that there was here a project which was very under-theorised or developed. All contributors felt the issue was a critical contemporary one for anthropology.

The always common and continuing presence throughout the period of collaborative writing and editorial work – because of his seminal writing on identity – was A.L. Epstein. Although he was not present at the workshop, and came to know of the volume only when it was nearly complete, Bill Epstein's work served as a guiding inspiration. The chapters are therefore intended as a tribute and acknowledgement of his many and profound contributions. He has taken the debate on social identity forward in a quite unique way and done so in a range of settings – in rapidly changing yet also culturally continuous urban and rural contexts and in ways that show how affect and identity and local, colonial and national politics are inter-digitated on the Zambian Copperbelt and among the Tolai of Papua New Guinea.

We benefited too from the active participation and generous suggestions of a number of other collaborators and colleagues. Richard Jenkins, a former colleague, read an article on Danish identity and their national flag at the Swansea workshop, and made many valuable suggestions on the individual chapters and for the introductory chapter. Margaret Kenna was generous with her time and suggestions and led the discussion on Michael Young's chapter as he could not attend the Swansea meeting in person. At an earlier stage, Karen Tranberg Hansen of Northwestern University had helped in the initial discussions which finally shaped the project. A seminar paper at Swansea by Robin Cohen on similar issues came at a very opportune time; we then benefited greatly from his insightful comments on the manuscript. Hazel Lewis administered the key workshop with her usual skill and efficiency and was the frictionless conduit through which John

Campbell and I organised editorial meetings and the flow of scripts. The single most important ingredient in the editorial process was John Campbell's commitment to and insight into the central ideas, his organisational skills and his persistence.

Alan Rew
Swansea, May 1998

For Bill Epstein

1 THE POLITICAL ECONOMY OF IDENTITY AND AFFECT

Alan Rew and John R. Campbell

In the latter half of this century the world has become increasingly one in ways that lack any precedent. Large-scale national and international government administration, transnational business practice, and intensified international transport and communication systems have all contributed an increased coherence and integration in the mounting global traffic in people and meanings. Yet the same contemporary world has also seen an increase in the scale and importance of 'neo-tribes' – instances of multiple local acts of self-identification with the tags of ethnic and geo-cultural allegiance (Maffesoli 1996; Bauman 1992: 136–7) together with self-recruitment to a great variety of other imagined and self-constructed communities. We live in a duplex or semi-detached mental habitat, one half of which is global and the other local and which must be linked if the habitat is to survive.

The commitment of the authors of this volume is to a real and imagined community of ethnographic writing seeking to describe and analyse the distinctive contemporary habitats that are born from the pairing and reproduction of local and global forces. The analysis of the interpenetration of forceful universality and embraced, resisted and tolerated cultural difference matters greatly to us. We recognise a pressing need to develop our skills and methods for analysing the coupling and products we perceive but do not fully understand. In this our concerns mirror a growing dissatisfaction in the literature (for example, Hannerz 1992) with the ways in which wider economic and political frameworks have rather offhandedly been brought into ethnographies. Sally Falk Moore (1986: 329) has criticised that two-system model in which only the extremes of scale, the largest and the smallest, are considered and linked largely by theoretical formulae.

We need therefore to replace the fractured and poorly adjusted binoculars that have been given to us in the 'global–local' instrument of vision with finer, more powerful and yet more sensitive illuminations of the complex uniformities and diversities that result. The anthropologists in this volume have found alternative and better calibrated instruments in the concept of *identity* and in an exploration of the affective self-constitution of the agents and energies of our modern (and postmodern) world.

SOCIAL NETWORKS: MODELS AND METAPHORS IN THE ANALYSIS OF COMMUNICATIVE ACTION

Hannerz has noted the need for a macro-anthropology of world culture while warning about the customarily high level of generality in the 'rhetoric of global-babble' and suggests that the concept of networks still has much to contribute to our knowledge of global cultural processes through its use in 'an orderly build-up of ethnography and analysis' (1992: 34). His reference to a concept that first gained widespread use in the 1960s and 1970s highlights the fact that there was already at that time a not-quite-conventional corpus of anthropological writing on self-determinations and social relationships generated by a variety of fieldwork circumstances in which the ethnographer had found a notable absence of any 'principal coordinating agency' able or wanting to license allowable difference or to set rules and institutionalise moralities. A brief review of the origins and uses of 'social networks' shows why we think it important to further develop the components of identity construction.

The concept of 'social network' was especially helpful in the Norwegian countryside, in part because of the confessional and domestic basis of Norwegian political alignments (Barnes 1954, 1972), and where social relationships were forming in the rapidly growing cities of Africa (Epstein 1961, 1992a; Mitchell 1969) and Melanesia (Rew 1975; Levine and Levine 1979). Social network analysis showed how conventions were being generated and transmitted in circumstances where the rules of any principal coordinating institutions were lacking or excluded from consideration. The breakdown of society through anomie and lack of norms was not threatened because of the lack of overarching institutions of political and social coordination transferred from the countryside or from the colonial power – rather, it was that individuals were actively creating new norms and institutions from the bottom up through linked dyadic relationships.

In these circumstances, the idea of the social network appealed because it lent support to social anthropology's need to maintain the primacy of society in determining behaviour. The legacy of Durkheim had strictly demarcated the realm of the social from the psychological and required comparative sociology to demonstrate the role of social convention and social structure in socialising individual behaviour. Networks provided the link and mechanism for conceptualising sociality in an otherwise fluid milieu. The content and overall social salience of those individual choices and socialisation in the networks, however, was referred back to tried and trusted social lineaments. First, there was the political analysis of contrasted life chances and commitments underlying networks – for example, Epstein's analysis of conflict between African trade union members and leaders and colonial, industrial management (Epstein 1958). Second, an anthropological approach to social classificatory systems was employed to discuss those components of social networks which involved urban ethnicity (Mitchell 1969). Finally, the content of networks became inseparable from the analysis of either 'strategising man' – involved in constant games of trading and exchange, and the tactical use of political rhetoric and obligations (Kapferer 1972) – or of 'significations' – involving the speech acts and non-verbal acts carried by the human nodes of the communication network.

In these classic analyses of the social network, individuals moved from the status of active informants in notebooks to become, in theoretical terms, rather passive human nodes carrying the norms and exchanges of the emerging society and culture that was flowing along a chain of interconnected nodes. In reaction to tensions of this kind between the live agency of the informant in the field notebook and the shallow view of the self in the abstracted theoretical model, A.P. Cohen has stressed the complex interrelationship of individual and society. He has identified the consequences of the neglect of self in anthropology and shows the complexity of the analytical task. He refrains from presenting an alternative schema – in part because his own self chooses to focus on irregularities in behaviour (Cohen 1994: 162) and he sees no reason to regulate this choice.

The problem that A.P. Cohen and the network theorists have faced is how much and what kind of volition and creativity to allow the individual actors in the interpretation of the cultural content. Cohen (1994: 21), for example, complains that in Giddens' theory of identity in *Modernity and Self-Identity* (1991) the 'agency which Giddens allows to individuals gives them the power of reflexivity but not of motivation'. The agents become 'perpetrators but not architects'. In Cohen's view, Giddens remains in the Durkheimian mode, treating society rather than self as an ontology which somehow has become independent of its members. Our own view is that his frustration arises because, although reversing the order from the Durkheimian one, the central problematic remains that of mid-century anthropology – the relationship between individual and society. Strathern (1992: 88–9) describes the central problematic at that time as follows:

Social levels were conceived as of a different order from persons concretely imagined as so many individuals ... an individual person was a potentially holistic entity – but for the anthropologists only from the perspective of another discipline such as psychology. From anthropology's own disciplinary perspective, the concept of society stimulated the 'more' holistic vision.

A fluid social organisation that posed a problem for that prevailing paradigm was the Melanesian society of the Garia as reported by Lawrence (Berndt and Lawrence 1971). There were no lineages, localised descent units or comparable groupings among the Garia. The social organisation provided, rather, a network of cognatic kin within which could be found 'security circles' – clusters of kin with whom an individual had safe relations – and then a collection of some 200 named cognatic stocks associated with bush deities. Strathern terms Lawrence's description of the Garia's ego-centred social organisation 'a scandal' to the sensibilities of the political–juridical theorists of unilineal descent systems – 'by contrast with what made a Garia a person it seemed in the 1950s impossible to discern what made a Garia a member of society' (Strathern 1992: 81). The analysis was shocking since it failed to identify rules and groups that could maintain social continuity and cohesion.

Scandal arose in part because of the underlying modernist imagery of society in mid-century social theory. That imagery makes us see persons as parts cuts from a whole (Strathern 1992): we must either somehow find the whole or allow a different holism at the level of the person. Strathern's account of the reception of Lawrence's anthropology of the Garia is a nice piece of professional irony showing how the leadership code of the anthropological neo-tribe at that date was offended by its person-centred findings. From the perspective of 1990s anthropology, the appropriate contrast with the Garia proves to be not the Tallensi, the Enga, the Mekeo or even a Melanesian cognatic system but the English, at least in the conceptualisation of parts (persons) to wholes (society)!

The problem of parts and wholes remains with us at the end of the century – but less in structural homologies or disciplinary levels than in the complex intertwining of political economy and cultural meaning. The 'after modernist' imagery is of fragmentation, scattering and hybridisation – a break in the ordering of the vision of society, a loss of unifying authenticity, the scattering of traditions, the recombination of their diverse elements, and the kaleidoscopic recombination and merging of local authenticities in dissolving habitats. Indeed, Castells in his *The Rise of the Network Society* (1996) takes this issue a step further by arguing that it is the technological transformations fostered by capitalism in the form of information technology (through its impact on communication and social organisation) which is radically restructuring space and time. The end result is, according to Castells, the creation of a new culture ('virtual reality') within tens of thousands of computer-linked 'virtual' communities worldwide at a time when primary identities, institutions, organisations and nation-states are experiencing fragmentation, dissolution and decay. From this loss of master narratives and whole visions, Marcus (1992) draws a political rather than an intellectual conclusion. Local identities emerge as a compromise between elements of resistance to incorporation into large wholes and elements of accommodation to the larger order. The task for anthropology becomes to show how distinctive identities are created from scattering, fragmentation, diversity 'and the localised intensification of global possibilities and associations'.

Scattering, separation and diversity is also central to Appadurai's (1990b, 1997) treatment of globalisation as the complex layering and disjuncture between the 'scapes' flowing into local societies from global visions. For example, the separate flows of ideas in 'financescapes' and 'technoscapes' arise from world financial systems and from the spread of IT and other global technologies; 'ethnoscapes' arise from global flows of people, whether refugees from civil strife and famine, 'development-induced refugees' (see for example, Rew 1996), labour migrants or world tourists and pilgrims. These cultural flows, together with flows from the mass media ('mediascapes') and from the visions and ideas of world ideological systems ('ideoscapes') are laid over local and national societies. Experience of them, argues Appadurai, is largely that of disjuncture.

STRUCTURE AND VOLITION, ORDER AND (INTER-) SUBJECTIVITY

Despite ethnographic discoveries in the politicisation of identities and local authenticities, the grand theories of social science continue to have difficulty with inter-subjectivity. In succession, *each* of successive analytical approaches – structuralism, modernism and postmodernism – has placed the *irrelevance* of subjectivity and identity at the very cornerstone of their account of social formation (Lash and Friedman 1992). We have already seen that Giddens' view of self-identity is highly circumscribed within parameters of social continuity. In Foucault's work we have a vision of 'subject positions' created only by the systems of dispersion that constitute the unity of discursive formations.

To describe a formulation *qua* statement does not consist in analysing the relations between the author and what he says (or wanted to say, or said without wanting to): but in determining what position can and must be occupied by any individual if he is to be the subject of it. (Foucault 1974: 95–6)

Bauman (1992: 71) concludes that, in Foucault's work what matters 'is not the personality and the will of the author of the statement, but the *possibility* of authoring a statement belonging to the discursive formation ...'.

This has, undoubtedly, been a seminal insight. Yet it is also deeply contradictory to the modernist tendency. In modernity social space opened up the way for an autonomous definition of identity, as God and moral certainty and the political certainties of kingly and grand-design socialist rule disappeared. Identity therefore becomes a meeting point of distinctly modern responsibilities – those of responsibility for one's own actions in an increasingly complex society and responsibility for ordering one's own life courses and careers.

Bauman (1992) places those heavy responsibilities at the heart of the postmodern condition. The kind of society that we now call modern arose from the discovery that human order was vulnerable and without sound, unshakeable foundation. The response to this frightening discovery was a sustained effort to design an order that was solid, obligatory and had eliminated the haphazardous and spontaneously disruptive. As Bauman (1992: xiv–xvi) notes, to create order means neither to encourage nor to eradicate differences. It means licensing them, and most importantly, implies the actions of a licensing authority. Obversely, it means also de-legalising unlicensed differences since the subversive power of unlicensed difference resides precisely in its spontaneity and unpredictability and its grey area of ambivalence.

Modernity in other words is both a continuous and uncompromising effort (and the range of detailed tasks necessary) to cover up the void threatened by any collapse in order and in the universality-claiming truths. The postmodern condition on the other hand lies in the recognition that the void is here to stay and that the authority of the central coordinating institutions for licensing difference has been dismantled. And thus, in the postmodern condition, people are left alone, privatised, with the fears that modernity created (Bauman 1992: 201–2). It is now the neo-communities that are expected to shelter people from these fears, not the state. Postmodernity, having privatised modern fears and the anxiety of living with them, had to become an age of *imagined* communities (1992: xviii, 198). These communities of belief and imputed importance depend, in the absence of institutional support, on the affective commitment of their self-appointed participants. At moments of crystallisation and the condensation of energy the commitment can be very intense – a source of *communitas* perhaps? The implication for the construction of identity is that no design can be taken as foolproof – each life-project consists of successive trials and errors and since it lacks a benchmark against which to measure progress, the identity of the agent is marked by the incessant activity of self-construction.

Epstein also sees identity as essentially a concept of synthesis, integration and action:

It represents the process by which the person seeks to integrate his various statuses and roles, as well as his diverse experiences, into a coherent image of self. (Epstein 1978: 101)

The awareness of self combines with inter-subjectivity and involves a continuum of social categorisation and self-ascription. Identity concerns what you consider you belong to, both at the level of ideas and explanation but also in terms of emotional experience and the expression of affect. The passions and heightened mutual susceptibility involved transcend the calculus of power and carefully calculated interest, either at the level of a rhetoric and vocabulary of emotions (Bailey 1983) or, as in the case of Epstein's interest, in the composition of affect. As identity assembles experiences of resistance and incorporation, or sets of commitments to imagined 'tribes' and other communities, it links political economy and cultural meaning by intertwining the global and local, whether these reflect the experience of modern designs and projects or the trials and terrors of postmodern conditions.

A focus on identity as an organising concept of research and explanation also avoids the dangers of a postmodernist anthropology which is unable to make comparisons between cultures. Do we really wish to accept arguments about the arbitrary, non-rational, declarative nature of the culture of postmodernism when history demonstrates the power of the non-rational in Auschwitz and over ethnic cleansing in Bosnia? The anthropological investigation of the intertwining of political economy and cultural meaning within specific identities and sites helps avoid that closure or break in historical time that postmodernism seeks to impose in the third quarter of the twentieth century (or post-1968, depending on who is defining it) in order to mark a different political and cultural reality. The postmodern world is, we worry, suddenly one in which tradition, history and time are eclipsed by a new cultural dominant of personal style, aesthetics, value (Docherty 1993). In such a world how do we understand and learn not only from the Holocaust but also from the 'racial terror' that is instituted in slavery and extended to the present day in the form of racism and ethnic genocide? There are problems here of affect – of anger, rage, fear, guilt, horror and outrage – and also of the aggregation of lived experience through identity formation to wider questions and statements of social concern and policy analysis.

The use of identity as a synthesising and integrating concept implies an emphasis on micro-events and the translation of apparently global and national structures into their micro-constituents. Appadurai (1989: 271) raises exactly these questions about rural standards of living in India. Is there a class of events that is a sensitive *micro*-indicator of poverty – an extensive phenomenon – and the impairment of everyday entitlements to livelihood, welfare and well-being? He finds the potential answer in actual labour contracts, attempts to gain access to credit and in specific acts of out-migration. Each would have a significant impact on lived experience and identities but also of course on trends in political economy if we can solve the conceptual challenge of how these micro-events can be aggregated.

This will seem an uncomfortable conclusion to the key professional protagonists in the debate on poverty – the economists and national development planners. They increasingly recognise the need for a social contextualisation but do not know how to integrate that context with their policy aims. Appadurai (1989: 273) recognises that to do so there would need to be a shift in attention from the *distribution of the net outcomes* of the social processes – seen largely in the measurable bundles of goods and services of households – to *relational processes* involving the *movements* of goods, services and communications between individuals, households and larger social categories and groups. The contrast between the perspectives may be, furthermore, as much epistemological as simply technical (1989: 276) and difficult to reconcile. Difficult or not, the search for methodological solutions in technique and approach is now recognised as a high priority in both disciplinary and practical policy terms for the on-going 'conversations between economists and anthropologists' (Bardhan 1989).

BEYOND SOCIAL CLASSIFICATION: CONTEXTUALIS-ING IDENTITY AND ITS EXPERIENCE

Methodological contrasts also dominate thinking in the literature on ethnicity (Despres 1984). On the one hand, structuralists tended to reify ethnic groups as 'real', objectively existing social groups, and ethnicity is seen as the expression of the primordial loyalties of its members; on the other hand phenomenologists stress the subjective, instrumentally oriented, cognitive aspects of ethnic behaviour. This objective/subjective dichotomy has long pervaded anthropological thinking and it is only recently that new approaches seeking to combine structural *and* phenomenological[1] concerns have developed, notably in work on culture (Shweder and Levine 1984), the body (Lock 1993), language (Besnier 1990) and music (Feld and Fox 1994). Recent work on social identity and on 'emotion' also illustrates the conceptual problems involved. Whether because of a fragmentation of the world system which is causing cultural fragmentation (Friedman 1989), or because of growing epistemological tensions within anthropology which have made problematic the basic premises of method and theory (Chapman et al. 1989), social identity is very much at the forefront of current research.

Wolf, for example, has recently drawn our attention to the concept of race, reminding us yet again of its recent (eighteenth-century) origin in European social classification (1994). He notes the variety of permutations which arise from a 'conflation of physical traits, temperament and political–moral behaviour' and from the correlation of biology with culture which gave rise to popular forms of racial essentialism that remain with us today (Wolf 1994: 4–5). If 'race', as such, is no longer a concern of anthropological study, its contemporary equivalent 'ethnicity' remains very much in vogue even if little definitional consensus has been achieved.

The terms 'ethnic' and 'ethnicity' demonstrate a similar socio-linguistic usage as 'race' in the sense of providing 'a rich moral vocabulary, laid out along dimensions of inclusion and exclusion, dignity and disdain, familiarity and strangeness' in which conceptions of biology, culture and language are used to classify and attribute identity to foreign 'Others' (Chapman et al. 1989: 13). When employed at 'home' in Europe and North America, as the same writers observe, the discourse about ethnicity becomes a concern of the majority population with the presence of minorities living in their midst (Chapman et al. 1989: 18), which is to say with a relationship of super- and sub-ordination and with maintaining the boundary between 'us' and 'them' (Eriksen 1993: 10).

Since an identity – racial, ethnic, religious, sexual, gender, and national – cannot exist in isolation and must take its meaning from the Other, and because every individual possesses a number of identities not all of which are relevant in every context, a particular identity is situationally defined in the course of social interaction. The power to attribute identity to minorities often becomes tied up with a questioning of the dominant scheme of classification and with a relentless search by minorities for 'an identity'. Outstanding examples would include, in the UK, the quest among Ulster Protestants for a history and identity as defined against the background of Unionist–Nationalist 'Troubles' (Buckley 1989); and in the USA, one implication of 200 years of racism against Black Americans has been a continuous 'unsettling and persistent struggle to find a suitable name' for themselves through an internal debate over the significance of race, colour, class and nationality (Collier–Thomas and Turner 1992).

The attribution of social identity, therefore, involves the power to impose an identity, naming the Other by reference to the dominant group's classification. This act of social categorising may be consensual, and may validate the Others' internal self-definition, or it may be imposed (Epstein 1978). At the same time, however, and implicated directly in the process of external definition, identity may be based on a process of self-definition or ascription which generates a subjective, experiential element. As Jenkins points out, identity is located precisely in an interactive social process; sociologically speaking an important distinction between category and group is involved wherein a 'group ... is rooted in processes of internal definition [that is, the nature of relations between members, editors], while a category is externally defined' (1994: 200). Acknowledgement of this distinction is important as it provides a way through a literature that has been overly concerned with the categorical, that is, with cognitive and situational dimensions of identity to the relative neglect of affect, the powerful charge of emotions that lies at the centre of the process of identification involving one's sense of self (Epstein 1978, 1992b).

Ethnicity, we have said, involves an attribution of identity to a minority by the majority; a relation and process intimately connected to issues of power, hierarchy, stratification, indeed to the nation-state. In an excellent review of research on ethnicity and class, Williams argues convincingly that the concept of ethnicity is most useful with regard to identity formation in a single political unit, a context

where the precepts of nationalist ideologies presume to link nation to state through a homogeneity of culture and person in civil society, [where] the introduction of an ethnic element into political discourses about rights and obligations is not likely to increase distributive justice [but is] ... more likely to produce an increasingly objectified and 'biological' view of differences and inequalities. (B. Williams 1989: 423)

The objectification of ethnic difference represents a use of cultural and biological criteria as significant social diacritica and is linked to a broader struggle with important material and political implications. For Williams ethnicity and race are varieties of a 'sub-national' identity[2] generated by nationalist efforts to construct an objective 'history' and authentic culture (B. Williams 1989: 429). The invention of this scheme of classification is based on a conflation of biology and culture in which

the magic of forgetfulness and selectivity, both deliberate and inadvertent, allows the once recognizably arbitrary classifications of one generation to become the given inherent properties of reality several generations later. (1989: 431)

Alonso brings us closer to the salience of ethnicity in her discussion of the tropes employed to substantialise the collective identity of ethnic and racial minorities (1994). For example, idioms of kinship are used to define membership in (and therefore exclusion from) the nation as well as to define morality as a function of one's place in the hierarchy, while constructions of gender and sexuality objectify and define one's 'nature' and one's subordination. While some work on social stigma exists (Epstein 1978; Goffman 1963), work on the experience of racism would need to explore the impact on the individual of so comprehensive a rejection of personal worth as to result in an internalisation of the negative evaluations of others resulting in the deprecation of one's culture and person. Race and ethnicity, along with gender, tend to be defined as categorical or terminal identities since they are defined as fixed or unchangeable across all social contexts of a society.

Constructions of *sexuality* – masculinity, femininity, hetero- and homo-sexuality – are also intrinsically social identities in the manner in which our understandings about gender are systematically expressed and communicated via language, dress, defined standards of behaviour, overt symbolism, indeed in the very organisation of social life with its distinctions between public and private spheres. In some societies such an organisation of social life results in the production of distinctive gender cultures (Barth 1983: ch. 20).[3]

The political use of culture to construct a *national identity* and a nationalist 'myth of election' has been widely commented upon in the literature, once again however the stress has been on the cognitive aspects of this identity and its situational and instrumental deployment rather than on the experience of inclusion or exclusion from citizenship (Smith 1994). Whether in 'ethnic competition ... inheritance of the right amount of blood becomes a euphemism for inheritance of the state' (B. Williams 1989: 432), or conversely whether a nation bases its legitimacy on its claims to be a culture, there is little doubt that nationalism 'reifies culture enabling people to talk about their culture as though it were a constant' (Eriksen 1993: 103). Nationalist ideologies harness tropes (for example, of metaphoric kinship), and create identity narratives using myth and 'history' to bring to fruition a political project of an 'imagined' political community whose aim is to encompass its culture within its national boundaries.

AFFECT AND IDENTITY

To summarise the argument so far, we hold that all social identities – racial, ethnic, gendered, sexual, religious and national – find their definition in relation to significant Others just as they articulate ideas of self or selfhood which are communicated and given meaning through social interaction. Since every individual has several identities to choose from, the identity communicated depends in part on negotiation which takes place in specific social contexts and which takes place according to recognised cultural conventions (Eriksen 1991). Recognition of difference and similarity is, therefore, based in part on shared understandings of particular cultural expressions of difference in which the very act of narrating one's own identity may be instrumental in attributing an identity to others (Martin 1995). Because of the subjective, experiential dimension of identity, effective identity narratives such as those deployed by (ethnic) nationalism are exercises in the mobilisation of emotion through a selective drawing upon affective elements, for example a contextually defined sense of exclusion, fear and anxiety vis-a-vis significant Others.

The problems involved in the analysis of social identity are shared with work on the anthropology of emotion/affect, though the two have usually been treated separately. Why this has occurred is best understood by examining how anthropology has sought to understand rationality and irrationality cross-culturally. Shweder traces the history of this debate in anthropology to two competing and irreconcilable conceptions deriving from Enlightenment thinking and the romantic rebellion against reason (1984). In anthropology the division is between those who advocate the intendedly rational nature of the human mind (bound by the dictates of reason regardless of time, place, culture and race) and those who argue that cultures are radically differing frameworks or self-contained worlds (with a stress on the non-comparable, arbitrary nature of culture).

This division is expressed in terms of an Enlightenment search for underlying universals in human behaviour, 'the idea of natural law, the concept of deep structure, the notion of progress or development' (Shweder 1984: 28). Romanticists, on the contrary, argue that ideas and practices are 'non-rational' and best understood through the analysis of local context and cultural frames.

The differentiation between rationality and irrationality, reason and meaning, extends into work on culture and emotion. In an early and influential paper entitled 'What is an emotion?', William James argued that 'bodily changes follow directly from *perception* of the exciting fact, and that our feeling of the same changes as they occur *is* the emotion' (1884: 189–90). In short, James distinguished between perception and the physiological state associated with it, arguing further that perception precedes and triggers or unlocks a nervous, emotional predisposition commonly recognised as emotional.

This embodiment[4] of emotion gives it an explicit physiological basis and results, as Solomon observes, in the substitution of a hydraulic metaphor for a theory (1984). For if emotion is an 'inner feeling', then it is unobservable and inaccessible to anthropology, furthermore an understanding restricted to biological terms results in the view that emotions are universally experienced despite the accumulation of considerable ethnographic data to the contrary (Shweder and Levine 1984). A theory of emotion which dichotomises physiology and culture is, Solomon argues, fallacious and incomplete; instead, emotions should 'be construed as cultural acquisitions, determined by the circumstances and concepts of a particular culture as well as, or rather much more than, by the functions of biology' (Solomon 1984: 239–40).

A subsequent overview of research on the anthropology of emotion concluded along similar lines that the

view of emotion which gives primacy to inner bodily experiences has held sway ... because it is solidly consistent with our highly individuated concepts of person and motivation. The result ... has been a relative neglect of the phenomenological and communicative aspects of emotion. (Lutz and White 1986: 429)

Lutz and White argue instead for an approach which explicitly focuses on the social context within which specific cultural formulations of emotion are expressed, a view which would renew emphasis on 'the public, social, and cognitive dimensions for emotional experience'.

If we reject the Jamesian argument concerning the universal physiological nature of emotion, must we not also reject empathy/rapport ('introspection') as a method for understanding it? It becomes necessary to ask 'how the anthropologist can read beyond the expression to the emotion?', to which one answer would be that an 'emotion is not a feeling (or a set of feelings) but an *interpretation*', (Solomon 1984: 246). In short, physiological reactions are a necessary but insufficient basis for differentiating between emotions. Indeed, Solomon argues for a theory of emotion as cultural construct in which an

emotion is a system of concepts, beliefs, attitudes, and desires, virtually all of which are context-bound, historically developed, and culture-specific (which is not to foreclose the probability that some emotions may be specific to *all* cultures). (Solomon 1984: 249)

To argue for the cultural construction of emotion is to link it to an interpretive understanding of culture *and* to social structure, that is the social positioning of individuals and groups who use language *and* emotion to structure the social and moral order, in part through the use of feelings 'to understand and communicate about social events' and social relations (Lutz and White 1986: 430). A cognitive, structural and phenomenological approach rests, therefore, on the problem of the 'self' and the Other if, by this formulation, we understand the self to 'be conceptualized as both an individual mental representation and a cultural or collective representation', personhood and selfhood (Shweder and Levine 1984: 14). These conceptions differ fundamentally but are implicated in each other in part through the requirement that through socialisation individuals are equipped with cognitive abilities, skills and competences that make for effective social participation, and enculturated into an understanding of the implicit or tacit meanings, knowledge and expectations which underwrite cultural communication and interaction (Poole 1994).

This approach to emotion and its link to the self brings us back to our earlier discussion of experience in that now we can foreground our argument in the tensions of 'lived experience' (Bruner and Turner 1986). On the one hand, individuals tend to work at developing basic

social competences which are required if they are to be effective
social actors, they invest something of themselves in the roles they aspire
to perform; on the other hand individuals are frequently caught up in
social situations which create tension. Two problems arise from this
disjuncture: (1) at the personal level, the experience of conflict between
individual and collective senses of self (for example, Cohen 1994: 56–7);
and (2) the problem of cultural continuity, including socialisation and
the maintenance of 'tradition' (Barth 1984).

The resolution of both problems lies in an appreciation of reflexivity
or inter-subjectivity which operates through a scanning for meaning,
and through the interpretation of shared meanings, making possible
the discussion and negotiation which are vital to an individual's ability
to make sense of his or her personal experience.

G.H. Mead's work on symbolic interactionism, and in particular
the role of symbols in the 'conversation of gestures' – which includes
the language of speech, of hands and of countenance – demonstrates
the social and transactional process through which meaning is
communicated (1972: 147 and passim). Though anthropology has
primarily been concerned with the representational function of
meaning, D'Andrade reminds us that meanings also 'create cultural
entities, direct one to do certain things, and evoke certain feelings'
(1984: 96).

Normally the four functions interpenetrate or overlap. For example,
the meaning of a taboo is a culturally acquired knowledge accompanied
by specific tacit entailments regarding its performance (Epstein 1978).
In addition, elements of the meaning system come to have a directive
force for individuals through a combination of attachment to specific
social values and/or for personal reward. Finally, 'ideas, feelings, and
intentions are all activated by symbols and are thus part of the
meaning of symbols' (D'Andrade 1984: 99). To put it somewhat
differently, what

is essential to communication is that the symbol should arouse in one's self
what it arouses in the other individual. It should have that sort of universality
to any person who finds himself in the same situation. (Mead 1972: 149)[5]

Recalling our discussion of identity as a two-way process of
categorisation and ascription, we are now in a better position to take
up Epstein's discussion regarding the potency of specific symbols of
identity as this relates to cultural continuity (1978: 109ff.). He makes

the point that categorisation may provoke a response by the categorised group resulting in their stressing or becoming attached to certain forms of behaviour that come to serve as 'symbols of exclusiveness' which 'intensify and reinforce the sense of identity' (1978: 110). Epstein then discusses how such symbols may become so internalised as to be transmitted as part of the group's identity, its 'intimate' culture. Typically, this might include highly affective meanings attached to specific forms of family life, marriage, types of food and dress.

The domain of family and kinship, which contributes centrally to the emotional salience of identity, provides a crucial link between socialisation and enculturation and cultural continuity. There is now compelling evidence demonstrating how the family, as the locus of 'intimate' culture (that is, relationships with parents and kin), provides the context, the model and the means by which key understandings regarding personhood, selfhood and individuality are learned and internalised by children (Poole 1994).[6]

Given the long period of physical dependence and neuro-biological maturation, the context within which cultural knowledge is imparted to children is clearly crucial (Poole 1994). Within the home, and through learning and defining relationships with family members, children begin the process of actively distinguishing between different social contexts and persons, and assessing the relative value of differing types of learning, knowledge, relationships and experience. It is in the early years that a sense of identity begins to emerge in children, in which the gradual accumulation of experience assists in the development of the reflexive ability to see themselves as others see them.

It is through socialisation that children are initiated into their society as adults and participants. It is at this time that their bodies are inscribed with cultural significance, children's sense of self becomes embodied as they are taught how to realise basic social values through their experience of what it means to be a social person (Mauss 1973; Lock 1993).[7] As in the conceptualisation of identity and emotion, anthropology has tended to focus upon the cognitive nature of socialisation without addressing the experiential dimension of what becoming a participant or belonging to a group means. Yet it is the intensely felt emotions aroused within individuals by social maturation which calls into conflict the difference between selfhood and personhood (Cohen 1994: ch. 3). Furthermore, identity and affect are obverse sides of self-consciousness – that is, there can be no social identity which does not possess an affective component. In seeking to recognise the social construction of affect within identity and to contextualise its expression we are, however, brought face to face with the question of what anthropological methods are available for the investigation (Epstein 1992b: ch. 1)?

While anthropology has been concerned with identity for some time, a near exclusive focus on ethnicity and an emphasis on cognition have resulted in the privileging of speech and language as methodological keys. Why this should be so is not difficult to understand given the importance of language in participant observation as well as its role in communication and socialisation (for example, Ochs and Schieffelin 1984). A development of this approach is to examine social discourse which treats speech as a kind of social 'code' the meaning of which emerges in public performances through its use by social actors (Abu-Lughod and Lutz 1990). The situational context and the relative position of the different actors provides the cues with which to decode a discursive meaning. One key to an anthropological analysis of these meanings lies in the appreciation of basic 'affective devices' (Besnier 1990) such as: special lexicons used to label or mark culturally significant areas of affect or experience (for example, emotion words and colour categories); the importance of synecdoche, metonymy and metaphor to make certain kinds of statements; and the role of idiophones and onomatopoeia. Such analyses depend on specialist socio-linguistic skills.

More commonly, however, anthropologists tend to examine varieties of cultural expression such as everyday conversation, poetry, song, laments, prayer, story telling, and myth-making. In short, the usual analysis is of any verbal narratives which are performed publicly and which embody statements or representations of shared social experience (Abu-Lughod and Lutz 1990; Abu-Lughod 1990; Bruner and Turner 1986). They also survey other forms of standardised public performance such as dance, vernacular culture and ritual. These may be viewed as structured narratives expressing meaning for audiences as well as devices for (re)defining the group in relation to significant Others.

These kind of performances are not static but function to interpret and rewrite the past, legitimate change (including devaluing the Other by objectifying difference), and mark and celebrate the participants' own culture (Martin 1995; Gilroy 1993). Such narratives are, by definition, sequentially organised and internally structured symbolic codes. Appreciation of the narrative flows from the audience's specific cultural aesthetics and cultural standards of performance and meaning. These cultural expressions also serve to reintegrate individuals into the group (for example, by creating a 'community of sentiment'; Appadurai 1990a) and can revivify tradition by generating strong emotional commitment through the performative act and the potency and polysemy of the symbols.

Social understandings will differ depending on: context (for example, public v. sociable settings); whether performance produces solidarity; the nature of participation (for example, passivity v. antiphony, call and response, role playing); on how it is culturally coded (for example, semantically or through music and rhythm); on what is coded (for example, specific emotions, statements about inequality or relationships); and the extent to which it permits of multiple and possibly conflicting interpretations (for example, insiders v. outsiders, and amongst insiders, distinctions based on gender, prestige and wealth).

While the methodological problems involved in the study of identity and affect are not inconsiderable, we wish to make clear our commitment to an anthropology which subscribes to the tenet that 'other people's truths are contained in their own classifications and understanding, and that our own culture offers no self-evidently privileged standard of verity' (Chapman et al. 1989: 10). The concept of 'culture' is thus central to an understanding of identity and affect as for all of social life (Barth 1984; Cohen 1994: 118ff.; Friedman 1994: 206ff.; Hannerz 1992). Structural–functionalism deployed culture as something which integrated the separate institutions and, through the enculturation of its members, achieved individual conformity with general social values and expectations. More recent work has tended to see culture as distributive, that is, as a communicative process which derives its significance through and permits social interaction. In this latter view, culture does not determine individual behaviour but rather individuals produce their own culture in the sense of a framework of meaning which allows cultural similarity and difference to be established as part of the process of social interaction.

These two contrasting views of 'culture' – as something that is supra-individual and based on shared values, premises and experience *versus* a variably distributed corpus of ideas, propositions, meanings which inform behaviour – has important implications for analysing a world of flux, movement and social complexity. For if we accept the latter view, then we are forced to question assertions about holism and integration, and approaches to culture based on a search for underlying deep structures. This is not an argument for a retreat into empiricism. Instead it is a call for the empirical testing of propositions about the relative interdependence of specific elements of a society, not a (re)discovery of coherence but an exploration of the range of variation in meaning, behaviour and values across a society which permits both general social communication and interaction *and* participation in 'different, partial and simultaneous worlds' which may only partially overlap or intermesh (Barth 1989: 130).

Two lines of reasoning can be adduced to support an argument that cultural frames are not so arbitrary or diverse as to elude rational understanding (Spiro 1984). First, though the range of cultural propositions or frames are theoretically unlimited, in fact only a limited range of types exist which suggests that an explanation of their distribution and their meaning *is* possible. Second, if we attend not only to the *conscious* or surface meanings of cultural frames (those which actors are reflexively aware of), but also to the *unconscious* awareness of meaning (as revealed, for example, in dreams) which are unconscious precisely because they arouse anxiety, shame, guilt, outrage and fear then we must accept that a universal (that is, rational) standard for judging the adequacy of the ideas is possible. Such a standard (of logic or evidence) rests on the recognition that cultural frames comprise a hierarchy of 'cognitive salience' in which the learning and understanding of cultural frames operates at a different level than the internalisation of beliefs and values which guide behaviour. As Spiro notes, the internalisation and incorporation of a frame as part of a person's personal beliefs links it to personal motivation, 'it arouses strong affect (anxiety), which in turn, motivates him to action' (Spiro 1984: 328). Nor does the analysis of unconscious meaning have to depend upon the Western cultural constructs of psychiatry. An alternative approach would be to use the cultural tropes in different societies to provide clues to the principles underlying classes of meaning and affect. Cultural propositions *and* human physiology intimately tie culture to affect.[8]

SCALE, CULTURE AND CONTEXT: ANTHROPOLOGI-CAL EXPLORATIONS IN THIS VOLUME

At the heart of our debate about identity is the validity of anthropology's claim to name and interpret the Other. Marcus has argued that contemporary ethnography must problematise notions of space, time and perspective/voice if it wishes to break with increasingly discredited 'meta-narratives' and remain relevant (Marcus 1992). This means that the locale of social activity is not a determinant of social identity but is only one among many contexts in which it is performed or produced by individuals and groups. Second, the process by which identities are produced does not conform strictly to a linear, historical notion of time or history; on the contrary 'scanning', 'memory' and subjective experience also contribute to emergent identities. Finally, the imposition of structure or order to a society reflects the authority of the anthropologist to recognise or privilege a particular perspective or voice at the expense of the richness and diversity of relationships, experiences and persons that compose that society.

While it is correct that the anthropologist/ethnographer shares some identities with her/his subjects and may participate in their lives to varying degrees, we do *not* feel a need to develop new research methods (for example, dialogics). Indeed, we would argue that good anthropology is already aware of the need for a careful exegesis of meaning obtained through 'coevalness' (Fabian 1983) – a relation of respect and equality between ethnographer and informant in which the identity of the former is also factored into the analysis – and reliance on sound research method.

Anthropological fieldwork underlines a commitment to empirical research and to the task of interpreting culture and identity, one's own as well as that of others. The contributors to this volume, for example, have occupied diverse research sites and roles. Long-term research for some contributors has resulted in a qualitative shift in their role from observer to participant, and from anthropological outsider to insider and friend, blurring the distinction between subject/object and between the ideals of detachment and objectivity in research.

While fieldwork tends to blur the injunction regarding detachment, traditional conventions of ethnographic writing have sought to reimpose it by stressing the relatively unique and bounded – in time and space – nature of our subjects and their day-to-day lives. Yet the objective of fieldwork, to understand a culture from the 'inside', is potentially frustrated by conventions of writing which, through a reductive model of culture, filter out the experiential component (Bruner and Turner 1986; Levine 1984). However, whether the focus is on specific symbols of identity, historically stable forms of identity and experience, or the impact of shifting contextual factors on the expression of affect, the contributors to this volume demonstrate an awareness not only of the complex and interdependent relation between local, national and global processes which impact on social identity but also of the central place of affect and emotion in any consideration of culture and identity. Awareness of Other, as the chapters show, is intimately connected with a sense of self and of belonging to a larger social collectivity which often provides a strong affective component in the experience and imagination of community and membership.

A shared concern with identity and affect immediately raises a host of problems for the anthropologist which the chapters in this book only begin to address. First, identity – including that of the anthropologist – is implicated in both the narrative account about a society and in terms of the experience and consciousness of local actors as lived out at several interconnected levels: as participants in local arenas who are, simultaneously, actors in an increasingly interconnected global culture, perhaps as members of a cultural diaspora or of a transnational culture. Making sense of one's experience and of one's world requires reflexivity, an ability to make sense of the present as performed in a range of different social domains, some of which are more meaningful than others (Bruner and Turner 1986). Consciousness (of self and of others) is achieved inter-subjectively through inference and interpreting shared experience or its 'expressions' through representations, performance and texts, in effect through a constant process of scanning for meaning or significance (1986: 11–13).

The anthropological task is, therefore, one of understanding the contexts within which, and social processes by which, meaning is interpreted and generated. For a start, this requires an open-ended inquiry which combines structural and phenomenological approaches. Such a political economy of identity and affect is predicated on an awareness of difference born of experience and knowledge of the social relationship(s) in which one participates. Social action, itself a product and producer of experience, hinges upon such knowledge and an appreciation of how individuals and groups are positioned vis-a-vis one another, that is on the relative power which individuals employ as they engage in pragmatic social action. Finally, experience acquires its salience precisely through its location and performance in public life, and it is precisely the public, political expression of affect and identity which anthropology is best equipped to understand (Abu-Lughod and Lutz 1990: 7; Barth 1989).

There are very public expressions of political identity in the chapters in the first part of the volume which, at the same time, also restate intimate relations and can envelop critical stages in individual life-projects.[9] Case studies in the first part of the volume highlight examples of continuing and changing identity formation. In the religious processions and disorder of late nineteenth-century Colombo, Sri Lanka, R.L. Stirrat shows the beginnings of an expanding scale of conflict and violence in the public expression of religious and ethnic identity of Colombo's streets. The identities being formed in the last years of the nineteenth century continue to this day in the politics and terror of Sri Lanka. And although the ethnic labels of 1883 look very similar to the ethnic tags of today the identities expressed are never complete. In the historical dimension of the account we see the imprint of both colonial and other global relations and the changing affective dimension of subscription to Buddhist and Catholic ritual. The identities of both Catholics and Buddhists had crystallised around the public display of images and it was selfhood that was threatened by the riots, rumours and scandalising that Stirrat explains.

David Mosse examines the responses of *Harijan* castes in Tamil Nadu to their subordination and harijan people's identities as Catholics, Hindus and members of the 'Untouchable' or *Dalit* political movement. In contrast to dramatic shifts in the historical importance of united-Catholic and Buddhist-nationalist identities in Sri Lanka, David Mosse's analysis shows major streams of substantial continuity in the identities of Tamil harijan households and castes. The *theoretically* available interplay of roles arising from self-recruitment to pan-Indian and Tamil-wide modern political movements and from continuing involvement in religious and caste hierarchies is usually finally integrated in, and overlaid by, more quotidian identities. The weight of selfhood seems buried in sub-caste service relations within the village and in caste association struggles.

The interment and even total absorption of identity does actually take place in Michael Young's account of amity and enmity in Kalauna, in the Massim region of eastern Papua New Guinea. Feasts with friends and revengeful (cannibalistic) feasting on enemies are compared. The reconstructions of the last *miwa* (cannibal feasts) to be held show extreme measures taken to secure revenge, including, in one area, an imperative to consume a miwa victim down to the very last morsel – revenge here was literally all-consuming. With the coming of colonial government cannibalism ceased and a local leader is credited with the innovation of substituting competitive food exchange – fighting with food – for the consumption of enemies. The social construction and symbolic expressions of food, nurture and love, aggression and body wastes are then analysed for their implications for passion and shame and on group identities.

Other forms of amity and enmity are explored for a different part of Papua New Guinea, and within the context of studies for planned economic and political change, by Alan Rew. He examines how cultural identities in the province of East New Britain are given public expression. Each relationship is paired and has a 'history' of prior contexts while contemporary contests are located in, for example: genealogies and ideas of kinship stocks; reconstructions and legends of pre-colonial and colonial subordination; and neo-tribes of order and utopia. Viewed in terms of the contemporary nation-state, social relations are marked by anxiety over present and future inequality, the increasing scale and purpose of micro-nationalist and social reform movements among the more peripheral peoples of the province, and the force of the divide between them and the dominant ethnic group, the Tolai. The sense conveyed in the ethnographies written on the Tolai, on the other hand, is that they remain largely unaware of the self-constructions of the ethnic 'others' around them or of the passions that are aroused by their economic and political success. The majority of Tolai are largely comfortable with their identities and the specific cultural 'flags' which represent their cultural continuity. In the Pomio-Bainings area of East New Britain, histories of subordination lead them to search energetically both for new self-constructions and for other tags and flags.

Tracing the results of 'external' influence and the displacement of affect into alternative institutional and expressive forms emerge as themes in all the essays in this first part of the volume. The impact of forces seen as external to the society and on-going social relations and institutional forms varies considerably, for example, in the two case studies from Melanesia. In Kalauna, colonial justice and peace have been absorbed to imply an almost seamless continuity in local values and affectual relations. There have been profound institutional displacements, following the imposition of colonial rule, from revenge cannibalism to aggressive and humiliating food gifts; but the emotional ethos continues throughout the history that Young has accessed for us. The dominant passion of Kalauna society seems to be simmering anger, with grass skirts swished aggressively and yams thrust under rivals' noses. Anger also features in the case study of the Pomio-Bainings – it is directed at the perceived denial of brotherhood by the Tolai. A social movement based on cargo-thinking among the Pomio and the Bainings has led to new identities incorporating strangers into a new intense solidarity of politics and sociability. It has also created, through the moral rearmament of the periphery, new affective and moral spaces. 'Mismeetings' at missions and government centres are displaced into mismeetings in development planning and representative politics. They are also stated in the flying of the Australian flag in some Bainings villages to symbolise a new pan-Bainings solidarity based on nostalgia for the securities of colonial administration.[10] Jenkins (1995) records in a similar vein how, for contemporary Denmark, the usual symbol of European nationalism and territorial claims – the national flag – is also displaced to 'fly' symbolically over babies' birthday parties and sales of consumer goods. The Danish flag is at once an icon of domestic relations and of the distinctiveness of Danish civil institutions in a small northern European state that has come to terms with the history of contraction from a once greater and glorious Scandinavian empire.

In commissioning the chapters that comprise this volume, we wanted to re-present two broad kinds of identities. First, we wanted to explore identity in situations where territorially based national or local definitions of social coherence and purpose were still salient and in counterpoint to alternative identities based on ethnicity, race, religion and class. Was 'identity' simply a 'softer', fuzzier version of classic concepts such as role, status, group and network which was of mildly interesting but passing topicality? The chapters in the first part of the book say 'no' to this question and do so by examining identities and affect in nation-states and local societies which have strength in their central coordinating institutions (whether government rules or rules on systematic food exchange) but also in alternative social bases and visions. Second, we wanted the book to focus on self-image and the moral and affective space of individuals defined contextually as figures and subjects in habitats, neo-communities and in global classificatory systems rather than in national or territorial terms. In many of the urban, migration and industrial contexts in which we had worked, the idea of nationalism and its alternatives was tangential in the extreme.

Subjects appeared, rather, as: perpetual strangers; mediating agents; members of a cultural diaspora and/or dispersed occupational elites; and as Third World development evangelists. The chapters in the second part deal with habitats and figures such as these. 'Social networks' had previously served as one useful organising concept for our studies of these phenomena; we felt that Bill Epstein's ideas on identity and affect could provide another. A central task for anthropological theory is how to describe and analyse experience and culture that is re-forming and hybridising after dispersal or is found in those occupational habitats where meaning and integration have to be recreated after institutional and economic shifts or collapse. As an integrating concept, 'identity' appeared to us well able to capture both the underlying cultural fragmentation and the emotional basis of lived experience in these more dispersed sites and cultural compilations in which we found ourselves.

The idea of *cultural diaspora* has been used to capture the narratives and memories of dispersal after the metropolitan, receiving, colonial or independent nation-states have failed to satisfy the demand for the new identities they were normatively expected to deliver. The failure to provide the identities needed was because of racism, ethnic or colonial exclusions (as in the chapter by Campbell on Asians in East Africa) or because the modernist industrial framework creates, momentarily, privileged islands of self-identification (as in the chapter by Grillo on Ugandan railwaymen and their work role commitments) but then moves on to other cultural and material terrain.

The cultural rupture imposed, or self-imposed, by exile sets the problem of how continuity and identity are achieved in a diaspora when the dispersed may be continuously in motion and its identity is perceived as constantly under threat (Appadurai 1990b). One outcome is a creative interpretation of the imposition of rupture and oppression. In *The Black Atlantic* Paul Gilroy analyses the role of 'black' musical performance in creating a 'distinct counterculture of modernity' (1993: 36). In Gilroy's view, black music is a discourse which provides a running, historic commentary on their racialised existence. Through a combination of sound, singing, antiphony, mimesis, gesture, kinesis and costume, a coded public communication is created which creates cognitive, moral and affective space for black people *and* restates their demands. This 'politics of transfiguration' not only draws upon historical experience of slavery and racism but also emphasises the emergence of qualitatively new desires, modes of association and interpretations of resistance. Another outcome of diaspora is a contest for the *ownership* of culture. For example, there are rival narratives and claims regarding 'the possession of national identities, histories and cultures' by the Republic of Macedonia and the Macedonian minority in Greece which have implications for human rights and for territorial claims (Danforth 1993: 10).

'Narrative' – whether produced by a 'community' or social science – is central to constructions of identity in the diaspora because it stakes the key claims to authenticity. Anne-Marie Fortier answers, for Italian exiles in London, a question asked by Michel de Certeau: 'How can readers resist discourse that tells them what is or what has been?' They cannot, is the implication – if, that is, the narrators can identify the tropes that can lead *through cultural production* to the unique character of the habitat and neo-tribe in question, even if they claim 'only' to reproduce events and characters. Narrative and the icons, core symbols and other representations it contains are not static and immutable but are continually changing as the dispersal and recombination of exiles and cultural elements continues. Boundaries shift, the cultural 'stuff' which characterises a group changes, and individuals move in and out of groups as circumstances alter. The key chapter that illustrates such responses to historical and life-chance change is by John Campbell. His account of Asians in Tanzania shows the evolution in their social organisation from ethnically defined patron–client ties, to ethnic networks based on affinity, to corporate ethnic associations. There are major changes to the signifiers and cultural content of the constituent social relations. Religious membership, language, domestic customs and relations, and caste all play their parts at different times and in different contexts. The identity-supplying drives of the colonial and independent state sculpted these significations of religion, caste, kinship affinities, assets and memberships into three racial strata; Africans and Europeans failed or refused to recognise any other markers and persistently racialised Asians into a single, 'Asian' identity. The anti-Asian character of African nationalism was put in place and led to the exodus of East African Asians to Britain and elsewhere in the early 1970s.

Ralph Grillo reminds us of the distinctively privileged islands of modernity in the colonial and immediately post-independence Third World. One of these islands was large-scale industry and infrastructure. The African railwaymen of Grillo's description internalise identities derived from their work roles and show a high level of commitment to their employment within the 'aristocracy of African labour'. Only part of this identification can be explained by concepts such as the social reproduction of labour power. The railwaymen in Grillo's study identify so strongly with their occupational grading as 'Running Shift Foreman' or 'Accident Clerk' that we come to think of their work roles as 'callings' or vocations almost. This, and other accounts of occupational and work role identifications,[11] are needed to counterbalance the tendency to treat 'identity' as equal to 'ethnicity' or 'gender'. Grillo wonders if these work role identifications arise from the co-location of work and residence, as in the traditional working-class communities based on deep mining, railway and dock working industry.

'Coal Valley' is Leonard Mars' pseudonym for a south Wales industrial community with memories of all the archetypal solidarities and oppositions expressed in Grillo's characterisation of 'traditional working-class communities'. Based for a century or more on coal mining, the last of Coal Valley's three collieries ceased operations in 1983. What had been an island of labour strength in the early twentieth century has now become a disposal site for redundant men and machines in the rust-belt of industrial de-development. The mine winding gear no longer operates and the doctor at the centre of the social situation Leonard Mars analyses is also retiring after a life-time of service in the valley. The central tropes in the retirement ceremony focus on nostalgia for miners' and valley solidarity, and for a stranger doctor's egalitarian style of professional community service. And it is these multiple identities and relations that create the 'structures of feeling' – in this case seen as Welsh – that Raymond Williams sought to narrate *despite* the paucity of institutions that could be distinguished from those in the rest of the United Kingdom (Williams 1989).

Grief about a lost vision also figures in Philip Quarles' analysis of the occupational world of international development planning. In the chapters by Campbell, Fortier and Mars, any loss of identity is followed by aspects of recovery. Philip Quarles presents a further instance of 'de-development', and also non-recovery, in the very development agencies themselves. Purpose is being lost; the milk of human kindness is turning sour; the discovery of unimplementable programmes at the organisational base is transferred (the 'metastasis') as illness to the organisation's head and its woefully inadequate heart. Whereas it used to be accepted that 'incrementalism' in policy and intervention was the norm, and policy pronouncements and visions were secondary or even epiphenomenal, the almost hysterical imposition of central management visions and neo-liberal policies has resulted in turbulence and disorder. In place of the current organisational metaphors of 'construction', 'war' and 'politics', Quarles argues that we need new metaphors of birth, pain and suffering and a new morality of effort. But does delirium signify *only* danger; are there not circumstances and individuals in which it can lead to creativity as well? The postmodern mood means a loss of purpose and the growth of turbulence (at least in the Netherlands) while postmodern creativity seems absent or aborted in the development agencies that Quarles examines. Is this a terminal and widespread condition, or a limited case of Dutch Disease?

The book as a whole confirms the need to link individual experience with broader social and historical process. In providing this link, the contributors also demonstrate an understanding of moral economy and emotion as dimensions essential to, and ever present in, sociality, not as something separate from social life. The Durkheimian tradition in social theory has set questions of identity and affect aside and treated them as 'psychology' or as a purely internalised state of mind inaccessible to the anthropologist and social historian. The chapters which follow show that we can research identity. Accounts of structure, social choice and loosely structured habitat can all gain from analysis of the public expression and resolution of those moral and affectual tensions that stem from an individual's contradictory memberships, emotions and imaginings.

NOTES

1. Anthropologists have employed a variety of terms in drawing attention to this dichotomy: objective/subjective (B. Williams 1989), group characteristics versus social process (Eriksen 1991) and universalist/interpretative (Lutz and White 1986).

2. Fox defines the term 'nationalist ideologies' – alternatively 'nationalisms', 'subnational identities' and 'ethnic nationalisms – to mean an ideology of peoplehood premised on the requirement of an independent state or autonomous territory for its realization (1990: 2–3).

3. Some writers would argue that social theory, particularly rationalist theory and philosophy (e.g. Protestantism and Marxism), are premised on specific forms of masculinity and femininity defined in terms of a denial of self as 'an emotional, somatic and spiritual being' (Seidler 1994).

4. Though James does admit a role for cultural or social variability through the need to learn appropriate bodily responses, this tends to be de-emphasised both in his article and in subsequent work on the topic.

5. Discussing the sincerity of affective displays, Besnier notes that 'so long as members of a culture "agree" to match particular emotion labels to particular displays, and as long as this agreement remains tacit, the display is sincere' (1990: 430).

6. The variability in the form and organisation of the 'family' need not be explained as historical deviations from a universal form, since socialisation does not require that family or kinship provide children with a specific type of significant Others (for example, both parents) but only with some significant Others which are appropriate in the child's cultural milieu.

7. Part of socialisation involves 'conditioning children's senses to the cultural norm' (Classen 1993: 8). However, we should not forget that, though the basic sensory paradigm through which we configure experience and knowledge is predominantly visual and aural, other societies organise and articulate their identity and knowledge through smell, heat, sound, colour or a combination of the senses. Cross-cultural variations in the role and significance of the senses should remind us that cognition and knowledge may be intimately linked to the social and moral order in a variety of ways, some of which are radically different from our own.

8. Spiro suggests that synecdoche would be worth pursuing, and gives as an example a form of transference between a patient and his therapist based on the unconscious meaning of maternal nourishment (1984: 338–9). But see his earlier discussion of Ilongot head-hunting (pp. 330–4). Fernandez (1986) makes a similar argument for analysing the interplay tropes.

9. In a paper presented at the workshop, Jenkins discussed how 'flying the flag' describes the ubiquitous use of the Danish flag, the Danebrod, to sacralise family rites, retail sales and national heroes and events. The paradox in the Danish flag is the public expression

it gives to commonplace family celebrations and the compressed and comfortable character it symbolises in Danish state institutions (see Jenkins 1995).

10. Bauman (1993: 154–60) takes the idea of *mismeeting* from Martin Buber. He also argues the need for aesthetic, moral and cognitive spaces when presenting any social mapping of a human population.

11. Rew (1975: ch. 3), for example, gives an almost equivalent example of work role identification in urban New Guinea.

REFERENCES

Abu-Lughod, L. 1990. 'Shifting politics in Bedouin love poetry', in J. Abu-Lughod and C. Lutz (eds) *Language and the Politics of Emotion*. Cambridge: Cambridge University Press, pp. 24–45.

Abu-Lughod, J. and C. Lutz (eds). 1990. *Language and the Politics of Emotion*. Cambridge: Cambridge University Press.

Alonso, A.M. 1994. 'The politics of space, time and substance: state formation, nationalism, and ethnicity', *Annual Review of Anthropology* 23: 379–405.

Appadurai, Arjun. 1989. 'Small-scale techniques and large-scale objectives', in P. Bardhan (ed.) *Conversations between Economists and Anthropologists: Methodological Issues in Measuring Economic Change in Rural India*. Delhi: Oxford University Press India, pp. 250–82.

—— 1990a. 'Topographies of the self: praise and emotion in Hindu India', in J. Abu-Lughod and C. Lutz. (eds) *Language and the Politics of Emotion*. Cambridge: Cambridge University Press, pp. 92-112.

—— 1990b. 'Disjuncture and difference in the global cultural economy', in M. Featherstone (ed.) *Global Culture*. London: Sage.

—— 1997. *Modernity at Large: Cultural Dimensions of Globalization*. Delhi: Oxford University Press.

Bailey, F.G. 1983. *The Tactical Uses of Passion: An Essay on Power, Reason and Reality*. Ithaca, NY: Cornell University Press.

Bardhan, P. (ed.). 1989. *Conversations between Economists and Anthropologists: Methodological Issues in Measuring Economic Change in Rural India*. Delhi: Oxford University Press India.

Barnes, John. 1954. 'Class and committees in a Norwegian island parish', *Human Relations* 7: 39–58.

—— 1972. *Social Networks*. Reading, MA: Addison-Wesley.

Barth, F. 1983. *Sohar: Culture and Society in an Omani Town*. Baltimore, MD: Johns Hopkins University Press.

—— 1984. 'Problems in conceptualizing cultural pluralism, with illustrations from Somar, Oman', in D. Maybury-Lewis (ed.) *The Prospects for Plural Societies*. Proceedings of the American Ethnological Society. 1982. Washington, DC: AES, pp. 77–87.

—— 1989. 'The analysis of culture in complex societies', *Ethnos* 54 (3–4): 120–42.

Bauman, Zygmunt. 1992. *Intimations of Postmodernity*. London: Routledge.

—— 1993. *Postmodern Ethics*. Oxford: Blackwell.

Berndt, R.M. and Peter Lawrence (eds). 1971. *Politics in New Guinea*. Nedlands: University of Western Australia Press.

Besnier, N. 1990. 'Language and affect', *Annual Review of Anthropology* 19: 419–51.

Bruner, E.M. and V. Turner. 1986. *The Anthropology of Experience*. Urbana: University of Illinois Press.

Buckley, A. 1989. '"We're trying to find our identity": uses of history among Ulster Protestants', in M. Chapman, M. McDonald and E. Tonkin (eds) *History and Ethnicity*. London: Routledge, pp. 183–97.

Castells, M. 1996. *The Rise of the Network Society, Vol. 1: The Information Age: Economy, Society and Culture*. Oxford: Blackwell.

Chapman, M., M. McDonald and E. Tonkin (eds). 1989. *History and Ethnicity*. London: Routledge.

Classen, C. 1993. *Worlds of Sense: Exploring the Senses in History and Across Cultures*. London: Routledge.

Cohen, A.P. 1994. *Self-Consciousness: An Alternative Anthropology of Identity*. London: Routledge.

Collier-Thomas, B. and J. Turner. 1992. 'Race, class, nationality and color: the African American search for identity', Philadelphia, PA: Center for African American History and Culture Occasional Papers series no. 1.

D'Andrade, P. 1984. 'Cultural meaning systems', in R.A. Shweder and R.A. Levine (eds) *Culture Theory: Essays on Mind, Self and Emotion*. Cambridge: Cambridge University Press, pp. 88–122.

Danforth, L. 1993. 'Claims to Macedonian identity', *Anthropology Today* 9 (4): 3–10.

Despres, L.A. 1984. 'Ethnicity: what data and theory portend for plural societies', in D. Maybury-Lewis (ed.) *The Prospects for Plural Societies*. Proceedings of the American Ethnological Society. 1982. Washington, DC: AES, pp. 7–29.

Docherty, T. 1993. *Postmodernism: A Reader*. London: Harvester-Wheatsheaf.

Epstein, A.L. 1958. *Politics in an Urban African Community*. Manchester: Manchester University Press.

—— 1961. 'The network and urban social organization', *The Rhodes-Livingstone Institute Journal*, 29: 29–61. (Reprinted in J. Clyde Mitchell 1969, and A.L. Epstein 1992a.)

—— 1978. *Ethos and Identity*. London: Tavistock.

—— 1992a. *Scenes from African Urban Life: Collected Copperbelt Essays*. Edinburgh: Edinburgh University Press.

—— 1992b. *In the Midst of Life*. Berkeley: University of California Press.

Eriksen, T.H. 1991. 'The cultural contexts of ethnic differences', *Man* 26: 127–44.

—— 1993. *Ethnicity and Nationalism: Anthropological Perspectives*. London: Pluto Press.

Fabian, J. 1983. *Time and the Other: How Anthropology Makes its Object*. New York: Columbia University Press.

Falk Moore, Sally. 1986. *Social Facts and Fabrications*. Cambridge: Cambridge University Press.

Feld, S. and A.A. Fox. 1994. 'Music and language', *Annual Review of Anthropology* 23: 25–53.

Fernandez, J. 1986. 'The argument of images and the experience of returning to the whole', in E.M. Bruner and V. Turner (eds) *The Anthropology of Experience*. Urbana: University of Illinois Press, pp. 159–87.

Foucault, Michel. 1974. *The Archaeology of Knowledge*. London: Tavistock.

Fox, R. (ed.). 1990. *Nationalist Identities and the Production of National Cultures*. American Ethnological Society Monograph Series no. 2: Washington, DC: AES.

Friedman, J. 1989. 'Culture, identity, and world process', *Review* 12 (1): 51–69.

—— 1994. *Cultural Identity and Global Process*. London: Sage.

Giddens, Anthony. 1991. *Modernity and Self-Identity*. Cambridge: Polity.

Gilroy, P. 1993. *The Black Atlantic: Modernity and Double Consciousness*. London: Verso.

Goffman, E. 1963. *Stigma*. Englewood Cliffs, NJ: Prentice-Hall.

Hannerz, U. 1990. 'Cosmopolitans and locals in world culture', in M. Featherstone (ed.) *Global Culture*. London: Sage.

—— 1992 'The global ecumene as a network of networks', in A. Kuper (ed.) *Conceptualising Society*. London: European Association of Social Anthropologists and Routledge, pp. 34–56.

James, W. 1884. 'What is an emotion?', *Mind* 9: 188–205.

Jenkins, R. 1994. 'Rethinking ethnicity: identity, categorization and power', *Ethnic and Racial Studies* 17 (2): 197–223.

—— 1995. 'Nations and nationalisms: towards more open models', *Nations and Nationalism* 1 (3): 369–90.

Kapferer, B. 1972. *Strategy and Transition in an African Factory*. Manchester: Manchester University Press.

Lash, S. and J. Friedman (eds). 1992. *Modernity and Identity*. Oxford: Blackwell.

Levine, Hal and Barbara Levine. 1979. *Urbanisation in Papua New Guinea: A Study of Ambivalent Townsmen*. Cambridge: Cambridge University Press.

Levine, R.A. 1984. 'Properties of culture: an ethnographic view', in R. Shweder and R.A. Levine (eds) *Culture Theory: Essays on Mind, Self and Emotion*. Cambridge: Cambridge University Press, pp. 67–87.

Lock, M. 1993. 'Cultivating the body: anthropology and epistemologies of bodily practice and knowledge', *Annual Review of Anthropology* 22: 133–55.

Lutz, C. and G.M. White. 1986. 'The anthropology of emotions', *Annual Review of Anthropology* 15: 405–36.

Maffesoli, Michel. 1996. *The Time of the Tribes: The Decline of Individualism in Mass Society*. London: Sage.

Marcus, G. 1992. 'Past, present and emergent identities: requirements for ethnographies of late twentieth-century modernity worldwide', in S. Lash and J. Friedman (eds) *Modernity and Identity*. Oxford: Blackwell.

Martin, D.-C. 1995. 'The choices of identity', *Social Identities* 1 (1): 5–20.

Mauss, M. 1973. 'Techniques of the body', *Economy & Society* 2: 70–88.

Mead, G.H. 1972. *Mind, Self, and Society*. Chicago: Chicago University Press. (Orig. 1934.)

Mitchell, J. Clyde (ed). 1969. *Social Networks in Urban Situations*. Manchester: Manchester University Press.

Ochs, E. and B. Schieffelin. 1984. 'Language acquisition and socialization: three developmental stories and their implications', in R.A. Shweder and R.A. Levine (eds) *Culture Theory: Essays on Mind, Self and Emotion*. Cambridge: Cambridge University Press, pp. 276–322.

Poole, F.J.P. 1994. 'Socialization, enculturation and the development of personal identity', in T. Ingold (ed.) *Companion Encyclopedia of Anthropology*. London: Routledge, pp. 831–59.

Rew, Alan. 1975. *Social Images and Process in Urban New Guinea*. St Paul, MN: American Ethnological Society.

—— 1996. 'Policy implications of the institutional ownership of resettlement negotiations: examples from Asia of resettlement practice', in C. McDowell (ed.) *Understanding Impoverishment*. Oxford: Berghahn, pp. 201–221.

Seidler, V. 1994. *Recovering the Self*. London: Routledge.

Shweder, A. 1984. 'Anthropology's romantic rebellion against the enlightenment, or there's more to thinking than reason and evidence', in R.A. Shweder and R.A. Levine (eds) *Culture Theory: Essays on Mind, Self and Emotion*. Cambridge: Cambridge University Press, pp. 27–66.

Shweder, R.A. and R.A. Levine (eds). 1984. *Culture Theory: Essays on Mind, Self and Emotion*. Cambridge: Cambridge University Press.

Smith, A.D. 1994. 'The politics of culture: ethnicity and nationalism', in T. Ingold (ed.) *Companion Encyclopedia of Anthropology*. London: Routledge, pp. 706–33.

Solomon, R.C. 1984. 'Getting angry: the Jamesian theory of emotion in anthropology', in R.A. Shweder and R.A. Levine (eds) *Culture Theory: Essays on Mind, Self and Emotion*. Cambridge: Cambridge University Press, pp. 238–56.

Spiro, M. 1984. 'Some reflections on cultural determinism and relativism with special reference to emotion and reason', in R.A. Shweder and R.A. Levine (eds) *Culture Theory: Essays on Mind, Self and Emotion*. Cambridge: Cambridge University Press, pp. 323–46.

Strathern, Marilyn. 1992. 'Parts and wholes: refiguring relationships in a post-plural world', in A. Kuper (ed.) *Conceptualising Society*. London: European Association of Social Anthropologists and Routledge, pp. 75–106.

Williams, B. 1989. 'A class act: anthropology and the race to nation across ethnic terrain', *Annual Review of Anthropology* 18: 401–44.

Williams, Raymond. 1989. *Resources of Hope*. London: Verso.

Wolf, E. 1994. 'Perilous ideas: race, culture, people', *Current Anthropology* 35 (1): 1–12.

PART I 'BECOMING ...'

Part I examines the impact of colonialism and colonial induced socio-economic and political change on 'local' societies and the manner in which individuals have experienced and expressed radically new social identities. One key issue is the increase in the scale of social relations which, in forcing a national and then global outward orientation, initiated a process of cultural redefinition and social realignment. In Sri Lanka the process of becoming a part of the modern world entailed the evolution of new, opposed forms of religious and ethnic identity which took their salience from the escalating scale of 'communal' conflict. Quite the opposite was experienced by the *harijan* of south India where marked cultural continuity with respect to caste identity occurred. Continuity has occurred despite the introduction of Christianity during the colonial period and attempts of the independent national state to create new 'ideoscapes' of social welfare and equity. In effect, new economic, social and religious identities were realigned to conform to the seemingly more enduring caste identities of concern in village and regional politics.

Colonialism imposed on the people of Kalauna in the southern Massim area of Papua New Guinea required them to fundamentally rethink the question of who they were and how and in what manner they should express their relationship to significant Others. The banning of cannibalism and its substitution by competitive food exchange allowed existing agonistic social relations between traditional enemies to remain unchallenged. The Kalauna people's all-consuming passion about identity remained even as the form of social exchange altered, a situation in marked contrast to relations between adjacent ethnic groups in East New Britain where new forms of social identity, based in part on cargo cults, arose. The salience of this new Pomio-Baining identity, itself an amalgam of diverse smaller groups, was defined by their historical subordination to the dominant Tolai, a group

37

largely unaware of their neighbours. Tolai disdain of the Pomio-Baining appears to have fanned the flames of indignation and resentment, and the case study illustrates the importance of this new form of solidarity forged before and during colonialism, and its displacement on to contemporary national politics and international development planning.

2 CONSTRUCTING IDENTITIES IN NINETEENTH-CENTURY COLOMBO

R.L. Stirrat

In *Ethos and Identity*, Epstein criticises certain earlier writers on ethnicity for viewing ethnic groups as cultural groups, and argues that 'a preoccupation with "custom" or "culture" leads to a blindness to social structural forms' (Epstein 1978: 92). Similarly, he argues that writers who have seen ethnic groups as a particular sort of interest group are also wrong, for whilst ethnic groups may have interests, to define these groups in terms of interests is 'to confuse an aspect of the phenomenon with the phenomenon itself' (1978: 96). Rather, argues Epstein, in the context of rapid social change, for instance in the Zambian Copperbelt or amongst immigrant Americans, we have to focus on questions which concern the ways in which 'ethnic identity is generated and transmitted, how it persists and how it is transformed or disappears, yielding to other forms of identity' (Epstein 1978: 96). Furthermore, ethnic identity is more than simply a social category. 'Because identity touches the core of the self, it is also likely to be bound by powerful affect ... The more inclusive the identity ... the deeper its unconscious roots and the more potentially profound the charge of affects' (1978: 101).

In this chapter what I want to do is explore a little further the relationship between 'identity' and 'culture' and the manner in which both 'touch the core of the self'. As with Epstein's work, the context is one of rapid social change, but here the focus is on a situation where identity is defined in terms of religion rather than ethnicity. In the previous paragraph I quoted Epstein's distrust of an approach to ethnic identity (and presumably identity more generally) which saw it simply in terms of contrasts between cultural groups. Yet there are ways of conceptualising culture which bring it much more into line with his approach to identity and which allow for culture and identity to be seen as two sides of the same coin. For Epstein's stress on the generation and transmission of identity, the processes which give rise to certain forms of identity becoming dominant at different times and in different places, is very similar to the ways in which Wolf and others conceptualise culture. For Wolf, 'a culture is ... better seen as a series of processes that construct, reconstruct and dismantle cultural materials' (Wolf 1982: 387).

This chapter focuses on one particular incident. On Easter Sunday, 1883, there was a riot involving Buddhists and Catholics in Kotahena, a suburb of north Colombo. By present-day Sri Lankan standards the level of violence was low and injuries few. Yet at the time the riot was seen as being of major importance and it marked the beginning of a series of violent clashes between groups defined in terms of religious identity which were to last for the next 40 years.

The data on which this chapter is based come from a book entitled, *Kotahena Riot 1883: A Religious Riot in Sri Lanka*, edited by G.P.V. Somaratne (Somaratne 1991).[1] Included in this fascinating volume is not only the report of the Commission of Inquiry appointed by the colonial government but also other relevant documents including official reports, copies of the correspondence between officials, and between officials and Buddhist and Catholic representatives, newspaper reports of the time and transcripts from the judicial inquiries. The volume concludes with Somaratne's own analysis of the events on which, in part, the argument of this chapter is based.

Within the confines of this short chapter it is impossible to do justice to the wealth of material collated by Somaratne. What emerges is an engrossing picture of life in Colombo in the late nineteenth century: a world of rumour and gossip; of condescending prejudice and casual racism; of administrative incompetence and official cover-ups. Rather, this chapter will concentrate somewhat narrowly on ways in which competing identities were generated and expressed, the symbols on which these identities centred, and the ways in which these identities 'touch the core of the self'. One of the themes which will emerge is the way in which the identities which were mobilised during this riot were constructed not just of local elements but as part of a global process, and that what in itself was a relatively minor and local event has to be understood as a moment in the complex processes involved in the European expansion and the spread of colonialism, not just British colonialism but also its predecessors. A list of those involved in one way or another in the riot displays its cosmopolitan nature. Although this chapter focuses on two groups, Catholics and Buddhists, many others were involved: Italian and French Catholic missionaries, British Protestant missionaries, American anti-Christian Theosophists, Protestant British and Sri Lankan administrators, European and Sri Lankan policemen of all ranks, and even an Irish Catholic regiment. Yet each of these groups has to be viewed not as an autonomous entity but rather as elements whose identities and self-images depended on their continual interaction with each other.

THE BACKGROUND

Under British colonial rule, the unification of the island, the growth of communications and most importantly the development of commercial estates led to a rapid transformation in the Sri Lankan economy. During the latter part of the nineteenth century the fastest growing town in Sri Lanka was the capital, Colombo. As well as being the administrative centre of the country, Colombo increasingly dominated foreign trade, and its growth attracted immigrants from all over Sri Lanka as well as from other parts of South Asia. As it grew, the city changed in character. Whilst Sri Lanka as a whole was predominantly Buddhist, Colombo in the early nineteenth century was dominated by non–Buddhists, mostly Muslims and Catholics. Although increasing numbers of Buddhists moved into Colombo, as late as 1881 the census reported that there were still only 25,379 Buddhists in the city compared with 27,518 Muslims and 28,638 Christians.

There had been a Catholic presence in Colombo since the days of the Portuguese who first came to Sri Lanka in the sixteenth century. During the Portuguese period, Catholics were a favoured group and the Church gained many converts although the majority were Catholic only in name. Despite periods of persecution under the Dutch a significant minority of the population along the west coast including the north Colombo area remained devout Catholics. By the late eighteenth century the Dutch authorities were allowing Catholics to practise their religion. Thus the church (later cathedral) of St Lucia in Kotahena, which will figure largely in what follows, is first mentioned in Oratorian documents in 1762. Dutch records mention a land grant of ten acres to the Church in 1779 on which a church was built (or rebuilt) in 1782, a few years before the British took over the Maritime Provinces of the island.

During the nineteenth century, the Catholic population of Colombo was concentrated in its northern suburbs. In Kotahena, over 50 per cent of the population was Catholic. Although there was a sizeable number of middle-class Catholics employed by government or in the private sector, the majority were relatively poor. Many were fishermen based in the Mutwal area; others worked in the markets, particularly the fish market, whilst still others were employed as carters, porters and labourers. In terms of caste and ethnicity, the Catholics of Colombo were highly mixed. Most Catholics were Sinhala-speakers, but there was a substantial number of Tamil Catholics, many of Indian origin, as well as people who claimed to be Sinhala yet spoke Tamil as their first language.

Under the British, missionaries were freely allowed to enter the country and Catholics were again allowed complete freedom of worship. The early missionaries were mainly Oratorians from Goa, but after the 1830s increasing numbers of European missionaries became active in Sri Lanka. Although not averse to converting non-Catholics and non-Christians, the missionaries concentrated on regularising the religious activities of the laity. Not surprisingly, the style of religiosity they encouraged was based on current European ideas of correct Catholicism. Thus particular stress was placed on the role of Christ and the importance of the Virgin Mary. Various styles of devotion were encouraged as well as cults, feasts in honour of the saints, pilgrimages and processions. To attain their goals, the missionaries created an extremely well organised parish system through which priests were able to exercise a good deal of control over the lives of the laity. The message of nineteenth-century European Catholicism was spread through schools, through preaching and pamphlets, through enforcing attendance at mass and the major feasts of the liturgical year.

Besides attempting to create a particular style of religiosity, the missionaries also encouraged Sri Lankan Catholics to think of themselves as separate from, and superior to, adherents of other religions in Sri Lanka. The result was a remarkably self-confident and at times arrogant group of co-religionists that defined itself in terms of its religious affiliation. Yet at the same time, Catholics saw themselves as a potentially endangered minority which had to protect what it perceived as its rights.

On the one hand, the government was dominated by Protestants. On the other, Catholics were increasingly aware of the numerically superior Buddhists who were becoming more and more self-assured in the mid to late nineteenth century.

The second half of the nineteenth century saw a rapid resurgence in the confidence of Buddhists in Sri Lanka. Although the 'Buddhist revival' can be traced back to the eighteenth century, from the 1850s onwards there was a growth in what has since been called 'Protestant Buddhism' (Bond 1992; Malalgoda 1976; Gombrich and Obeyesekere 1988; Obeyesekere 1975). Amongst other things this involved an attempt to 'cleanse' Buddhism and Buddhist practice from 'accretions', the active involvement of the Buddhist laity in forms of religious practice which were previously the monks' domain, and the establishment of new *nikaya*, orders of monks, who upheld this sort of approach to Buddhism.

Much of this revival was centred in the southwest of Sri Lanka, particularly along the coast south of Colombo. In this area, members of various castes who had traditionally been viewed as relatively low in the status hierarchy took advantage of the new commercial opportunities created by British rule. 'Protestant Buddhism' proved particularly attractive to this rising bourgeoisie not only because of its style of religiosity but also because it provided a focus around which their claims to status could be advanced (Roberts 1982). As their wealth and power increased, Low Country groups came into conflict with members of the Goyigama caste, traditionally the dominant caste in the island. One arena in which this conflict was worked out was through the sponsorship of Buddhist institutions and festivals as well as through the creation of new *nikaya* in opposition to the Goyigama–controlled *Siam Nikaya* which dominated the interior of the island (Wickremeratne 1969: 136).

If on the one hand the Buddhist revival of the nineteenth century was the result of endogenous forces, at the same time it was also a reaction to Christian missionary activities. Protestant missionaries, having a much smaller base than their Catholic counterparts on which to build, were much more active in their attempts to convert non–Christians, and their evangelical efforts encouraged a Buddhist reaction. Yet at the same time, the Buddhist revival freely borrowed from and used the techniques of the missionaries such as the establishment of various organisations to promote Buddhism, the use of the printing press, a renewed interest in the Buddhist texts and the development of a Christian-influenced style of sermons and debate. Much of the character of 'Protestant Buddhism' was based on Western formulations of what was 'true Buddhism'. The ensuing conflict involved pamphlet wars and a celebrated series of public debates, the most famous being the one held in Panadura in 1873. This attracted the notice of Theosophists in Europe and America. The American Theosophist Colonel Olcott arrived in Sri Lanka in 1880 and became a central figure in espousing the interests of Sri Lankan Buddhists with government. Not only did he provide new organisational skills but also gave physical evidence of Europeans opposed to the teachings of the Christian Churches.[2]

As the Buddhist population in Colombo grew, temples began to be built. It appears that as late as the 1830s there were no Buddhist temples in the city, the nearest being the ancient temple of Kelaniya a few miles away. In 1830, however, Buddhists bought a plot of land for a temple in Kotahena, about two furlongs from the Catholic cathedral. On this site a temple known as the *Dipaduttama Vihara* was constructed by a monk called Sinigama Dehirakande Terunnanse who belonged to the *Amarapura Nikaya*, one of the new *nikaya* founded by groups from the southwest of Sri Lanka. This monk died in 1842 but in 1858 the temple came under the control of his sister's son, Mohottiwatte Gunananda, also known as Migettuwatte Gunananda Thera, who was to become a central figure in the Kotahena riot.

Gunananda was born in 1823 and like his mother's brother came from southern Sri Lanka. He had been originally ordained when only 12 years old, but had left the robes, came under the influence of a Protestant catechist, and attended school in Kalutara where he learnt some English and the basics of Christianity. After school he moved to Colombo where he worked for a newspaper, the strongly pro-Christian *Observer*, but after his mother's death he was reordained by his mother's brother. Rather than receive higher ordination, he remained a *samanera*, a novice, for the rest of his life.

For the period, the trajectory followed by Gunananda is archetypical involving a movement from the relatively homogeneous Buddhist-dominated south to the heterogeneous world of Colombo. Not surprisingly, Gunananda became active in the Buddhist revival. He was the main Buddhist spokesman at all the Panadura debates as well as being active as a pamphleteer against the Christian missions. In 1849 he was instrumental in setting up the *Bodhirajah Samitiya*, a society to protect Bo trees, and in 1862 he helped found the *Sarvajna Sasanabhivurdhidayaka Dharma Samaga*, a society to propagate Buddhism (Somaratne 1991: 397). During the Panadura debates he was the major speaker for the Buddhists and afterwards became associated with Colonel Olcott, although the relationship was somewhat uneasy. That he was involved in such activities marks him off from the more traditional monks, particularly those of the *Siam Nikaya*, but besides the world of religion, he was also active in the secular world. He was engaged in business as a trader and a money lender, and was seen by many as attempting to accumulate a fortune (Somaratne 1991: 400).[3]

Although the British authorities in Sri Lanka were predominantly Protestant, and although they were under continual pressure from Evangelical Christian groups in England, this was a period when the government was relatively sympathetic to Buddhists. Governor Longden recognised the dominant role which Buddhists played in Sri Lanka and was reportedly on good terms with Gunananda. In part this was a recognition that although 'Protestant Buddhists' may have been opposed to Christian missionary efforts, they were not anti-British per se. Thus in many temples, including Gunananda's own, a royal coat of arms was displayed above the statue of the Buddha invoking the traditional image of royal protection for Buddhism.

THE LEAD-UP TO THE RIOT

By 1883, tension was rising between Buddhists and Christians throughout Sri Lanka, but particularly in Colombo. Here, a number of factors were important. Given its administrative and economic importance, increasing numbers of Buddhists were drawn into the city. The presence of Gunananda was a further factor. Rumours were current amongst the Catholics that he had stamped on a Bible, and his declamatory sermons at Kotahena *vihara*, coupled with equally aggressive sermons from Catholic missionaries, raised tension amongst both the Buddhist and Catholic laity. Finally, government actions which could be interpreted as supportive of Buddhism – the attitude of the governor and his support for the return of certain relics from India – only increased tension amongst both Catholics and Protestants.

In Kotahena, the new *vihara* was improved and enlarged during the 1870s and 1880s. Although there was another *vihara* in Kotahena under the control of the *Siam Nikaya*, the *Dipaduttama vihara* was by far the most popular. When festivals were held, Buddhists came from all over the island as well as from the villages around Colombo in what were described as boisterous and elaborate processions (Somaratne 1991: 118). In theory, all processions had to receive permission from government, and usually these permits banned the use of drums when the processions were passing religious buildings (Roberts 1990). It seems that the ban on drumming was frequently ignored and rumours circulated in Colombo that Queen Victoria had given Gunananda an open permit to have what processions he liked in whatever manner he chose.

In the early 1880s a new statue of Buddha was constructed at Kotahena, and in January 1883 Gunananda announced that an eye-setting ceremony was to be held at the *vihara* on 12 February.[4] However, there was a minor smallpox epidemic in north Colombo, and so the government asked that the ceremony be delayed. Gunananda agreed to the authorities' request that no processions be held until after 31 March, but later the priest considered that this delay had been engineered by the Catholics, and so he continued to hold processions (with, it seems, government permission) which would reach their climax on 31 March, an auspicious day. To this ceremony a vast number of priests, 500 in all, was to be invited. It was planned that they would read 500 sections of the *Tripitaka* and receive 500 *atapirikara*. Furthermore, it was planned that leading up to this grand ritual, *pirit* would be chanted and *bana* read each night starting on 8 February.[5] It just so happened that 8 February 1883 was Ash Wednesday, the start of Lent, and that the Buddhist festivities would reach their height at Easter itself. As we shall see later, it is unclear as to whether the timing of the ceremonies at Kotahena were being driven by the Christian or the Buddhist calendar.

Already, there was confusion on the part of the government authorities: whilst the civil authorities had asked for the festivities to be delayed owing to the smallpox epidemic, the police were still granting permits for processions. This confusion became worse over the Easter period. In early March, the Catholic authorities as usual made applications to hold processions on Palm Sunday, Good Friday and Easter Sunday, but owing to administrative failures, these licences were not immediately issued. However, a licence was granted for a Buddhist procession to be held on Palm Sunday.

On Palm Sunday, 18 March, a Buddhist procession to the *vihara* at Kotahena took place. The route took it near St Lucia's, and as it passed the turning to the cathedral it was attacked by a group of Catholics and a statue in the procession was stoned by some boys. But the police were present and kept the crowd in order, although much to the Buddhists' chagrin, none of the stone throwers was punished.

The next stage was for the Buddhists to apply for licences for processions on 23 March (Good Friday), 24 March and 25 March (Easter Sunday). All of these were turned down by the authorities 'out of respect for Catholic feeling' (Report, para 13). This led the Buddhists to reapply for permission to have a procession on 25 March, arguing that they had forgone two days owing to government regulations, and that the 'moon was right' on 25 March despite full moon falling on 23 March. On the evening of 18 March the police decided to consult the Catholic Bishop. He agreed not to oppose any procession held after midday on Easter Sunday.

This did not satisfy the Buddhists. On 20 March there was a further application for a Buddhist procession to be held on 23 March, Good Friday. This was at first refused, but when the police were told that 'the proposed *perahera* [procession] would be a very quiet one, consisting merely of women carrying flowers, unaccompanied by music and that it would take a route which would not bring it near the cathedral' (Report, para 14) they acceded to the request. However, the permit was issued without a ban on music, and on the grounds that music might offend the Catholics, the civil authorities revoked the permit on the evening of Thursday 22 March.

Revoking the permit, whilst it did stop the procession, was too late to prevent a rise in tension. To quote the official Report on the riots:

the Buddhists appear to have been so elated at obtaining their licence, notwith-standing the opposition of the Roman Catholics, that they openly taunted the latter by sending them anonymous letters, three of which – all much to the same effect – have come into our hands. The following is a translation of one of them: 'You fools! You tried to stop our wedding procession on the funeral day of that God of yours! You couldn't do it! We will come in with the procession on Friday – stop it if you can.' (Report, para 15)[6]

On Good Friday, it appears that most Roman Catholics still believed the Buddhist procession was to take place, and a crowd of Catholics gathered at St Anthony's church, Kochchikade, on what was thought to be the processional route.[7] They announced that they would stop any procession which attempted to pass. The crowd dispersed once they had been assured by the police that there would be no procession but they reformed later. Although there was no trouble, Buddhists were once more annoyed that the police had made no effort to charge people.

THE RIOT

Given the preceding events, it is not surprising that trouble was expected on Easter Sunday. Yet just as police incompetence had made things worse in the days leading up to Easter, so their actions on Easter Sunday exacerbated the situation.

The Buddhist procession consisted of two groups, one starting at Borella, the other at Kollupitiya. They met at Maradana, about two miles from the temple at Kotahena. Before it left Maradana the procession was inspected by the police, led by Inspector Holland, himself a Catholic, to make sure that it did not include anything which might offend the Catholics as had happened on Palm Sunday. Nothing was found. However, accompanying the procession was a group of between 20 and 25 men dressed as 'soldiers' and carrying sticks. These men were disarmed. The procession itself consisted of a series of floats pulled by bullocks accompanied by groups of men, women and children. The whole procession set off for Kotahena at 1.30 p.m. escorted by a force of two inspectors and twelve policemen.

In Kotahena all was quiet after the Easter morning service. Then just before 1.00 p.m. according to the Commission's Report, or around 1.15 p.m. according to one police sergeant (Somaratne 1991: 283):

the neighbourhood was alarmed by the sudden and violent ringing of the cathedral bell, followed at once by the ringing of bells in all the Roman Catholic churches in the neighbourhood, and without delay, as if at a preconcerted signal, large bodies of men already armed with clubs, and marked on the forehead and back with white crosses, began to assemble at St Lucia's corner. (Report, para 20)

The police at Kotahena attempted to disperse the crowd of Catholics, but as they were heavily outnumbered they failed. Meanwhile the Buddhist procession kept advancing towards Kotahena. Rumours spread amongst the Buddhists that a monk had been assaulted, and there was a rush to grab weapons from a timber yard on the processional route. The police made a final attempt to disperse the Catholic crowd, but this also failed. On the same spot that the trouble had taken place on Palm Sunday the two crowds clashed. The aim of the Catholics was to disrupt the procession and destroy the images in the carts. In this they succeeded. As well as destroying the carts and the images, five bullocks were killed. During a lull in the fighting the Assistant Inspector of Police managed to persuade a few of the Catholics to accompany him to the cathedral, and there the priests persuaded at least some of the Catholics to disperse. Perhaps more importantly, it started raining and the fighting died down. The police had summoned troops, but the Royal Dublin Fusiliers arrived after the fighting had ceased. The Buddhists withdrew and by 5.00 p.m. there was general peace in the area except for a little fighting and stone throwing around the Buddhist temple.

Not surprisingly, tension remained high. On Easter Monday in Kotahena, a Catholic priest was assaulted by a group of Buddhists, whilst two processions were reported approaching Colombo and aiming for Kotahena. The army was called in by the civilian authorities to keep these processions under control.

The first of these, from a village about 12 miles south of Colombo, was unarmed and included women and children. After discussions with the authorities the Buddhist monk who was leading it attempted to persuade the participants to return home. However, 'some Colombo roughs ... became violent' (Report, para 25) and the military had to stop the procession.

The second procession which started from Peliyagoda, a village to the north of Colombo, was rather different.

[T]he persons composing it were armed with clubs, swords, and other weapons, about a dozen men being dressed as soldiers in uniform, and armed with muskets, which were afterwards found to be loaded. (Report, para 26)

However, when the military called on them to lay down their arms they did, and the procession ended peacefully without entering Colombo.

Although tension remained high for some time after the event, there was no more violence in Colombo although there were some minor incidents elsewhere. Instead there was a series of inquiries, hearings at the coroner's court, newspaper articles and so on all concerned with either trying to discover the 'truth' about what had happened, apportion blame for the events, or cover up administrative and other failures.

DISCUSSION

Processions were a common feature of religious life in nineteenth-century Sri Lanka amongst both Catholics and Buddhists. By the middle of the century, the potential that such processions had to be the occasion of conflict was recognised by the British and a series of regulations was drawn up. In these regulations particular attention as paid to activities which might cause offence to religious groups, most notably the use of 'tom toms' when passing the religious buildings of other religions.[8] From then on, in theory at least, permits had to be obtained before processions could take place. The failure of the authorities to implement these regulations was in part responsible for the riot in 1883.

In some respects, processions played a similar role in both the Catholic and the Buddhist communities. They were a means by which claims to status and power and displays of material success could be made by individuals and groups. At a collective level, processions were means through which identity could be claimed, affirmed and strengthened.

Thus at Kotahena, each individual procession was sponsored by one or two prominent Buddhists, and of course was a source of status for the individuals involved. Furthermore, the series of processions to Kotahena temple in the early months of 1883 was a deliberate effort orchestrated by Gunananda to display and mark the status not just of his *vihara* but also of the Buddhist community in Colombo. They were a particularly visible part of the process by which Buddhists saw themselves as reclaiming the city for so long under the domination of non-Buddhists. In this sense, then, it could be argued that the clash at Kotahena, like many other clashes in the late nineteenth and early twentieth centuries, was concerned with Buddhists expanding their 'sacred space' (see Rogers 1987: 181).

Certainly this was an element in the events of 1883. Kotahena was after all a Catholic stronghold, and the series of processions into the temple from the environs of Colombo were a manifestation of Buddhist revitalisation. But this is not the whole story. There had been processions to the Buddhist temple at Kotahena for many years prior to the riot, and even in 1883 during the weeks before Holy Week there were no attacks by the Catholics on the processions which went to the temple. Whilst space was important other factors were also crucial.

The first of these was time. Originally, it seems that Gunananda had planned to complete the ceremonies at the temple before Easter. It was only because of the outbreak of smallpox that the rituals were delayed at the request of the civil authorities. However, it appears that he later interpreted the request to delay the celebrations as a Catholic ploy and so deliberately moved the eye-setting ceremony forward from the previously agreed date of 31 March. Given his experience of Christians and the long period he had been resident in Kotahena, he must have been aware that this would lead to a temporal clash with the Easter rituals at the cathedral. Whether or not the timing of the Buddhist processions was a calculated act to provoke the Catholics is impossible to ascertain. Certainly the Catholics thought so, and the Buddhist attempt to hold a procession on Good Friday which would pass so close to important Catholic churches was seen as a deliberate affront.[9] But Buddhists claimed that there was no such deliberate planning, and Governor Longden agreed with them. After all, if it had not been for the ban on processions owing to the fear of smallpox, all the processions would have been over long before Easter. At the same time, it may be significant that the climax of the Buddhist rituals was not held, as might be expected, on a full moon Poya day which would have cut down the possibilities of a clash between the two groups.

No matter whether or not Gunananda deliberately attempted to time the rituals to coincide with Easter, the result was certain to offend the Catholics. Now it was not just a matter of processions past the cathedral to the temple, but rather of celebratory processions at the most solemn time in the Catholic calendar. And this is what the Catholics took exception to, not Buddhist processions in themselves.

If the timing of the processions was seen by the Catholics as a deliberate affront, a much more serious insult took the form of the images carried, or rather, reportedly carried in the processions. Here we enter a world of rumour and accusation basically concerning two images, one which could be interpreted as a parody of the Virgin Mary; another which parodied Christ on the Cross.

The first of these was an image which the Buddhists claimed was Mahabamba. According to the Buddhists, this was simply an image of Brahma, and was carried in the procession 'to amuse the public', although it should be added that presumably this figure was a parody of the statues carried in Hindu processions. But according to the Catholics, this image was a parody of the Virgin Mary. To quote the *Examiner*, a paper which supported the Catholics:

Among other things [the procession on Palm Sunday] contained the huge figure of a female dressed in blue and, to a Catholic mind, suggestive of the Virgin Mary. According to authentic evidence, both Catholic and non-Catholic, the procession halted for a moment near the turn to the Catholic Cathedral, and the female figure was slightly turned to it in mockery, while the people cried *sadhu*. With regard to this it is answered that the figure was *Mahabamba* – one of the characters in Buddhist legends. But it is to be noted that *Mahabamba* was a *male*, not *female*. That was the beginning of the arousal of Catholic feeling. (Somaratne 1991: 118, emphasis in original)

Another description, this time from Inspector Gunerame,[10] who was a Protestant, is slightly different:

The figure was from 15 to 20 ft. high with a man's head, skirts with a kimono like that of a woman's. The Dress I think green or blue, I cannot say which but there was a great (mustache) of red in it. The head was movable. The figure was carried by men and halted several times to rest the bearers. I did not see anything unseemly pass, but heard afterwards that the R.C. had taken offence at the figure halting in front of the Cathedral on its way to the temple. (Somaratne 1991: 256)

A third description is different again, this time from Inspector Marshall who was in charge of the police force detailed to accompany the Palm Sunday procession:

The body was white with blue sleeves and the skirts an ordinary sarong red white and black. The head was not movable. (Somaratne 1991: 260)

Finally, a description from a Catholic called Sampayo who saw the procession from his verandah is different again:

It appeared like a female figure with a veil and a gown and dressed in green. The face I believe had a beard but the figure was certainly a female figure, calculated as I thought to represent the Virgin Mary. The figure had not a sarong cloth: it had a green dress and a veil not covering the face but hanging down the back. (Somaratne 1991: 299)

Whatever this image actually looked like, it is clear that the Catholics took exception to it, and that by carrying it in their procession on Palm

Sunday the Buddhists were seen as mocking the Catholics. Clearly the image was ambiguous: it could be interpreted as the Virgin Mary or it could be interpreted as Mahabamba. And even it was not meant as an insult to the Catholics, they interpreted it as such, and the reaction of some Catholic spectators on Palm Sunday was to use violence.

But Mahabamba was only part of the story, and on Easter Sunday the statue was not carried in the procession. In the procession certainly was a series of floats: a huge cobra, a bungalow, a bird. On this all agree, and according to the Buddhists they were there to entertain the crowd. Much more serious were the rumours which spread amongst the Catholics that included amongst the images carried in the procession were some which parodied Christ. According to the *Observer*, the procession included:

two images of the Lord Jesus Christ, one representing the crucifixion, and the other of his burial. These images were carried in a sort of pagoda which was fixed on a bullock cart. (Somaratne 1991: 131)

The *Observer* (26 March 1883) claimed that on Easter Sunday dead monkeys tied to crosses were carried in the Buddhist procession:

Most respectable witnesses are prepared to swear that they saw it in Borella, before the procession came to Maradana police station, and there is equally indubitable testimony, that it was with the procession in Skinner's Road, and it was seen just before the fight. (Somaratne 1991: 131)

However, what is striking is that besides these reports, there is very little evidence that anyone did see monkeys nailed to crosses and even the *Catholic Messenger* admitted at the time the Commission of Inquiry published its Report that there was no proof of such images. Rather, what stands out is the way that rumours of the presence of such images swept through the Catholic community in north Colombo on Easter Sunday 1883, and how these led to the attack on the Buddhist procession.

During the riot, most of the violence of the Catholic crowd was directed towards the images and the carts in which the images might be secreted. The reports of eye witnesses describe how the carts were attacked and destroyed. Thus a carter called Don Cornelis, who gave evidence at one of the judicial inquiries held after the riot, described in great detail the attack on his cart and his bulls which were involved in the procession, but fails to mention any attacks on people. The aim of most Catholics was to destroy what they believed to be blasphemous parodies of the core symbols of their religion, not to attack or kill Buddhists themselves. Otherwise one might expect a much higher death toll than the one Buddhist who was killed.

We do not know whether there were images of Christ in the Buddhist procession. Even so, it is clear that the Buddhists, or at least some of them, knew enough about the Catholic religion to fix on symbols – the Virgin Mary and Christ – and times – Easter – which were particularly powerful for Catholics, and thus guaranteed to produce a strong reaction in the Catholic community. Rumours of images which parodied the Virgin Mary and Christ struck at the heart of Catholic teaching, dogma and identity.

'TOUCHING THE CORE OF THE SELF'

One of the features of the events at Easter 1883 was the importance of rumour. Reading the documents collected by Somaratne, the overriding impression is of groups of people easily swayed by stories of attacks and tales of provocation. Given the climate of suspicion on both sides, particularly amongst Catholics, the smallest incident or the most minor rumour appears to have been sufficient for crowds to form on the street and arms to be taken up.

This air of mutual suspicion appears to have been closely related to the manner in which religion had become, by the late nineteenth century, a crucial component of personal identity amongst large sections of the population in the coastal provinces of Sri Lanka. The ways in which this developed amongst the Buddhists have been traced by writers such as Obeyesekere (1975, 1979) and Malalgoda (1976). Both argue that it was a response to colonial rule on the one hand and traditionally dominant Sri Lankan groups on the other, and that a sense of Buddhist identity was most strongly developed amongst rising mercantile groups who took advantage of the new economic opportunities created by colonial rule. Primarily, the Buddhist revival promised such groups a sense of self-respect and self-worth as heirs to a great and historical tradition of Buddhism. Furthermore, the form that this religious revival took was one which stressed 'respectability' and order. As Obeyesekere has pointed out, much of the content of the revival took the form of an adoption of Victorian bourgeois values, and in such a context violence was to be abhorred. Thus almost all the descriptions of the Buddhist processions in 1883 stress their non-violent nature and the presence of sizeable numbers of women and children. Whilst the Buddhists may have wished to assert their moral and religious superiority over the Catholics, it does not seem that physical violence was on the agenda until after the events at Kotahena on Easter Sunday. Indeed, the style of Buddhism espoused by the revivalists, ruled out violence as an option for a 'good Buddhist'.

The situation amongst the Catholics was rather different. Here, from at least Palm Sunday, violence was on the agenda. Crowds gathered ready for physical combat. It is clear that preparations to attack the procession were in place on the morning of Easter Sunday. Weapons – clubs, sticks, stones, fish gaffes, swordfish teeth – were amassed at the junction near the cathedral. Women are notably absent from the descriptions of the Catholic crowds, and the men were marked with white crosses in preparation for what was expected to be a physical clash.[11]

That the Catholics were willing and prepared to attack the Buddhists does not necessarily mean that their religion 'touched the core of the self' to a greater degree than was the case amongst the Buddhists. Rather, it should be interpreted as a difference in the way in which religious identity was constructed amongst the Catholics, and perhaps also it says something about the social composition of Catholics in north Colombo at that time.

Conversions to Catholicism in Sri Lanka were from the beginning strongly concentrated amongst relatively marginal groups of people along the western coast. Many of these appear to have been relatively recent immigrants from south India, and were never fully integrated into the structures of Sri Lankan society (Roberts 1980). This process of immigration was still continuing in the late nineteenth century and Catholicism offered, amongst other things, a solid identity in an otherwise unstable world. This was particularly marked in north Colombo where most Catholics were part of a highly unstable world of daily paid labour, small-scale activities in the fish market, petty street trading and so on. This indeed is the picture which emerges of those involved in the riots whose occupations are mentioned in the documents. Within such a world, the only solid and continuing identity was allegiance to the Catholic Church, and any attack on the Church and its teachings, whether it took the form of violence or, as in this case, trespass on what Catholics considered their time and their space, was a threat to the Catholic self.

Yet perhaps most important of all was the form that Catholicism took. The missionaries of the nineteenth century stressed devotion and faith. To be a true Catholic was to practise an unquestioning faith in the Church and its teachings. Central to this were various cults surrounding images of holy beings: Christ, the Virgin Mary, the saints. Given the strength of devotion and allegiance to the Church, almost any image carried by the Buddhists could have been interpreted as a parody of such central symbols of Catholic identity. In effect the Buddhists had gained the moral high ground, and there was little that the majority of Catholics could do except respond violently. What non-Catholics saw as unthinking zealotry was to the Catholics only a manifestation of their faith and an expression of their commitment to their religion. For them there was no alternative but violence, a physical manifestation of their personal identity.

Here it is worth mentioning that other Christians did not react in the same way to the Buddhist celebrations in 1883. An Anglican church, St James, was even closer to the Buddhist temple than was the Catholic cathedral. Although Anglicans did complain that the noise disturbed their devotions, there was no attempt at a violent reaction. In part this can be seen as linked to the small numbers of Anglicans in Kotahena, but it was also linked to the social origins of Anglicans – a more middle-class constituency than the Catholics – and much less stress on devotion in the Anglican tradition than in the Catholic Church.

Yet Buddhist and Catholic identities were not the only identities at stake in the context of the 1883 riot. If one can talk of 'causes' and 'responsibility' for the riot, a central role has to be given to the colonial authorities. In a sense, the proximate cause of the riot was administrative confusion over the granting of permits for processions, and a failure to effectively police the procession on Easter Sunday. Certainly, as Somaratne points out, the press at the time put much of the blame on the administration in general and the Governor in particular (Somaratne 1991: 412–13). Somaratne goes on to argue that the Commission of Inquiry was 'economical with the truth'; that its primary goal was to shift responsibility for the riot on to the Catholics and away from the civil authorities, and that in doing so it downplayed the responsibility of the Buddhists.

Even if Somaratne is perhaps too sympathetic to the Catholics, there is evidence to support his analysis. The Commission of Inquiry consisted of three men: Saunders, the Government Agent in charge of the Western province which included Colombo; Duncan, the officer commanding the Royal Dublin Fusiliers; and de Saram, the District Judge of Kurunegala. All three were government employees with certain interests to defend – the first two were involved in the events surrounding the riot – and all three were Protestants. Whilst Saunders and Duncan were British, Somaratne reports that de Saram was a Eurasian. Given the need not to further alienate the majority Buddhists who were already outraged in what they interpreted as a failure to deal with the rioters, it is not surprising that the Report was relatively uncritical of the Buddhist involvement.[12] Furthermore, in their Report there was a general tendency to downplay reports of Buddhist actions and stress the Catholics' resort to violence.[13] Whilst there were criticisms of the administration, these were relatively minor.

Looked at from a different point of view, the treatment of the colonial administration by the Commission of Inquiry was more than just a whitewash but also an attempt at restoring the self-confidence and self-image of the European administration. The riot threatened that sense of superiority and unfailing competence essential to the identity of any colonial regime. What the Report did was to assist in the reconstruction of a sense of identity of the colonial administration formed around an unquestioned ability to rule. It was all the fault of the Catholic hierarchy who had failed in their mission.

The reaction of the Catholic hierarchy to the criticisms contained in the Report and to later correspondence with the police authorities was, not surprisingly, somewhat mixed. Whether or not they had been involved in organising the attack on the procession, they were forced to identify themselves to some extent with their co-religionists and defend their actions as the result of gross provocation. Yet at the same time they implicitly accepted one of the interpretations of the riot which became popular after the event: that it was fomented by 'men of the lowest rank who deliberately assembled and inflamed with drink attacked an inoffensive crowd' (Somaratne 1991: 352). In the end both missionary and colonialist could continue in their role of civilising agent whose task it was to transform the nature of the 'lower orders'. That set of binary oppositions – order versus disorder, civilisation versus savagery, control versus chaos, knowledge versus ignorance – which were crucial to the identity of both colonialists and missionaries was reinforced.

But the contrast between the layman on the streets outside the cathedral defending what he saw as his rights through violence, and the priests and bishops engaged in exchanges of more or less polite letters with the Inspector General of Police, highlights one very important aspect of the nature of identity in Sri Lanka in the late nineteenth century. Although the riot was and is presented as a clash between Catholics and Buddhists, not all Catholics in Colombo were involved nor were all Buddhists. Within each community there was a broad spectrum of opinion, belief and practice, and by no means all Catholics in Kotahena were involved in the riots. The behaviour of those Catholics who were involved in the riot may have helped to generate stereotypes amongst the Buddhists (and also Protestants) of the ignorant and uncivilised nature of Catholics, but at the same time for the Catholic bourgeoisie it reinforced their sense of superiority over the lumpen masses of north Colombo.

CONCLUSION

In her article discussing violent clashes between Catholics and Protestants in sixteenth-century France, Natalie Davis discusses the various forms of violence employed by the two groups. One of the suggestive themes which emerges in her work is the way in which Protestants engaged in iconoclasm in response to what they saw as the 'wrongful use of material objects' (Davis 1987: 174). In nineteenth-century Sri Lanka the situation is clearly very different. In Kotahena the Buddhists made no attempt to physically destroy Catholic images. Instead they turned them into objects of ridicule. And whilst in early modern Europe the Catholic reaction was to turn to violence against the putative destroyers of their sacred objects, in nineteenth-century Sri Lanka the violence was primarily directed towards destroying the parodies of their sacred objects.

It would, of course, be going much too far to see the clashes between Catholics and Buddhists in Sri Lanka during the late nineteenth and early twentieth centuries as simply a reworking of the religious wars of Europe, or the Buddhists who took part in the processions at Easter 1883 as being the dupes of Protestant missionaries. Yet there is a sense in which sixteenth-century Europe and nineteenth-century Sri Lanka are related.

The most obvious is the way in which images were of crucial importance for Catholics in both sixteenth-century France and nineteenth-century Sri Lanka. As far as the Catholics of Colombo were concerned, it was around these images of Christ and the Virgin Mary that their identity was crystallised. These images set Catholics apart from other groups in Sri Lanka and were core symbols of what it meant to be Catholic. By parodying these symbols, particularly at Easter, Buddhists were attacking what was central to being Catholic. By making fun of images of Christ and the Virgin Mary the Buddhists were also making fun of the Catholics and thus threatening the Catholics' idea of selfhood.

The Catholic core symbols were only too clearly of European origin and the identity which Catholics were defending was in large measure the result of the work of non-Sri Lankan missionaries. Yet even the Buddhists were heirs to a European tradition, although in a rather more complex manner. The competition between Protestant and Catholic missionaries was a continuation of the struggle in Europe which had begun with the Reformation. Protestant attacks on Buddhism intersected with both the pre-existing Buddhist revival and the attempts by groups from southern Sri Lanka to assert their own identity in response to other Buddhist groups in the country as well as against the missionaries. The result was that a particular form of Buddhism became a central element in their attempts to create their own identity out of both a Buddhist past and European (including Christian) influences.

As Rogers (1987) remarks, the Catholics at Kotahena gained only a Pyrrhic victory. The 1883 riot in Kotahena was only the first of a series of violent clashes between Catholics and Buddhists which lasted for the next 40 years. As the Buddhists gained ground, so there were more clashes which involved space and time and the claims to 'respect' which each group demanded from the other. But as Epstein points out, identities are transformed or disappear, yielding to other forms of identity. In the twentieth century, the Buddhist revival became more and more closely associated with the nascent nationalist movement, itself in part a response to a new set of global forces. Over time, identities constructed in terms of 'race' and 'nation' became more important and Buddhism became one element in these new forms of conceptualising identity (Nissan and Stirrat 1990). Furthermore, such were the strengths of these new ways of constructing identities that a century after the Kotahena riot, Catholics had ceased to be a unified group. Just as Sri Lankan Catholics were the heirs to one phase of Western influence introducing one way of conceptualising identity, so they became the victims of another moment in the spread of Western categories of thought. This is another story (see Stirrat 1998).

NOTES

1. Secondary sources on the riot include Dep (1969), Rogers (1987) and Tambiah (1996) whilst additional information is available in Roberts (1990) and Stirrat (1992).
2. Colonel Olcott is perhaps best known for his 'Buddhist Catechism', modelled on Christian catechisms, as well as being the originator of the Buddhist flag. After the 1883 riot he was centrally involved in putting pressure on the British authorities to further the interests of the Buddhists and visited London on behalf of the Buddhist Defence Committee (Sumathipala 1969–70).
3. One of the sub-plots in the events surrounding the riot concerns a loan made by Gunananda to Inspector Gunerame, the officer in charge of the police station in Kotahena. After the riot Gunananda, irked by what he saw as official favouritism towards the Catholics, implied that Gunerame had hinted that the loan should be treated as a bribe to ensure support for the Buddhists. (He also claimed to have evidence that bribes had been offered by the Catholics.) Later he withdrew this accusation. Whatever the truth of the matter (and the whole incident becomes more complicated as Gunananda's niece was married to Gunerame's nephew), Gunerame was demoted after the riot.
4. A description of this ritual is given in Gombrich (1966).
5. The *Tripitaka* consist of the Pali canon, and the *atapirikara* are the eight requisites of monks. *Pirit* consists of ceremonial chanting of certain texts from the Pali canon, whilst *bana* are sermons.
6. The texts of two other letters ostensibly written by Buddhists and sent to Catholics is given in Somaratne (1991: 267): 'Fool on the funeral day of your God is our wedding, our *perahera* is coming. Stop it if you can', and, 'Fools, you tried to stop our wedding on

account of your funeral but you failed. We are coming by the Kochchikade church. Stop it if you can.' However, these were given by a Catholic witness before the Commission of Inquiry, and allowance has to be made for the possibility that these were manufactured to support the Catholic position before the Commission.

7. St Anthony's church, Kochchikade, was and still is one of the most popular churches in Colombo. It was visited by the Pope during his 1995 visit to Sri Lanka.

8. Roberts (1990) deals with these regulations at some length.

9. Elsewhere in Sri Lanka there were other clashes on Easter Sunday between Catholics and Buddhists in Ratnapura, Balangoda and Galle. This further fuelled Catholic suspicions that there was deliberate Buddhist provocation. It was rumoured that a student of Gunananda organised the Buddhists in Ratnapura.

10. See note 3 above.

11. Another fascinating item in Somaratne's collection is the statement of a Buddhist who became involved with the Catholic crowd prior to the riots and, at the behest of a Catholic friend, was painted with a cross on his forehead.

12. Surprisingly, there were no convictions in relation to the riot despite both criminal and civil proceedings. It appears that the accused were discharged on advice from the Queen's Advocates' Department.

13. There is also the curious case of Kutch Appu. The Commission's report mentions only one death in the context of the riot – Juan Naide, a Buddhist. Intriguingly he was killed before the riot started. There is no mention of the death of the Catholic, Kutch Appu, who also appears to have been killed during the riot. At one point Inspector Gunerame was accused of killing him.

REFERENCES

Bond, G.D. 1992. *The Buddhist Revival in Sri Lanka*. Delhi: Motilal Banridass.

Davis, N.Z. 1987. *Society and Culture in Early Modern France*. Cambridge: Polity Press.

Dep, A.C. 1969. *A History of the Ceylon Police* (1866–1913), Volume 2. Colombo.

Epstein, A.L. 1978. *Ethos and Identity: Three Studies in Ethnicity*. London: Tavistock.

Gombrich, R. 1966. 'The consecration of a Buddhist image', *Journal of Asian Studies* 26: 23–36.

Gombrich, R. and G. Obeyesekere. 1988. *BuddhismTransformed*. Princeton, NJ: Princeton University Press.

Malalgoda, K. 1976. *Buddhism in Sinhalese Society, 1750–1900*. Berkeley and Los Angeles: University of California Press.

Nissan, E. and R.L. Stirrat. 1990. 'The generation of communal identities', in J. Spencer (ed.) *Sri Lanka: History and Roots of Conflict*. London: Routledge.

Obeyesekere, G. 1975. 'Sinhala–Buddhist identity in Ceylon', in George de Vos and Lola Ross (eds) *Ethnic Identity: Cultural Continuities and Change*. Palo Alto, CA: Mayfield Publishing Company.

—— 1979. 'The vicissitudes of the Sinhala–Buddhist identity through time and change', in M. Roberts (ed.) *Collective Identities, Nationalisms and Protest in Modern Sri Lanka*. Colombo: Marga.

Roberts, M. 1980. 'From southern India to Lanka: the traffic in commodities, bodies and myths from the thirteenth century onwards', *South Asia* 4: 36–47.

—— 1982. *Caste Conflict and Elite Formation*. Cambridge: Cambridge University Press.

—— 1990. 'Noise as cultural struggle: tom–tom beating, the British, and communal disturbances in Sri Lanka', in Veena Das (ed.), *Mirrors of Violence*. Delhi: Oxford University Press.

Rogers, J.D. 1987. *Crime, Justice and Society in Colonial Sri Lanka*. London: Curzon Press.

Somaratne. G.P.V. 1991. *Kotahena Riot. 1883*. Colombo: no publisher.

Stirrat, R.L. 1984. 'The riots and the Roman Catholic Church in historical perspective', in J. Manor (ed.) *Sri Lanka in Change and Crisis*. London: Croom Helm.

—— 1992. *Power and Religiosity in a Post-Colonial Setting*. Cambridge: Cambridge University Press.

—— 1998. 'Catholic identity and global forces in Sri Lanka', in Tessa Bartholomeusz and Chandra R. de Silva (eds) *Buddhist Fundamentalism and Minority Identities in Sri Lanka*. Albany: State University of New York Press.

Sumathipala, K.H.M. 1969–70. 'The Kotahena riots and their repercussions', *Ceylon Historical Journal* 19: 65–81.

Tambiah, S.J. 1996. *Levelling Crowds: Ethnonationalist Conflicts and Collective Violence in South Asia*. Berkeley and Los Angeles: University of California Press.

Wickremeratne, L.A. 1969. 'Religion, nationalism and social change in Ceylon, 1865–1885'. *Journal of the Royal Asiatic Society* (Ceylon Branch) 56: 123–50.

Wolf, E. 1982. *Europe and the People without History*. Berkeley and Los Angeles: University of California Press.

3 RESPONDING TO SUBORDINATION: THE POLITICS OF IDENTITY CHANGE AMONG SOUTH INDIAN UNTOUCHABLE CASTES

David Mosse

This chapter focuses on social groups which are ascribed an inferior social identity, namely India's lowest or Untouchable castes (also labelled *Harijans* 'children of God', the Scheduled Castes or *Dalits* 'the oppressed or broken'),[1] and examines the social responses to these negative identities. In public and academic discourse Untouchable caste groups in India are increasingly attributed distinct nation-wide political identities, for example as Dalits. In colonial times, Untouchables also gained new identities, often religious ones as Christians (and Muslims and later Buddhists). However, the acquisition and use of new and emancipatory social and political identities is often constrained by local relations of power. Indeed, more universally valid social and political identities stand in contrast to caste identities defined by local hierarchical social relations. This chapter examines various ways in which low-caste groups manipulate existing and new identities as a means to acquire new political and symbolic resources. In other words, it examines the local politics of identity change.

Drawing on village-level evidence from the southern state of Tamil Nadu, the chapter addresses a number of questions. First, what defines the social inferiority of Untouchables? Here (in the next section) I examine the cultural construction of subordinate social identities and the idioms through which inferiority is expressed and reproduced. I will also look at differentiation within the broad category of Untouchables, and at the separate Untouchable caste identities which exist in one village. The second question is, what are the *self*-identities of Untouchable castes and do they significantly revise or redefine collective ascriptions of their identity? Third, what are the social and political responses to ascriptions of inferiority? I will examine the way in which identities have been abandoned, changed or renegotiated in one village, and the political and symbolic resources employed.

The third section of the chapter examines the importance of new religious identities, and specifically conversion to Christianity among Untouchable groups in colonial south India. Today, Christian identity in Tamil Nadu is not a substitute for caste; rather it provides a distinctive religious identity superimposed on, but largely secondary to, the social order of caste. However, Christian identity has, at key moments, provided new symbolic resources which have changed the way in which different Untouchable castes operate within the local caste system. It has provided opportunities for assertions of rank or autonomy, and for the renegotiation of social relations and meanings. In often complex ways, Untouchables have both drawn on alternative religious identities *and* manipulated the very institutions and symbols which conventionally define their inferiority in order to assert new status, independence and respect.

Untouchable identity is not, however, pliable at will. Since, as will be shown, it is inextricably bound to service and dependency, the ability to acquire and sustain alternative identities, or to redefine the meaning of symbols of inferiority, depends crucially upon having the power and resources to change existing relations of dependence. In short, identity change is caste politics. A central theme, then, is the interplay of power and identity.

Alternative identities for Untouchables have been generated and adopted in historically specific contexts. Christian conversion, a central idiom of mobility in the late nineteenth and early twentieth centuries, lost its relevance in post–colonial Tamil Nadu. Other religious and political redefinitions of Untouchable identity also, have lost ground to the post–Independence bureaucratic emphasis on welfare categories rather than social identities. The fourth section of the chapter examines some examples of the articulation of identity among Untouchable castes in the context of increased targeted benefits from within and outside the state system. In Tamil Nadu, Untouchables have failed (even by comparison with some other states in India) to develop a unifying political identity. The final section indicates some of the wider obstacles to the generation of such overarching identities.

RELATIONAL IDENTITY AND THE CULTURAL
CONSTRUCTION OF SUBORDINATION

This section examines the transactional contexts which define inferiority
within caste society. The ethnographic setting is a multi-caste village
(Alapuram) in the dry eastern plains district of Ramnathapuram in Tamil
Nadu having a sizeable Untouchable caste population (654 in 1983).[2]
There are several different Untouchable castes within Alapuram (Pallar,
Paraiyar, Chakkiliyar, and so on), occupying different positions within
the social order. The relationship of all of these castes to 'upper' castes
and to each other is, however, articulated in a common language of
control and dependence, which will be considered first.

Untouchable castes in Alapuram, as more generally in Tamil Nadu,
have long been dependent labouring clients of higher castes. Historically,
this dependence has been based upon the possession of inferior rights
to primary resources: land and water. Today, for example, Untouchable
castes, if not landless, cultivate smaller and inferior land holdings
(often as share crop or land mortgage tenants); and their rights to water
from irrigation sources (such as tanks) are often circumscribed by
'shares' systems which give privileged access to dominant castes at times
of shortage (Mosse 1995, 1997b). Economic relations based on property
ensure the reproduction of social relations of dominance and
dependence. They do not, however, define the idioms of subordination,
the symbolic forms in which power (or its absence) is expressed and
the social identities which are generated. The cultural construction of
Untouchable subordination has considerable regional variations within
Tamil Nadu, let alone within India as a whole.[3] Among other things
these reflect different production systems and models of caste dominance
(Ludden 1985). In dry-zone Alapuram, for example, where the model
of caste dominance is royal and martial rather than priestly or
Brahmanical (as in wet-zone river valley villages) Untouchable status
is expressed more in idioms of feudal service than those of ritual
impurity. Nevertheless, historical and ethnographic evidence from
Alapuram helps highlight some elements of a more general discourse
of subordination.

Several specific transactional contexts define Untouchable social
identities in Alapuram. First, most (67 per cent) Untouchable households
were formerly party to hereditary relationships of service (*atimai*) and

mutual obligation with high-caste landowning households (*aiyavitu*, the lord's house), which can be recorded for at least three generations (Mosse 1986: 526ff., 1994a). The dependent client households are referred to as *kalampudikkira vitu*, literally, 'the house which takes from the threshing floor'. This refers to the collection of sweepings from the 'lord's' threshing floor after each day's harvest. This grain is not a wage, but a prestation which signifies the subordination of the Untouchable family, the patron's rights over their time and labour, and the client's right to patronage, subsistence and protection, as well as their obligation of service. These obligations include ritual services at life-crisis ceremonies – a second transactional context defining subordinate identities. Services include a range of roles which are culturally defined as polluting, for example, drumming at funerals, grave digging, the acceptance and removal of substances polluted by death – cooked food and the shroud of the corpse.

At life-crisis rituals (puberty, childbirth or death) popular Tamil culture conceptually and ritually distinguishes positive from negative elements – separating the auspiciousness, coolness, order and purity of valued social statuses, from the inauspiciousness, danger, heat, disorder and impurity of transition (Good 1991; Mosse 1997b). By assigning negative and inauspicious elements to Untouchables as low-status ritual servants (dealing with impurity and danger), this hierarchical opposition provides another idiom for social subordination, dependence and inferiority (Dumont 1980). Where Dumont's (1980) structuralist analysis of caste ideology is mistaken, however, is in taking the purity–impurity opposition (one idiom) as definitive of the whole system, and in assuming impurity to be the defining feature of untouchable identity, separable from the relations of power of which it is a sign (Dirks 1990). In other words, Untouchables in Alapuram are not 'low because their *tolil* [caste-specific occupation] associates them in a number of ways with the death of higher beings – of humans and cows [as removers of carcasses] in particular' (Moffatt 1979: 111). They perform these negative ritual roles *because* they are socially subordinate. This polluting work then contributes to their inferior social identity. Purity and power are inseparable.

This subordination is/was expressed in several further idioms, for example those of kinship, deferential terms of address, clothing, physical posture, restrictions on food exchange and so forth. For example, in fictive kin terms, the Pallar (untouchable caste) are the 'sons' of Carpenters, Necavar Paraiyars (another Untouchable caste) are 'nephews' of their Vellalar patrons. All Untouchable castes refer(red) to high castes as *cami* (lord) or *nacciyar* (mistress), *aiya* (grandfather) or *atta* (mother, father's mother) and with respectful second-person pronouns *irrespective of age* (Mosse 1986: 232–6; cf. Levinson 1982). Hierarchical transactions set up a series of separations, which excluded Untouchables from commensality, the use of common drinking water sources and so forth.

In Tamil villages, the subservience involved in individual relations with high-caste patrons was generalised, and defined a caste-wide public code of conduct for Untouchables. They were, for example, formerly forbidden to ride bicycles, wear sandals, or carry umbrellas in high-caste streets, were excluded from public places such as temples and teashops, and from honourable public roles such as being donors at temple or church festivals (Mosse 1997a). Further, members of Untouchable castes officially held certain menial *village* service roles: the *vettiyan* or Pallar caste woodcutter and grave digger; the *totti* or Paraiyar caste 'sweeper' and drummer; and the *pakatai* or Chakkiliyar caste leather worker. These public roles defined the identity of these particular castes in a more general and public sense, and affirmed their (low) status within the village as an ordered social hierarchy ordained by the king, or for the service of the village deity (cf. Hocart 1950). This was dramatically signified in the roles Untouchable castes played, and the prestations they received, at the annual village festivals. Here servitude and ritual impurity were combined in public assertions of caste identity and ceremonial rank.

Untouchables lack autonomous caste identities, that is identities apart from service. Dependence and service do not simply describe the social relations into which they, as social actors, enter. Dependence and service ideologically constitute Untouchable caste identity within village society. In the discourse of caste dominance and power, Untouchables personify dependence (Dirks 1990); their identity and their institutions are derivative of those they serve. The internal organisation of Untouchable castes (for example, lineage and clan groupings), their status and even the pattern of conflicts within Untouchable communities have all been extensions of the order of dominant groups (Dirks 1990: 274–5, 279). While various rights and honours define status for high castes and artisans, in themselves, or in relation to the overlord – the king or the deity (Hocart 1950) – Untouchable rights (to subsistence and so on) have only existed in relation to service rendered to patrons and to the wider village. Untouchables are the objects of ordering principles of others, they are 'far from the ordered centre' (Dirks 1987) and associated, symbolically, with the dangerous forces of disorder (Deliège 1992: 279; Pfaffenberger 1982: 58–9). Indeed, disorder, danger and impurity are, at the general level of Indian cultural semantics, idioms of subordination, just as control and order are idioms of dominance (Dirks 1987). Finally (and this is an important insight from Dumont), the identities of Untouchable and high castes are structurally related; the inferiority of dependent Untouchable castes itself contributes to the status, honour and ultimately the identity of upper-caste patrons (Dumont 1980; McGilvray 1983; Pocock 1962). Untouchable social identities are 'relational', then, in the sense that they are defined and reproduced by relations of dependence and subordination. For this reason, as evidence from Alapuram testifies, autonomous definitions of identity and independent institutions among Untouchables have been strongly and violently proscribed by upper castes.

The status of the various named Untouchable castes in Alapuram (Pallar, Paraiyar, Chakkiliyar and so on) is differentiated (a) in terms of the type and range of services they offered (and offer), and (b) the status of the castes to whom they offered these services (Mosse 1986). The least economically dependent group are the Pallars, whose public roles were those of grain measurer (*kutumpan*), tank sluice operator (*nirpaccai*), and grave digger (*vettiyan*). Service relations (*atimai*) existed exclusively with dominant upper-caste households and were later abandoned to Paraiyars. Paraiyars had (and still have) fewer assets and a greater degree of dependence and obligation. There are two Paraiyar sub-castes – Necavar (weavers) and Totti Paraiyars. Only the latter held the public office (*totti*) and only they provide specialist 'impure' ritual services such as drumming, horn blowing, funeral services (announcing death, wailing, carrying burning pots), and the removal of dead cattle. Paraiyars rank below Pallars. Their greater subordination brings into play a wider range of polluting and servile ritual actions, and they offer services to lower-status groups (washermen, toddy tappers). Two further Untouchable castes in the village, the Potera Vannar (Untouchable washerman) and the Chakkiliyar (cobbler) occupy the lowest social positions on account of their position as servants to Untouchables (in fact to a Pallar Untouchable elite). Chakkiliyar are the 'children of Pallars'. They have the highest degree of dependence on menial labour, inferior ritual service and free hand-outs.

If Untouchable caste identity is collectively defined and publicly articulated in terms of subordinate inferiority, to what extent do their self-images comply with these definitions? Here, it is necessary to separate (a) the question of Untouchable consensus with (or counter-cultural rejection of) a given model or idiom of dominance and subordination, from (b) the question of Untouchable castes' response to *their* own subordination. The first question is the subject of separate discussion (Mosse 1994a). Briefly, evidence from Alapuram suggests that there is indeed a broad consensus with the dominant cultural idioms of subordination and inferiority. However (to address the second question), agreement that certain actions signify social inferiority does not, of course, imply acceptance of positions of inferiority by those who occupy them, or preclude active struggle to escape or redefine such positions. This is the issue addressed here.

There is not space to describe the nuances of identity and responses to subordination among the different Untouchable castes, expressed in anecdote, proverb or caste myths of origin (Mosse 1986: 237–64). But some conclusions from the review of such material are the following. First, all Untouchable castes account for their particular inferior social position in terms of poverty and humanly instituted and enforced servitude (rather than inherent impurity, karma and suchlike). Second, their subordination is viewed as undeserved, resulting either from misfortune, migration and historical accident, or (more commonly) from the treachery, robbery, witchcraft and illicit gains of the better-placed groups who exploited the Untouchables' qualities of generosity and honesty to deprive them of their inheritance. Third, as the caste myths of origin make plain, the Untouchables (or rather particular castes) are suffering under mistaken identities. Their true and original identities, from which they have fallen, are, respectively, warrior rulers (Pallars, see below), Brahmans (Totti Paraiyars) and high-caste weavers (Necavar Paraiyars).

Fourth, Untouchable castes ascribe an inherent and deserved inferiority to those below them in the hierarchy. While those in superior social positions are cheats and frauds, and they themselves have fallen from greatness into forced servitude, inferiority inheres in those of lower social status and is manifest in impure work and habits. Even more than upper castes, Untouchables derive status and identity from not being quite at the bottom, and from the negative identities which they do *not* share with those below them. This elaboration of status discrimination at the bottom of the hierarchy is explored in detail elsewhere (Mosse 1986). For example, the status and identity of both Paraiyar sub-castes (Necavar and Totti) in the village are defined by the same relations of dependency and service. Nonetheless, Necavars, who do not perform lowering *tolils* (cattle scavenging, funeral service, drumming), emphasise their own Hindu orthodoxy and purity and the impurity of the Totti *tolil*. Interestingly, Alapuram Totti Paraiyar origin myths (Mosse 1986: 243–6) concede the inferiority (if not the impurity) of tasks such as cattle scavenging, funeral service or drumming. The myths also link the loss of Paraiyars' original Brahman status to the ultra-sinful and impure acts of killing of a cow and the eating of beef. But, as the story makes clear, there was a misconstrual of intent – bad actions were done with good intentions – and therefore the fall from status was undeserved. Paraiyars deny that their caste is inherently qualified to perform inferior roles and account for their doing so in terms of bad luck, trickery and the enforcement of village authorities. As will be explained later, today Totti Paraiyar self-images are tied up with their Christian identity.

There is one final point in relation to the cultural definition of Untouchable 'lowness'. These cultural constructions are not to be taken as representing some timeless tradition. Ideologies of caste are historically as well as regionally specific. There are grounds for believing that Untouchable castes in Tamil Nadu were incorporated into hierarchical dependency relations to an unprecedented degree as a result of changes effected by the consolidation of colonial power in the nineteenth century. These had a generally negative impact on the livelihoods of Untouchable labour. Washbrook, for example, argues that British policy 'centred on the progressive destruction of labour's independence and rights and share in the social product' (1993: 84). It made labour's grain share rights unenforceable, reduced alternative employment, enforced movement of labour back on to the land and drove down labour prices. Finally, and correspondingly, a Brahmanisation of caste ideology under British rule (Dirks 1987) helped to construct the identity of Untouchables as ritually impure.

INDEPENDENT IDENTITIES: CHRISTIAN CONVERSION AND SOCIAL MOBILITY

If Untouchable identity is culturally defined in negative relational terms (that is, as dependence, subordination), it is not surprising to find that Untouchable emancipatory and self-respect movements articulate non-relationally defined identities – identities not defined primarily in relation to service to high castes – and forms of action which go beyond the 'moral community' of the village, with its implication of hierarchy and subordination. The movements defining such autonomous identities for Untouchable castes in India are large in number and diversity (Mosse 1982). At their most radical and all-embracing they assert the historical, cultural and religious independence of the Untouchable castes from the dominant Hindu caste culture. There is, in fact, an influential argument that Untouchables have always been marginal to the dominant hierarchical values of caste society, and that they adhere to a pervasive egalitarian counter-cultural tradition (Miller 1966; Lele 1980; Nemade 1980). It is suggested that this egalitarian antithesis is manifest in recurring anti-caste movements, prominent among which are the early *bhakti* (monotheistic devotional) religious movements which stressed equality and social reform.

I have already suggested that there is much ethnographic evidence to dispute the notion that Untouchables are adherents to a separate egalitarian subaltern culture (Moffatt 1979). Correspondingly, there is little to support the notion of an historically and geographically pervasive counter-culture. Some of the arguments on devotional *bhakti* cults, for example, inadequately distinguish the historical context of these religious movements from their contemporary political significance, and that of their saint heroes who have become the symbolic focus for more recent political mobilisation. As far as the Tamil country is concerned, the *bhakti* tradition can be shown to have originated as an elitist (Brahman/Vellalar) synthesis, popularised, not because the equality it preached found mass grassroots support from low castes, but because it was adopted by rulers, and became institutionalised as an avenue for new forms of non-Brahman status mobility (Hardy 1983; Stein 1968; Appadurai 1977, 1981: 63–104).

Without denying the liberating role of the *bhakti* tradition (Lele 1980) or the existence of localised anti-caste protest in the Tamil country, it is probably true to say that only in nineteenth-century British Madras, and in large measure as the (unintended) result of Protestant missionary activity did movements redefining Untouchable social identity arise across the state.

CHRISTIAN MISSIONS AND UNTOUCHABLE CONVERSION MOVEMENTS IN COLONIAL INDIA

By the 1850s Protestant missions in India had reached a broad consensus that caste was a *religious* institution, and therefore fundamentally incompatible with the Christian gospel. As the conclusion to an inquiry by the Bishop of Madras, in 1845, put it, 'the distinctions [of caste] are unquestionably religious distinctions, originating in, and maintained by, the operation of Hindu idolatry' (cited in Forrester 1980: 39). Conversion required the utter rejection of caste identity and practice.[4] This position and the strong church prohibition on retaining caste-based exclusions reduced, and then reversed, the small trickle of individual high-caste converts. But it also marked the start of mass conversion movements among south Indian Untouchables.[5] Between 1851 and 1871 the number of Christians in the Madras Presidency increased from 74,000 to 300,000 largely as a result of group conversions from Untouchable castes (Richter 1908: 201). Low-caste conversions continued until Independence such that of the 11 million Christians given in the 1961 census over 62 per cent were Untouchables from the southern states.[6]

These largely rural 'movements' not only involved conversion on a large scale, but also conversion by *groups* of Untouchables rather than by individuals. They were often started by the conversion of individual Untouchable leaders, then spread first to the economically more independent sections of the community – those with assets (land, cattle), wider contacts (traders) and independence from high-caste sanctions – but then on to the more dependent sections. Typically, conversion was the result of a collective decision made, for example, through caste *panchayats* (councils). Once initiated conversions spread through kinship and marriage ties rather than direct evangelism. Conversion also moved across caste lines (between different Untouchable castes), although often where one caste converted to one Protestant denomination, its local status rival converted to an alternative mission in the area. Conversion movements, however, only rarely spread 'upward' to non-Untouchable castes.[7] Significantly, group conversion by Untouchables was not something Protestant missionaries either expected or intended. On the contrary, a process of 'downward percolation' of Christianity from individual and high-caste converts was widely assumed. 'Mass movements', in fact, often began in areas where missionaries were *not* active, and this new form of conversion prompted revision of missionary strategy (towards low castes). Mass conversions were, in short, caste-based social movements in which Untouchables redefined their religious identity and sought new patrons. There are several factors which might have prompted such identity change in the second half of the nineteenth century.

Conversions occurred at a time when socio-economic changes under colonial rule were particularly detrimental to Untouchable castes. While retaining low social status, these groups had lost certain compensatory rights and securities, becoming dependent on the market for the sale of their labour power to an unprecedented degree (Washbrook 1993, Oddie 1979: 128ff., Hjejle 1967: 116–18, Gough 1960).[8] At times of famine this generated acute need. But equally, there were new freedoms – from personal bonds and traditional obligations – to discover alternative patrons who could provide a new status, self-respect and an alternative religious idiom in which to express this.[9] Contrary to popular belief, relief and welfare do not appear to have played a major role in conversions. Many conversions occurred in the absence of material benefits (Clough 1914: 279), before or after rather than during famines (Fernandes 1981: 279), and conversion frequently did not lead to any improvement in economic or social status, but rather the loss of security through imposed sanctions, increased social ostracism of converts and supra-village organised high-caste resistance to further conversion. Rather, as Forrester puts it conversion movements were 'a kind of group identity crisis in which the group passes through a negative rejection of their lowly place in Hindu society to a positive affirmation of a new social and religious identity', an identity, specifically which does not depend on its acceptance and recognition by higher castes (1980: 77). The following sections return to Alapuram, where 74 per cent of the Untouchables are Christian converts, to examine the social significance of Christian identity in two Untouchable castes, Protestant Paraiyars and Catholic Pallars.

ASPIRATIONS OF AUTONOMY: PROTESTANT CHRISTIAN IDENTITY AMONG PARAIYARS

Totti Paraiyars (23 households in 1983) were group converts of the American Mission in Madurai and Ramnad in the 1940s. They provide a concrete example where Christianity has provided Untouchables with a new identity, independent of the service relations with high castes which earlier defined the group's inferior social position. Christianity not only provided Paraiyars with a new 'autonomous' (non-hierarchically defined) identity – symbolised in their own place and rituals of worship – but also generated an alternative self-respect social model. As argued elsewhere (Mosse 1994a: 86–9), for Totti Paraiyars, Christian identity implies a set of aspired-to relations of social independence and respect. In particular, the shift from Hindu to Christian identity symbolises and anticipates a move away from a set of actions, relations and prestations described loosely as *acinkam* – 'degrading, uncivilised, unclean' which include cattle scavenging, beef eating, *parai* drumming, funeral service, receiving threshing floor sweepings, extreme deference to patrons, and towards a contrasting set, described as *nakariyam* – 'civilised, polite, urbane' (Fabricius 1972: 595). This latter set includes contractual relations and cash payment for services, high-status ritual roles (playing prestigious temple drums and pipes (*melam, nakucuvaram*), respectful terms of address and so on). The *nakariyam/acinkam* distinction brings together the notions of purity and power which Dumont's analysis separated. It describes a contrast between, on the one hand, relationally defined actions and identities indicative of dependence and servitude (*atimai*), and, on the other, independent and autonomous identities. For Paraiyars, Protestant Christianity is *nakariyam*. In their own eyes, conversion brought an end to beef eating, uncleanliness and impurity, it marked a changed self-image and was, at the same time, a concrete statement of the aspiration for a change in status and identity.

While few Christian Paraiyars in Alapuram have the power to make this model a reality, its possibilities were established in the context of backing from pre-Independence American missionaries. These missionaries supported Alapuram Paraiyars in certain moves for independence from high-caste patrons and the abandonment of some of the practices symbolic of subordination. Initially missionary support focused on those traditional service roles and behaviours which they disapproved of on moral/religious grounds: village scavenging and eating carrion, drumming at Hindu temples, the denial to Paraiyar women of the right to cover their breasts in the presence of high-caste men (cf. Oddie 1975: 74; Fishman 1941: 12–14; Hardgrave 1968). Protestant missionary standards of Christian life required certain changes – status-enhancing in relational terms and therefore threatening to high-caste patrons – for which missionaries were prepared to intervene on Paraiyars' behalf. In fact, the nature of missionary social action expanded after the late nineteenth century as changes in theology and social attitudes resulted in a more world-affirming, socially oriented conception of Christianity prepared to engage in action for social change on behalf of Untouchable castes both locally and through campaigns, literature, the courts and the mobilisation of public opinion in Europe and America (Oddie 1979; Gladstone 1976).

While missionary intervention helped to define an independent identity as a set of social *possibilities* for Paraiyars, there were limits to its impact locally. Conversion itself produced very little sustainable social change among Alapuram Paraiyars. As with the vast majority of mass movement converts, they have remained low-status labouring clients and village servants.[10] The patronage of missionaries and the better access to police, courts and government which it implied effected a temporary shift in the local balance of power which allowed assertion of a new autonomous identity. However, with the post-Independence departure of foreign Protestant missionaries from Ramnad – a district which was in any case remote from the centres of Protestant mission and the schools, jobs and institutional support they provided (cf. Hardgrave 1969; Frykenberg 1976) – Christian Paraiyars in Alapuram were rapidly forced back into old service roles which had temporarily been abandoned. Christianity has not enabled Paraiyars to escape an inferior caste identity. Ironically, Protestant Christianity, represented only in the poorest Untouchable caste sections of Ramnad villages, has as elsewhere itself become an identifying marker of Paraiyar caste identity (cf. Wiebe 1970b: 300; Diehl 1965: 16).

Even though Christian identity has provided neither a radical challenge to the caste system, nor the basis for supra-village mobilisation among Paraiyars, it has generated self-respect and a world view which is consistent with and justifies an everyday renegotiation of subordination and the meanings attached to service roles among those excluded from more radical means of status mobility. Alapuram Christian Paraiyars have, in fact, gradually withdrawn from ignominious roles, or, where this is not possible or affordable, redefined these in ways which increase their sense of dignity, self-respect and autonomy. These moves, made possible through greater economic security (for example, migration incomes invested in land) have been described elsewhere (Mosse 1994a: 86–90). In brief, they involve first, restricting the degree of obligation both by abandoning generalised public service roles (for example, as village *tottis*), by restricting services to a few key patrons, and by accepting a reduced form of patronage – for example, claiming less than their full entitlement to hand-outs (for example, threshing floor sweepings). Second, where possible, Paraiyars negotiate status-neutral (*atimai illamai*, 'without servitude') contractual arrangements for performing traditional services such as drumming or funeral services, and insist on remunerative cash payment and gifts in kind of the sort given to high-status ritualists (raw food, betel, cloth) rather than hand-outs indicative of dependence and subordination. Significantly, in this context 'inferior' service roles have ceased to be polluting, and Christian Paraiyars have successfully renegotiated the meaning of key cultural components of their identity. Today, there is a highly complex pattern of Paraiyar dependence and service, less and less reflective of caste-wide identity and more determined by individual trade-offs between status and dignity and economic reward and security.[11] Underlying these individually negotiated service relations, however, there is a shared model of honourable service, of 'patronage which is not patronising' (Scott 1990: 197) and of respect for which Protestant Christian identity remains a key point of reference.

ASSERTIONS OF POWER: CATHOLIC PALLARS, CHURCH HONOURS AND MOBILITY

The majority (over 75 per cent) of the 83 Pallar households in Alapuram are Roman Catholic. Like the Protestant Paraiyars, Catholic Pallars found support from Jesuit missionary priests (resident in the village) during the twentieth century for their withdrawal from low-status dishonorific service roles (such as drumming and other services at Hindu temples, grave digging, service roles at funerals and festivals). They were also supported in challenging caste-based exclusions (such as, from drinking water sources in the village), prohibitions (on women covering their breasts in high-caste streets) and extreme forms of deference (for example, ritual prostrations at the feet of high-caste patrons). Indeed, among Roman Catholic Pallars these forms of protest began earlier (in the 1890s)[12] and were more successful than among Paraiyars.

Also, like the Protestants, the grounds on which Jesuit priests supported Pallars shifted from religious discipline (to ensure 'proper' Christian behaviour among converts) to social justice (Mosse 1994b: 96). These parallels are not coincidental. In fact, competition between the missions, and threats from Untouchable Church members to shift affiliation from one Church to another if appropriate interventions in disputes was not forthcoming, ensured some comparability in the support provided.[13]

These parallels notwithstanding, the social meaning of Christian identity for Alapuram's Roman Catholic and Protestant converts is by no means the same. Pallar mass conversions to Christianity occurred in pre-colonial Ramnad in the late seventeenth and eighteenth centuries in very different historical circumstances from the Untouchable conversions to Protestant missions in the nineteenth and twentieth centuries. Pallars in Ramnad were evangelised by Jesuit renouncer priests (*pantarawamis*) of the Madurai Mission whose converts were not required to abandon caste customs or adopt new cultural identities.[14] Where they converted along with their Maravar warrior-caste overlords, Pallars retained their status as a dependent service group (Mosse 1994b, 1996). Not only did the early Jesuit missionaries have no reason to challenge these caste relations, but also they had no political influence in the Ramnad kingdom with which they could have supported assertions of untouchable autonomy even if there had been any. In fact, there is much to suggest that the position of Untouchable labourers in the eighteenth century was far more favourable than in the late nineteenth century (Washbrook 1993).

The adoption of Christian identity at this time did not involve any aspiration to autonomy beyond caste relations. After all, both high and low castes joined the mission. Rather, converts placed themselves within an alternative (Catholic) religious and ceremonial system which articulated precisely the *same* relations of power and caste status.[15] However, unlike Hindu temples, this was a ritual system which did not exclude Untouchables by criteria of purity by birth. In fact, the Catholic Church and its festivals in Alapuram (an important local shrine) provided a hierarchy of statuses and ranked ritual roles within which Pallars in the nineteenth and twentieth centuries were able to stake claims to elevated caste status and honour. Thus, for most of the past 150 years, Catholic Pallars did not seek to deny an oppressive hierarchical order, but rather to advance their position within it. Through challenging exclusions, rearranging seating arrangements in the church, asserting the right to prestigious ritual roles (as donors at the festivals or recipients of church 'honours'), and by launching their own independent saint's festival, Catholic Pallars were able to use the Church's existing caste-based system of ceremonial privilege to assert a status commensurate with their growing economic power and independence (Mosse 1994a).

This is not to say that Christian identity was not important to redefining social position. First, Pallars were able to win support from the priests (who controlled the allocation of these ritual privileges) for their claim to equal honour and status with high castes, on the grounds that they should be treated equally *as worshipping Christians*. Second, unlike the Protestant mission patrons of Paraiyar Christians, the Catholic Madurai Mission could and did provide institutional support which helped initiate and sustain Pallar assertions of independence: access to education and to salaried employment locally (as teachers in Church schools from the 1920s) or opportunities further afield (jobs in the military, police or railways, migration to Burma and Ceylon). These factors go some way to explaining why the vast majority of Untouchable conversions in this area, and the most stable among them, have been to Roman Catholicism rather than Protestant Christianity, despite its retention of caste hierarchy.

Unlike Protestant Paraiyars, then, Catholic Pallars were able to make *positive* status claims within a widely acknowledged public system of ranking, not only asserting independence from inferior service relations, but laying claim to the signs and symbols of caste dominance. (Needless to say this was not achieved without strong and sustained high-caste resistance and often violent conflict over a period of more than 80 years; Mosse 1997a). Catholic Pallars did not abandon the symbols of caste rank and power, nor use Christianity to assert a separate and autonomous identity. Rather (and more ambitiously) they attempted to use these public signs of social hierarchy to have their caste honour and respect publicly recognised by high castes and so to shift from a position of subordination to one of dominance. However, defined in relational terms, enhanced status not only requires ritually marked equality with superior social groups, but also clearly defined superiority over inferior and dependent service groups. Arguably, this is precisely what an Alapuram Pallar elite achieved, gaining some measure of social standing and public status, first, by displacing markers of their own former inferior identity (such as grave digging) on to lower groups (Paraiyars), and second, by acquiring for themselves low-status dependent clients (Chakkiliyars and Harijan Vannars) who perform(ed) polluting tasks at their funerals and life-crisis rituals.[16]

The Protestant Paraiyar and Catholic Pallar cases do not exhaust all the forms of identity change and status striving within Alapuram. As indicated earlier, Hindu Necavar Paraiyars emphasise purity, Hindu orthodoxy and the establishment of independent cults in the village as idioms for their independence from the servile Untouchable identity (Mosse 1994a: 89–90). Significantly, while Catholic Pallars and Hindu Necavar Paraiyars have exploited opportunities for status gains within the system, emulating dominant (Catholic or Hindu) cultural norms. Totti Paraiyars, who are more intimately bound to inferior occupations, have fewer resources, greater dependency and therefore very limited opportunities for upward mobility, have chosen to adopt a quite separate religious identity. Chakkiliyars, at the very bottom of the hierarchy are the only group not to have attempted in any way to redefine subordinate and servile identity, but rather to have maximised the returns and security which such an identity can still offer. Finally, the different religious identities adopted by Alapuram Untouchables rejecting social inferiority are also responses to status competition between the different Untouchable castes themselves. Local configurations of Untouchable religious identity reflect local caste structures. Thus in nearby villages where their status rivals are Hindu, Necavar Paraiyars are Catholics; in all-Hindu villages, Totti Paraiyars may be Catholics, and so on. In the cases I know, religious identity is village-based (or patrilineal). Thus, Hindu Necavar Paraiyar daughters from Alapuram become Catholic when they marry into the nearby village where this is the sub-caste's religion.

POST-INDEPENDENCE: FROM SOCIAL IDENTITY TO WELFARE CATEGORY

In post-Independence Tamil Nadu there has been, on the one hand, a decline in the social mobilisation of Untouchables under alternative religious and political identities and, on the other, an increase in state benefits for 'ex-Untouchables'. Untouchability has become de-politicised and Untouchables identified with welfare and bureaucratic categories. This section explores some identities generated in this context.

After Independence the established Churches – Protestant and Roman Catholic – failed to generate new religious identities for Untouchables in Tamil Nadu. There was a marked decline in the growth of the Churches and some new disincentives to conversion: the Indian government took on a range of welfare and educational functions formerly undertaken by missions, Christian Untouchables were disqualified from privileged access to state benefits as Scheduled Castes;[17] and there was in general a 'nationalist' resistance to religious conversions and the activities of foreign missions (Wiebe 1970; Estborn 1961). The post-Independence Indian Protestant and Catholic Churches had anyway reoriented themselves away from the radical anti-caste, anti-Hindu evangelism of the colonial missions. Indian clergy (mostly from non-Untouchable castes) sought to free the Church from missionary paternalism and to develop a truly Indian form of Christian theology and organisation. There was an emphasis on Church consolidation rather than growth, and a more positive evaluation of Indian cultural traditions including caste (Mosse 1994b; Forrester 1980: ch. 7; Caplan 1980: 228). Only in more recent decades has the ecclesiastical leadership (Protestant and Catholic) taken a firmer stand against manifestations of caste within the Church. This is a matter both of caste in the organisation of Church worship and festivals (among Catholics, Mosse 1994b) and 'caste as an organising principle for political struggles within the [Protestant] church' (Caplan 1980: 228). In response to all-India directives, the Catholic priests in Alapuram have, in recent years, progressively dismantled the Church festival honours system and other ritual markers of caste status. In doing so they have both democratised Church institutions and removed the ceremonial system within which Catholic Pallars achieved and endorsed positive caste status and honour. However, persisting caste discrimination within the mainline Church has contributed to increasing numbers of Catholic Pallars in Alapuram joining Pentecostal sects in the area which emphasise a radical rejection of caste and all vestiges of priestly and episcopal rank and authority (Mosse 1994a, 1994b).

Several other radical anti-caste movements which began and contended with the nationalist movement in the first half of the twentieth century lost momentum after Independence. These were perhaps most fully expressed through the leadership of Dr B.R. Ambedkar, whose rejection of caste ideology and assertion of a new independent identity for Untouchables led him to convert to Buddhism in 1956 along with some millions of Maharashtrian Mahars and Lucknow Jatavs (Zelliot 1966; Ling 1980; Omvedt 1994). But Ambedkar's idea of a 'political Buddhism' with close alliance between new Buddhists and the Republican Party (an all-India Untouchable party founded in 1958) failed. While the figure of Ambedkar grew in importance as a national symbol of Untouchable caste honour, in political terms Harijans tended to be incorporated into regional electoral coalitions (Mendelsohn and Vicziany 1994: 67), and the Buddhist movement increasingly focused on a 'self-respect' identity and a new *religious* culture, unrelated to the wider political field (Ling 1980: 120–2, Miller 1967; Zelliot 1966: 207ff.). Indeed, the social experience of converted Buddhist communities finds a parallel with that of Protestant Christians in Tamil Nadu (ibid. Ling; Miller; and Zelliot).

The Buddhist movement was anyway of marginal influence in Tamil Nadu. Here, outside the Churches, the critique of caste took the form of a radical anti-Brahman movement. Under the leadership of E.V. Ramaswami ('Periyar'), the Dravida Kalagam (DK) movement in the 1920s and 1930s promoted an atheistic anti-caste movement which inverted sanskritic ideals, 'purified' the Tamil language of sanskritic elements, and challenged the elite position of Brahmans in Tamil society. In what was often perceived as a counter-nationalist movement, the DK identified Brahmans and Brahmanism rather than British colonial rule as the source of oppression of Tamils. Issues of untouchability had a symbolic and polemical significance: the DK took Untouchables into temples and employed Untouchable cooks at party meetings and conferences (M. Barnett 1976). However, as Barnett (1976) has skilfully demonstrated, the movement failed to generate liberating identities for Untouchables and, especially after Independence, progressively excluded this social category from its anti-caste egalitarianism. On the one hand, the early Dravidian movement was driven by the interests of a non-Brahman 'forward' elite who experienced a sense of *relative* deprivation vis-a-vis Brahmans under colonial administration (cf. Irschick 1969: 188). On the other hand, on entering electoral politics in the 1960s the movement (and its party the Dravida Munnetra Kalagam – the DMK) moved away from the agenda of social reform and focused on generating mass support in rural areas (through the use of popular drama and film; Hardgrave 1973) from 'backward' non-Brahmans. These castes, representing a new middle peasant elite, were precisely those locally dominant castes (such as the Maravars of Ramnad) who had most to lose from political gains by their Untouchable dependants and who offered strongest resistance to their social mobility.[18] Untouchables, who were always marginal to the women's programme of social reform, steadily lost political ground after the 1940s (M. Barnett 1976: 300).

In legal terms, Untouchables no longer exist in India, and most practices which define Untouchable social identity are now illegal. With the passing of anti-untouchability legislation, Untouchables potentially have the backing of the state in struggling against persisting social disabilities; and with state policies of 'compensatory discrimination' (job reservations for Scheduled Castes and targeted poverty alleviation programmes) considerable state resources are, in principle, available for their social advancement. Untouchables are now ascribed a legally and bureaucratically defined identity as 'Scheduled Castes'. This, rather than socio-religious or political identities, is articulated to secure state support and resources (where necessary, Christian Untouchables will adopt Hindu names to qualify for these state benefits). But, as Mendelsohn and Vicziany argue, the increase in bureaucratically administered state welfare for ex-Untouchables has gone along with a de-politicisation of untouchability and the conversion of a potentially radical social and political grouping into a bureaucratic and welfare category (1994: 64).

This contemporary situation presents two sorts of problems. The first is that while low-caste identities have been rejected or redefined in order to serve positive social and political ends, the state's positive discrimination policy means that 'the individual who seeks help in getting rid of his identity must proclaim it' (Isaacs 1965: 114) or 'a Harijan must assert that he is a Harijan if he is to mobilise the support necessary for his political advancement. And it is here that the demands of power and status come into conflict' (Béteille 1965: 27, cited in Rudolph and Rudolph 1967: 150). The second problem is that despite state support, the evidence strongly suggests that Untouchables have failed to lose their economic and social status as a subordinate people (Mendelsohn and Vicziany 1994). It is clear, for example, that in the absence of some external intervention on their behalf the sanctions of locally dominant castes, backed by their superior collective resources, have operated with more speed, force and certainty against Untouchable protest than has the law to support it. Untouchables still need external patrons willing to identify them as a political group. The final sections of this chapter address these issues: first, looking at how some Untouchables in rural Tamil Nadu have managed to articulate identities which allow them to claim and ensure access to state benefits – but with *dignity*; and, second, to examine new forms of patronage outside the state in rural Tamil Nadu and the identities and labels which these emphasise.

A CASTE MYTHOLOGY FOR MODERN TIMES: ALAPURAM PALLARS

From the late 1960s the Church and its festivals no longer provided the main context for Pallar mobilisation for social change in Alapuram. While the struggle for festival honours had brought an extended supra-local caste network into play, in 1969 this was used to organise a more direct protest against 'the oppression of untouchability', to break caste exclusions (such as entry to teashops) and to resist high-caste sanctions and reprisals (Mosse 1994a: 93–4). The protest demonstrated the efficacy of organised mass action in eliciting state support (police protection, intervention by the district authorities and by a state minister) for legally endorsed rights as 'Scheduled Castes' and 'citizens of India'. Even though other castes (Necavar and Totti Paraiyars) were only marginally involved, these identities gave Pallar stated interests a more universal validity by linking them to more general categories. These identities did not, however, express the distinctive identity and honour of the Pallar caste (as against other Untouchable castes) in the way that Catholic festival honours had. With the collapse of the Church honours system this required a new ideology for the validation of Pallar identity, one moreover that would go beyond the limited transactional context of the village.

This, Pallars (in particular the village youth) found in a state-wide caste association, the Teventira Kula Velalar Cankam, formed in 1983 specifically to petition government and promote the distinctive interests and political identity of Pallars. The discourse of the Cankam concerns the past. In particular, it claims for the Pallar caste an original and authentic supremacy as warrior kings (*muventar*) and original settlers of fertile river tracts (*velalar*). This claim is asserted and detailed through two 'historical' texts.[19] In this discourse contemporary struggles are represented as the recovery of a lost past and the reclamation of rights associated with an underlying superior social identity (cf. Cohn 1959: 207–8 and Lynch 1969: 70–4, 1972: 97–112). As with other reformist or 'sanskritising' Untouchable movements, the discourse is not anti-caste, and unlike other Dalit movements it is neither anti-Brahman nor anti-Hindu. Rather, the immediate source of oppression is located in the non-Brahman social groups presently wielding power within the Dravidian nationalist parties, and the locally dominant 'Backward Castes'. Moreover, wider Untouchable caste mobilisation is not encouraged. Indeed, the caste 'histories' serve to distance Pallars from other Untouchable castes who are implicitly identified with less cultured indigenous 'jungle tribes'.[20] The Cankam discourse provides a model of reality helping to resolve the contradiction of experienced change and mobility with the persisting fact of discrimination. However, its function as a model *for* reality, having dynamic and motivational power for change (Lynch 1972: 102) has been far more limited. The Cankam only generated local support briefly in 1984 during an ultimately unsuccessful campaign to place the new high school in the village under Pallar management (Mosse 1994a).

The Cankam does, however, express a view held by several Untouchable political leaders (including Dr Ambedkar), namely that a new and dignified identity is a pre-condition for the effective assertion of social and political rights. In the case of Pallars this identity enabled the caste to

stake a claim to a proportionate share of benefits under state compensatory discrimination for Scheduled Castes (vis-a-vis other Untouchable castes), without this being conceived either as recognition of lowness and inferiority or the receipt of charity, but as claiming back a small part of what is rightfully theirs. (Mosse 1994a: 96)

The Alapuram Pallar ability to mobilise support, organise direct action against social oppression and define new identity is unusual among Untouchable communities in Tamil Nadu. It resulted from an unusual degree of economic power, numerical strength, a widespread supra-village support network, strong leadership and, most importantly, 100 years of experience of organised action within the Catholic Church. For most Untouchables, external intervention of some sort remains necessary to challenge persisting dependencies and social subordination.

NEW PATRONS: NON-GOVERNMENTAL ORGANISATIONS AND UNTOUCHABLE 'DEVELOPMENT'

During the 1980s and 1990s 'rural development' rather than 'religion' or 'politics' has been the context within which a large number of Untouchable communities in rural Tamil Nadu have found patrons and resources to redefine social position and identity. Much of this takes place beyond state, Church or party. Indeed, the perceived failure of the state, the Churches and the political Left to deliver political and material benefits to Untouchables has promoted new agencies of rural change and also prompted Untouchables to see these as alternative patrons willing to identify them as a concrete interest group, to support access to new resources and freedom from dependency, and support expressions of autonomy and status. These agencies are non-governmental or voluntary organisations (NGOs/VAs), mostly financed by grants from European Church-based and secular donor NGOs (Christian Aid, Oxfam, HIVOS, NOVIB, and so on), whose numbers increased dramatically from the early 1980s. A shift, at this time, from welfare and service delivery approaches towards grassroots action for the poorest brought many NGOs in Tamil Nadu into closer contact with the economic and social disabilities of local communities of Untouchable castes, and in consequence NGO discourses of poverty and deprivation (analysis and action) became more and more influenced by these people's own caste-based interpretations.[21] Moreover, by the mid-1980s a significant number of small NGOs were led by individuals from Harijan castes.

Like earlier mission organisations, these local NGOs provide patronage and support to groups of Harijans. As a result of the influence they wield, together with the new organisational and material resources they bring, there has been – in certain localities – a shift in the local balance of power and an increase in the options for social mobility available to Untouchables. Concrete instances of this include Untouchable withdrawal from tied labour and low wages, withdrawal from low-status service roles, challenges to high-caste ritual exclusivity, and resistance to any resulting social and economic sanctions. At the widest level of generalisation, NGO support has helped provide certain Untouchables with new organisational resources and brought the machinery of the state and its laws on untouchability within grasp. In some cases, being part of an NGO *cankam* (self-help group) also provides Untouchables with new forms of group identity, the prestige associated with having a 'society' with its formal offices and meetings, written records and accounts, and symbols of power (not least the NGOs' jeeps and visiting foreigners), all of which back up assertions of social independence and resistance to high castes.

Within the dominant development discourse, however, caste discrimination and social disability are not currently valid policy themes.[22] In securing support Untouchables have therefore had to adopt a range of development beneficiary identities, as 'landless labourers', 'marginal farmers', 'water users', 'watershed managers', 'artisans' and so forth, rather than caste identities. Nonetheless, under these labels Untouchables have been able to advance 'strategic' goals, challenge dominant caste privileges and re-position themselves within local village society. Consider an example from irrigation development. Water rights in tank irrigation often remain a high-caste privilege in caste-based shares systems. Recently, NGOs working to 'sustainable water resources development' objectives have enabled Untouchable farmers to make inroads into these institutions of caste dominance and to negotiate positions of influence within new 'farmers associations' (Mosse 1995, 1997b; CWR 1991). In a few cases, notably in projects supported by Church-based NGOs, Christian identity (combined with new beneficiary labels) continues to generate development support among Untouchable communities.

For reasons related to the nature of local beneficiary organisations (*cankams*), and the type of patron–client dependencies which often develop between NGOs and 'their' village-level beneficiary groups, it seems probable that NGO programmes will remain highly localised and unable to contribute to wider mobilisation or new political identities. This is a source of concern to an articulate 'activist' section of the NGO movement in India, among whom there is a strong feeling that NGOs should move away from localised and project-based forms of action (which are partly seen as the product of foreign funding mechanisms) and begin to contribute more directly to political processes of change on behalf of the most subordinated sections of Indian society (Unia 1991; Stephen 1990).

Today, much ideological reflection focuses on the choice of social identities for popular mobilisation of 'the poor': should these be based on caste, class, gender or occupation? NGOs are divided. On the one hand NGOs are reappraising the wisdom of having established close links with Untouchable communities and are now advocating wider class, sector or gender-based forms of organisation and closer linkage with unions and Left parties (cf. Shah 1991: 283). On the other hand, caste and socio-cultural aspects of disadvantage are re-emphasised.

'DALIT' IDENTITIES AND THE POLITICAL CULTURE OF CASTE IN TAMIL NADU

While Untouchables remain subject to external definitions of subordination (in terms of caste/class and so on), this does not mean that identities generated by Untouchables themselves are absent from today's politics of caste. However, perhaps precisely because of the failure of Untouchable political mobilisation, and the muting of Untouchable interests within the major parties – Dravidian, Congress or Communist – there is a growth of Untouchable cultural politics *outside* mainstream political processes (Mendelsohn and Vicziany 1994: 107–14). This articulates broad counter-cultural *Dalit* identities (the term *dalit* meaning 'the oppressed, broken or downtrodden'). Dalit organisations, and the literature they generate, consciously assert socio-cultural identities which are separate from dominant Hindu culture. The movements are sympathetic to Christians and Muslims but also articulate indigenous non-sanskritic religious identities. These movements, which began alongside the nationalist movement, may also, as Omvedt suggests, be experiencing 'a second upsurge today in an era of the crisis of nationalities and of socialism' (1994: 13). However, the momentum of Dalit movements in Maharashtra and Karnataka, in particular, has not been replicated in Tamil Nadu. In this final section, I want to suggest that here the political culture of caste has not encouraged new independent political identities among Untouchables, but rather has reasserted and reified 'Untouchable' ('Harijan') as a subordinate identity. This comment needs to be set in context.

Recent historical and anthropological work on Tamil Nadu has revised some long-held assumptions about the fixity of caste. It is now known that there was, in pre-colonial times, considerable flexibility in caste identity and mobility in the social order (Dirks 1987; Bayly 1989). Economically successful groups acquired high-caste status, warrior kings issued caste titles and so forth. British rule transformed caste. Census categories and the new status of Brahmans within the colonial administration had a major impact in reifying caste identity and its Brahmanical underpinnings. Anthropologists of the 1960s and 1970s inherited a 'traditionalised' and localised image of caste articulated, as Dumont (1980) showed, around the opposition of the pure and the impure. Sub-caste identities were defined by transactionally maintained blood purity which distinguished an elaborate ranked order of castes at village level (S. Barnett 1976; Dumont 1980; Beck 1972). Untouchables simply occupied the lowest positions in the system as receivers, consumers and disposers of impurity.

This caste order was in collapse from the moment it was first conceptualised. Caste politics of the twentieth century demanded supra-local alliances, new 'caste associations', political interest groups and the like (Rudolph and Rudolph 1967). There was a shift away from localised transactionally defined identity among Tamil high castes towards a more simplified 'natural identity' (Barnett 1975, 1977). The abandonment of inter-caste restrictions on food/water exchange, seating arrangements and so forth is now very general. Caste identities remain, but they are, in Dumont's terms, 'substantialised'. The caste order characterised by ranked interdependence, has begun to shift to one 'in which caste appears as a collective *individual* (in the sense we have given to this word), as a substance' (Dumont 1980: 222). In describing change in the caste system as '... a transition from a structure to the juxtaposition of substances' (1980: 227), Dumont has in mind something akin to a shift between Durkheim's 'organic solidarity' and 'mechanical solidarity'. This type change in caste ideology, with its move away from transactionally maintained rank, clearly has implications for the status and identity of Untouchable castes.

What is striking, however, is that the erosion of interactive ranking has not extended to Untouchable castes. Changes in caste ideology have not erased, but have often enhanced, the distinction between 'caste-Hindus' and Untouchables. In rural areas of the state, increasing levels of 'atrocities against Untouchables', protests and conflicts, all indicate that much is still at stake in preserving the hierarchical nature of this social boundary. But what is also striking is the retention of separation and rank between different Untouchable castes themselves (in large mixed communities). Long after upper castes in Alapuram had begun interacting reciprocally (in food exchange, terms of address, and so on, in the 1940s) and when any discussion of relative rank between them had been rendered meaningless, separation and rank remained between Untouchable castes (Mosse 1986). The principle of exclusion and subordination of inferior groups – retained in caste-Hindu/Untouchable interrelations – was repeated within the Untouchable community.

If local power relations prevent rural Untouchables from extracting themselves from caste-based transactions and so prohibit the organised assertion of 'substantialised' identities, a study in Madras in the early 1970s suggested that this may even be so in urban areas where caste identities are most 'substantialised' and where castes most clearly exist as competing interest blocks rather than as complementary parts of a social whole. On the one hand, the study showed that Untouchable castes in Madras city had a distinct occupational profile (skewed towards menial and 'impure' tasks), high unemployment and were residentially segregated. On the other hand, it showed that caste-based transactions, which had been abandoned in most contexts, were retained between urban upper and Untouchable castes (Barnett and Barnett 1973: 395–6).[23] In the transition of identities (which the Barnetts characterise as from 'caste' to 'ethnicity'), '*Untouchables persist as a caste residue – the norms of purity and impurity as defining code of conduct still apply to them in urban transactions*' (1973: 396–7, emphasis in the original). But, further, the study suggested that the qualitative separation of urban Untouchables is increasingly perceived in 'racial' rather than caste terms, in the sense that difference is characterised in physical rather than behavioural terms: 'caste Hindus are coming to see Untouchables not as a separate caste, but as a distinct race' (1973: 397).

The use of concepts of 'ethnicity' and 'race' in the context of changed caste identities may abuse these terms as comparative analytical categories. Nonetheless two valid points are being made, first that

Untouchables' experience of change in the caste system is distinctive, and, second, that many Untouchable groups lack the power to define new and positive global identities.

SUMMARY AND CONCLUSIONS

Untouchable castes in Tamil Nadu have made a variety of responses to negative social identity. In particular they have manipulated non-Hindu religious identities to win patronage and to challenge the relations of dependence and service which customarily define their social inferiority. The significance of Christian identities has depended upon the resources and power available to Untouchable castes. Thus, while the better-placed Catholic Pallars of Alapuram used membership of the Church to lay claim to symbols of status and asserted a new dominance, Protestant Christianity provides poorer Paraiyars with an identity separate from those inferior service roles which they are still constrained to perform. But it also provides a self-respect model of service supporting micro-level renegotiation of these roles and their meaning. Untouchable identities have also been asserted in terms of relations between the different untouchable castes: Pallars asserted a new status by displacing the signs of their inferiority (such as grave digging) on to Paraiyars and acquired their own inferior dependent service group; Necavar Paraiyar Hindu orthodoxy asserted their superiority over Tottis and emphasised the ritual inferiority of the latter's role; and Tottis displaced such assertions from status rivals by becoming Christians.

The Christian Churches in Tamil Nadu have become less and less able to offer meaningful alternative religious identities to untouchables. This is not to say that religious conversion has no significance today. On the contrary, in the context of increased politicisation of religious identity in India, conversion has retained and increased its force as an idiom of Untouchable protest. In particular, group conversion to Islam by communities of Hindu and Christian Pallars in 1982 had the immediate and dramatic effect of focusing national media attention on the issue of caste discrimination (Mathew 1982; Khan 1983).

In post-Independence Tamil Nadu, however, non-religious bureaucratic and legal definitions of 'ex-Untouchable' identity have gained prominence as the means to acquire resources and challenge discrimination. In this context new identities are articulated to satisfy the combined need to lay claim to state resources for the socially subordinate, and to assert power, independence and dignity. Significantly, competition between Untouchable castes for limited state resources has ensured the retention or reaffirmation of separate Untouchable caste identities (that is, Paraiyar, Pallar, and so on). But at another level a pragmatic need to find new patrons and access to development resources diverts attention away from caste issues altogether.

There appear to be significant social constraints to the generation of viable overarching and politically effective identities among Untouchables in Tamil Nadu. The sort of local protests or the redefinition of service roles described here seem unlikely to translate into mass support for a wider Dalit movement. The reasons are complex but must in part concern the strong resistance to assertions of autonomy by Untouchables from locally dominant castes, and the lack of unity of identity among Untouchable castes. In the absence of broad political identities for Untouchables in Tamil Nadu, their political participation will be determined by the categories of mobilisation of others both within and outside mainstream politics. There is much uncertainty surrounding these today. Caste/class categories are being reassessed by the Churches, NGOs and more widely. The Left parties, for example, are reappraising issues of caste (Shah 1991: 333) – not least because of the experience that 'new class formations are grounded in caste' (Sheth 1984, cited in Prabhaker 1988: 37) – and caste-based Dalit organisations are broadening the concept 'Dalit' from its caste and ethnic origin. In India today much hangs on the articulation of identity and with new and powerful alignments dominating Indian politics in broader political terms there is much at stake.

NOTES

This chapter draws on fieldwork and archival research conducted in Tamil Nadu between 1982 and 1984, and intermittently between 1987 and 1991 while Oxfam Representative for south India in Bangalore, and again between 1993 and 1995. I should like to express thanks to informants in the village of 'Alapuram', to M. Sivan and to the ESRC who funded the research on which this chapter draws. Transliteration of Tamil words follows the conventions of the *Madras University Tamil Lexicon*.

1. There is no fully satisfactory value-free descriptive term to use in discussing Untouchables. All of these terms imply particular discourses on Untouchable identity. My use of the conventional term Untouchable (capitalised) as a general category embracing several different castes should not be taken to signify particular importance to restrictions on touch, which rarely exist in Tamil Nadu.

2. 'Alapuram' is a pseudonym for a village in which I carried out intensive fieldwork in 1982–84, visited intermittently 1987–91, and in which I again began research in 1993.

3. There is still comparatively little literature on Untouchable castes within India as a whole, although Untouchable castes in Tamil Nadu have received better attention. Among the most important general sources are: Moffatt (1979), Deliège (1988, 1992), Mahar (1972), Mosse (1994a), Cohn (1955, 1959), Hjejle (1967), Khare (1984), McGilvray (1983), Isaacs (1965), Juergensmeyer (1982), Lynch (1969).

4. On the development of the Protestant critique of caste during the nineteenth century see Forrester (1980), also Warren (1967: ch. 2), Richter (1908), Oddie (1969). This marked a departure from the more accommodating position taken by eighteenth-century pre-evangelical Protestant missionaries – the Dutch and Danish Calvinists and Lutherans (see Arasaratnam 1981) as well as the first Anglican SPCK and SPG missionaries. The Roman Catholic Church had a quite different view and accepted caste as a *social* institution. Being Christian was compatible with the retention of caste identity and practices (see below, Mosse 1994b).

5. The literature on mass conversion movements is extensive and has been reviewed elsewhere (Mosse 1982). Some of the most important sources are: Fernandes (1981), Fishman (1941), Forrester (1977, 1980), Frykenberg (1976), Goudie (1918), Kooiman (1989), Luke and Carmen (1968), Manickam (1977), Manor (1971), Oddie (1975, 1977a, 1977b), Pickett (1933), Richter (1908). Considerable scholarly interest has focused on these mass conversion movements and their interpretation is fraught with difficulties, not least of which is the employment of a consistent

understanding of the concept of conversion itself. Here conversion may be taken to mean the collective self-ascription as Christians – the adoption of a Christian identity – which may or may not involve change in world view, beliefs, practices, intellectual outlook, emotional condition or 'shifts in the perception of ultimate verities' (Frykenberg 1981: 122).

6. Significantly, several nineteenth-century Hindu reform movements, most importantly the Arya Samaj, aiming to justify but modernise caste, modelled themselves on Christian missionary organisations and hoped to contain Christian conversions by offering new 'sanskritic' Hindu identities to converts and Untouchables through purificatory 'reconversion' rituals (Arya Samaj, *suddhi* movement; Heimsath 1964; Jordens 1975, 1977, 1981; Rao 1974). Despite widespread influence in the north, in south India this did not compare with the impact of the Christian missions.

7. There is some conflicting evidence on this. See, for example, Manor (1971) and Oddie (1977).

8. Material deprivations resulting from changes under colonial rule contributed to several peasant uprisings in the second half of the nineteenth century (Gough 1974).

9. Significantly, in some areas egalitarian devotional (*bhakti*) Hindu movements were precursors to, or fed into, conversion movements (Fishman 1941: 69; Fuchs 1965: 260–3, Oddie 1975; Forrester 1980: 91).

10. For comparable observations on the social position of Protestant converts see Alexander (1972: 155–9), Diehl (1965); Koshy (1968: 51), Luke and Carmen (1968), Shiri (1977: 61), Wiebe (1970).

11. Fluctuating degrees of dependence and obligation of individual families not only depends upon their asset holding position, but is also influenced by crop failure, opportunities for migrant labour, marriage and dowry payments, and so on.

12. Detailed records of these changes are provided by entries into parish diaries maintained by Jesuit priests resident in Alapuram from the 1850s (Mosse 1986, 1997: 83ff.).

13. However, Jesuits would not intervene on Paraiyars' behalf if by doing so there was a risk of the Paraiyars' high-caste Catholic patrons leaving the Church in protest. Indeed, nineteenth- and early twentieth-century Jesuit priests operated within a delicate system of ordered hierarchy, the maintenance of which was

essential if high-caste Church membership was to be maintained. Direct intervention on behalf of the lowest untouchable castes (Paraiyars) in situations of conflict, or their inclusion in the Church was virtually ruled out. This restriction on support from Catholic priests is one important reason why Paraiyars became Protestant rather than Catholic Christians.

14. The mission was initiated in 1606 by the Italian Jesuit Roberto de Nobili, whose policy on 'accommodation' to Hindu cultural traditions was to achieve some notoriety within the Church hierarchy not only for its admission of caste in the Church, but also for the practice of having different 'castes' of renouncer missionaries serving different caste converts (*sanyasins* for Brahman converts; *pandaraswamis* for non-Brahmans, and for a period a third category serving untouchable converts). The Society of Jesus was eventually suppressed by Papal Bull in 1773, and the Jesuits were expelled from India on the grounds of these errant practices (Neill 1984; Dumont 1972: 250–1, 372).

15. The manner in which caste hierarchy has been reproduced through Catholic institutions – Church organisation, festivals, life-crisis rites, which all retain Hindu ritual forms – is described in detail elsewhere (Mosse 1994a, 1994b, 1996, 1997b).

16. Several studies of the Arya Samaj and similar Hindu reform movements in north India (and the Sri Narayana Guru movement in Kerala) suggest that these also offered opportunities not for the rejection of caste but the achievement of higher status within the hierarchy (Sharma 1976; Lynch 1969; Mahar 1960; Rao 1977; Cohn 1955). This also meant rejecting ideas of ascriptive status, and advancing the notion that caste rank is based on achievement or merit (Harper 1968: 64).

17. Since the passing of the Government of India (Scheduled Castes) Order in 1936, the state has implicitly held a *religious* theory of caste as a Hindu institution. The existence of Scheduled Castes is not admitted in non-Hindu convert communities (except Sikhs) who are, irrespective of caste of origin, categorised in the lower priority category of Other Backward Castes.

18. The political rivals of the Dravidian nationalist party (the DMK) were the Brahman-led Communist Party who gained support from untouchable landless labourers in selected districts (Béteille 1974), and Congress Party which mobilised untouchable votes in the 1960s

largely through vertical links and tied-labour relations (Barnett and Barnett 1973).

19. *Muventar Yar?* – 'Who were the three great Tamil kings?', and *Velalar Yar?* – 'Who are/were the Velalars?', both books written by Deva Asirvatam (1977, 1981).

20. The Teventira Kula Velalar Cankam has on a number of occasions passed resolutions to reject the government's attempt to change the collective term for Scheduled Castes to *Adi Dravida* ('original Dravidians'). They strongly reject the idea of Pallars as being inheritors of some pre-Tamil culture which would associate them with inferior 'jungle tribes'.

21. Despite diversity (in goals, origins, structure, funding, relation to government etc.) there are common strategies and methods revolving around forms of 'awareness raising' which draw loosely on the tradition of liberation theology and the writings of Paulo Freire, and the promotion of organised 'groups' (*cankams*) in Harijan villages and 'colonies'. These cankams provide a basis for collective action, petitioning for state resources or for separately funded economic programmes (based round credit, livestock, artisanal production, and so on).

22. Within the (Catholic) Church too, class, occupation or gender rather than caste are emphasised as the basis of social action. The Alapuram church's social programme is characterised by mixed caste youth and women's groups and the discourse revolves around class identities, economic exploitation and the injustice of government and the 'ruling classes' (rather than the local dominant castes). Continued action against the performance of polluting tasks emphasises *human dignity* not caste status. Wider organisation on a non-caste base began in the Alapuram parish in 1985 under the influence of some radical priests. There is now a structure over several southern districts capable of mobilising mass action from groups of labourers and women on issues such as water, wages and rape. While this movement has managed to generate mass support around unifying issues of the poor on a non-caste basis at a 'supra-local' level, locally caste often continues to be the primary basis of social mobilisation.

23. Similar observations have been made in urban north India (Gooptu 1993).

REFERENCES

Alexander, K.C. 1972. 'The neo–Christians in Kerala', in J.M. Mahar (ed.) *The Untouchables in contemporary India*. Tucson: University of Arizona Press, pp. 153–61.

Appadurai, A. 1977. 'Kings, sects and temples in south India 1350–1700 AD', *Indian Economic and Social History Review* 14: 47–73.

—— 1981. *Worship and Conflict under Colonial Rule: A South Indian Case*. Cambridge: Cambridge University Press.

Arasaratnam, S. 1981. 'Protestant Christianity and south Hinduism 1630–1730: some confrontations in society and belief', *Indian Church History Review* 15: 7–33.

Asirvatam, D.A. 1977. *Muventar yar?* (Tamil) Tanjavur: Irama Tevan Patippakam.

—— 1981. *Velalar yar?* (Tamil) Tanjavur: Irama Tevan Patippakam.

Barnett, M.R. 1976. *The Politics of Cultural Nationalism*. Princeton, NJ: Princeton University Press.

Barnett, M. and S. Barnett. 1973. 'Contemporary peasant and post-peasant alternatives in south India: the ideas of a militant Untouchable', *Transactions of the American Philosophical Society* 63: 385–410.

Barnett, S. 1975. 'Approaches to changes in caste ideology in south India', in B. Stein (ed.) *Essays on South India*. Hawaii: Hawaii University Press.

—— 1976. 'Coconuts and gold: relational identity in a south Indian caste', *Contributions to Indian Sociology* (N.S.) 10: 133–56.

—— 1977. 'Identity, choice and caste ideology in contemporary south India', in K. David (ed.) *The New Wind: Changing Identities in South Asia*. The Hague/Paris: Mouton.

Bayly, S.B. 1989. *Saints, Goddesses and Kings: Muslims and Christians in South Indian Society, 1700–1900*. Cambridge: Cambridge University Press.

Beck, B.E.F. 1972. *Peasant Society in Konku: A Study of Right and Left Subcastes in South India*. Vancouver: University of British Columbia Press.

Béteille, A. 1965. 'The future of the Backward Classes: the competing demands of status and power', *Perspectives,* supplement to the *Indian Journal of Public Administration,* 11.

—— 1974. *Studies in Agrarian Social Structure*. Delhi: Oxford University Press.

Caplan, L. 1980. 'Caste and castelessness among south Indian Christians', *Contributions to Indian Sociology* (N.S.) 14: 213–38.

Clough, J.E. 1914. *Social Christianity in the Orient*. New York: Macmillan.

Cohn, B.S. 1955. 'The changing status of a depressed caste', in M. Marriott (ed.) *Village India: Studies in the Little Community*. Chicago, IL: University of Chicago Press, pp. 53–77.

—— 1959. 'Changing traditions of a low caste', in M. Singer (ed.) *Traditional India: Structure and Change*. Philadelphia, PA: American Folklore Society, pp. 207–15.

CWR. 1991. *Alternative Approaches to Tank Rehabilitation and Management – A Proposed Experiment: Annual Report 1989–90*. Madras: Centre for Water Resources, Anna University.

Deliège, R. 1988. *Les Paraiyars du Tamil Nadu*. Nettetal: Steyer Verlag.

—— 1992. 'Replication and consensus: untouchability, caste and ideology in India', *Man* 27: 130–55.

Diehl, C.G. 1965. *Church and Shrine: Intermingling Patterns of Culture in the Life of Some Christian Groups in South India*. Uppsala: Acta Universitatis Uppsaliensis Historia Religionum 2.

Dirks, N.B. 1987. *The Hollow Crown: Ethnohistory of an Indian Kingdom*. Cambridge: Cambridge University Press.

—— 1990. 'The original caste: power, history and hierarchy in South Asia', in M. Marriott (ed.) *India through Hindu Categories*, Contributions to Indian Sociology, Occasional Studies 5. New Delhi: Sage, pp. 59–77.

Dumont, L. 1980 (1972). *Homo Hierarchicus: The Caste System and its Implications*, revised edn. Chicago, IL: University of Chicago Press.

Estborn, S. 1961. *The Church among Tamils and Telegus*. Lucknow: The National Christian Council of India.

Fabricius, J.P. 1972 (1779). *Tamil and English Dictionary*, 4th edn. Tranquebar: Evangelical Lutheran Mission.

Fernandes, W. 1981. 'Caste and conversion movements in India', *Social Action* 31: 261–90.

Fishman, A.T. 1941. *Culture, Change and the Underprivileged: A Study of the Madigas in South India Under Christian Guidance*. Madras: The Christian Literature Crusade.

Forrester, D.B. 1977. 'The depressed classes and conversion to Christianity 1860–1960', in G.A. Oddie (ed.) *Religion in South Asia: Religious Conversion and Revival Movements in South Asia in Medieval and Modern Times*. London: Curzon Press, pp. 35–66.

—— 1980. *Caste and Christianity: Attitudes and Policies on Caste of Anglo-Saxon Protestant Missionaries in India*. London: Curzon Press.

Frykenberg, R.E. 1976. 'The impact of conversion and social reform upon society in south India during the late company period: questions concerning Hindu–Christian encounters, with special reference to Tinnevelly', in C.H. Phillips and N.D. Wainwright (eds) *Indian Society and the Beginnings of Modernization c. 1830–1850*. London: School of African and Oriental Studies, pp. 187–243.

—— 1981. 'On the study of conversion movements: a review article and a theoretical note', *The Indian Economic and Social History Review* 17: 121–38.

Fuchs, S. 1965. *Rebellious Prophets: A Study of Messianic Movements in Indian Religion*. London: Asia Publishing House.

Gladstone, J.W. 1976. 'Nineteenth-century mass movements in south Travancore: a result of social liberation', *Indian Church History Review* 10: 53–65.

Good, A. 1991. *The Female Bridegroom: A Comparative Study of Life-Crisis Rituals in South India and Sri Lanka*. Oxford: Clarendon Press.

Gooptu, N. 1993. 'Caste, deprivation and politics: the Untouchables in U.P. towns in the early twentieth century', in P. Robb (ed.) *Dalit Movements and the Meanings of Labour in India*. New Delhi: Oxford University Press, pp. 277–98.

Goudie, C. 1918. 'Facts and figures of mass movements', *The East and the West* 16: 310.

Gough, K. 1960. 'Caste in a Tanjore village', in E.R. Leach (ed.) *Aspects of Caste in Southern India, Ceylon and Northwestern Pakistan*. New York: Cambridge University Press, pp. 11–60.

—— 1974. 'Indian peasant uprising', *Economic and Political Weekly* 9: 1391–412.

Hardgrave, R.L. Jr. 1968. 'The breast cloth controversy', *The Indian Economic and Social History Review* 2: 171–87.

—— 1969. *The Nadars of Tamilnad*. Berkeley: University of California Press.

—— 1973. 'Politics and the film in Tamil Nadu: the stars and the DMK', *Asia Survey* 13: 288–305.

Hardy, F. 1983. *Viraha-Bhakti: The Early History of Kṛṣṇa Devotion in South India*. Delhi: Oxford University Press.

Harper, E. 1968. 'Social consequences of an "unsuccessful" low caste movement', in J. Silverberg (ed.) *Social Mobility in the Caste System in India*. The Hague: Mouton.

Heimsath, C.H. 1964. *Indian Nationalism and Hindu Social Reform*. Princeton, NJ: Princeton University Press.

Hjejle, B. 1967. 'Slavery and agricultural bondage in south India in the nineteenth century', *The Scandinavian Economic History Review* 15: 71–126.

Hocart, A.M. 1950. *Caste: A Comparative Study*. London: Methuen.

Irschick, E.F. 1969. *Politics and Social Conflicts in South India: The Non-Brahman Movement and Tamil Separatism 1916–1929*. Berkeley/Los Angeles: University of California Press.

Isaacs, H. 1965. *India's Ex-Untouchables*. New York: John Jay.

Jordens, J.T.F. 1975. 'Hindu religious and social reform in British India', in A.L. Basham (ed.) *A Cultural History of India*. Oxford: Clarendon Press.

——— 1977. 'Reconversion to Hinduism: the Shuddhi of the Arya Samaj', in G.A Oddie (ed.) *Religion in South Asia: Religious Conversion and Revival Movements in South East Asia in Medieval and Modern Times*. London: Curzon Press.

——— 1981. 'Dayananada Sarasvati and Christianity', *Indian Church History Review* 15: 34–47.

Juergensmeyer, M. 1982. *Religion as Social Vision: The Movement against Untouchability in Twentieth-Century Punjab*. Berkeley: University of California Press.

Khan, M.A. 1983. *Mass Conversions of Meenakshipuram: A Sociological Enquiry*. Madras: Christian Literature Society.

Khare, R.S. 1984. *The Untouchable as Himself: Ideology, Identity and Pragmatism among the Lucknow Chamars*. Cambridge: Cambridge University Press.

Kooiman, Dick. 1989. *Conversion and Social Equality in India: The London Missionary Society in South Travancore in the 19th Century*. New Delhi: Manohar Publishers.

Koshy, N. 1968. *Caste in the Kerala Churches*. Bangalore: Christian Institute for the Study of Religion and Society.

Lele, J. 1980. 'The *bhakti* movement in India: a critical introduction', *Journal of Asian and African Studies* 15: 1–15.

Levinson, S. 1982. 'Caste rank and verbal interaction in western Tamil Nadu', in D.B. McGilvray (ed.) *Caste Ideology and Interaction.* Cambridge: Cambridge University Press.

Ling, T. 1980. *Buddhist Revival in India: Aspects of the Sociology of Buddhism.* London: Macmillan.

Ludden, D. 1985. *Peasant History in South India.* Princeton, NJ: Princeton University Press.

Luke, P.Y. and J.B. Carmen. 1968. *Village Christians and Hindu Culture: Study of a Rural Church in Andhra Pradesh, South India.* London: Lutterworth Press.

Lynch, O. 1969. *The Politics of Untouchability.* New York: Columbia University Press.

—— 1972. 'Dr. B.R. Ambedkar: myth and charisma', in J.M. Mahar (ed.) *The Untouchables in Contemporary India.* Tucson: University of Arizona Press, pp. 97–112.

McGilvray, D.B. 1982. 'Mukkuvar vannimai: Tamil caste and matriclan ideology in Batticaloa, Sri Lanka', in D.B. McGilvray (ed.) *Caste Ideology and Interaction.* Cambridge: Cambridge University Press.

—— 1983. 'Paraiyar drummers of Sri Lanka: consensus and constraint in an Untouchable caste', *American Ethnologist* 10: 97–114.

Mahar, P.M. 1960. 'The changing religious practices of an Untouchable Caste', *Economic Development and Cultural Change* 8: 279–87.

Mahar, M.J. (ed.). 1972. *The Untouchables in Contemporary India.* Tucson: University of Arizona Press.

Manickam, S. 1977. *The Social Setting of Christian Conversion in South India: The Impact of the Wesleyan Methodist Missionaries on the Trichy–Tanjore Diocese with Special Reference to the Harijan Communities of the Mass Movement Area 1820–1947.* Wiesbaden: Franz Steiner Verlag.

Manor, J.G. 1971. 'Testing the barrier between caste and outcaste: the Andhra Evangelical Lutheran Church in Guntur District, 1920–1940', *Indian Church History Review* 5: 27–41.

Mathew, G. 1982. 'Politicisation of religion in Tamil Nadu (Parts 1 and 2)', *Economic and Political Weekly* 25: 1027–34, 1068–72.

Mendelsohn, O. and M. Vicziany. 1994. 'The Untouchables', in O. Mendelsohn and Upendra Baxi (eds) *The Rights of Subordinated Peoples.* New Delhi: Oxford University Press.

Miller. R. 1966. 'Button, button ... great tradition, little tradition, whose tradition?', *Anthropological Quarterly* 39: 26–42.

—— 1967. 'They will not die Hindus: the Buddhist conversion of Mahar ex-Untouchables', *Asian Survey* 7: 637–44.

Moffatt, M. 1979. *An Untouchable Community in South India: Structure and Consensus*. Princeton, NJ: Princeton University Press.

Mosse, D. 1982. 'Hierarchy and equality in south India: a survey of literature relevant to the study of egalitarian ideologies and Untouchables in south India with particular reference to *bhakti*, the Dravidian movement and Christianity'. Unpublished thesis manuscript, Oxford University.

—— 1986. 'Caste, Christianity and Hinduism: a study of social organisation and religion in rural Ramnad.' PhD thesis, Oxford University.

—— 1994a. 'Idioms of subordination and styles of protest among Christian and Hindu Harijan castes in Tamil Nadu', *Contributions to Indian Sociology* 28: 67–106.

—— 1994b. 'The politics of religious synthesis: Roman Catholicism and Hindu village society in Tamil Nadu, India', in C. Stewart and R. Shaw (eds) *Syncretism/Anti-syncretism: The Politics of Religious Synthesis*. London: Routledge, pp. 85–107.

—— 1995. 'Local institutions and power: The history and practice of community management in the development of tank irrigation systems in south India', in S. Wright and N. Nelson (eds) *Power and Participatory Development: Theory and Practice*. London: Intermediate Technologies.

—— 1996. 'South Indian Christians, purity/impurity, and the caste system: death ritual in a Tamil Roman Catholic community', *Journal of the Royal Anthropological Institute* (N.S.) 2:, 1–22.

—— 1997a. 'Honour, caste and conflict: the ethnohistory of a Catholic festival in rural Tamil Nadu (1730–1990)', in J. Assagag and G. Tarabout (eds) *Alterité et identité: Islam et Christianisme en Inde*, Collection Purusartha, Vol. 19. Paris: École des Hautes Études en Sciences Sociales.

—— 1997b. 'The ideology and politics of community participation: tank irrigation development in colonial and contemporary Tamil Nadu', in R.L. Stirrat and R. Grillo (eds) *Discourse of Development: Anthropological Perspectives*. Oxford: Berg Publishers.

Neill, S. 1984. *A History of Christianity in India: 1707–1858*. Cambridge: Cambridge University Press.

Nemade, B. 1980. 'The revolt of the underprivileged: style in the expression of the *Warkari* movement in Maharashtra', *Journal of Asian and African Studies* 15: 113–23.

Oddie, G.A. 1969. 'Protestant missions, caste and social change in India', *Indian Economic and Social History Review* 6: 259–92.

—— 1975. 'Christian conversion in Telegu country 1860–1900: a case study of one Protestant movement in the Godavery-Krishna Delta', *Indian Economic and Social History Review* 12: 61–79.

—— 1977a. 'Christian conversion among non-Brahmans in Andhra Pradesh, with special reference to the Anglican missionaries and the Dornakal Diocese c. 1900–1936', in G.A. Oddie (ed.) *Religion in South Asia: Religious Conversion and Revival Movements in South Asia in Medieval and Modern Times. London: Curzon Press*, pp. 67–92.

—— (ed.) 1977b. *Religion in South Asia: Religious Conversion and Revival Movements in South Asia in Medieval and Modern Times.* London: Curzon Press.

—— 1979. *Social Protestants in India: British Protestant Missionaries and Social Reforms 1850–1900.* New Delhi: Manohar.

Omvedt, G. 1994. *Dalits and the Democratic Revolution: Dr Ambedkar and the Dalit Movement in Colonial India.* New Delhi: Sage.

Pfaffenberger, B. 1982. *Caste in Tamil Culture: The Religious Foundation of Vellalar Dominance.* New York: Maxwell School of Citizenship and Public Affairs, Syracuse University.

Pickett. J.W. 1933. *Christian Mass Movements in India: A Study with Recommendations.* Lucknow: Lucknow Publishing House.

Pocock, D.F. 1962. 'Notes on *jajmani* relationships', *Contributions to Indian Sociology* 6: 78–95.

Prabhakar, M.E. (ed.). 1988. *Towards a Dalit Theology.* Delhi: Indian Society for the Propagation of the Gospel (ISPCK).

Rao, M.S.A. 1974. 'Religious Movements and Social Transformation in India', in Marga Institute, *Religion and Development in Asian Societies.* Colombo, Sri Lanka: Marga Publications, pp. 130–45.

—— 1977. 'Ideology of a protest movement: Sri Narayana Guru Swamy: Philosophy', in P.K.B. Nayar and J. Kattakayan (eds) *Perspectives in Sociology.* Trivandrum India: The Kerala Sociological Society.

Richter, J. 1908. *A History of Missions in India,* trans. S.H. Moore. Edinburgh: Oliphant, Anderson and Ferrier.

Rudolph, L.L and S.H. Rudolph. 1967. *The Modernity of Tradition: Political Development in India*. Chicago, IL: University of Chicago Press.

Sharma, U.M. 1976. 'Status striving and striving to abolish status: the Arya Samaj and the low castes', *Social Action* 26: 215–36.

Scott, J.C. 1990. *Weapons of the Weak: Everyday Forms of Peasant Resistance*. Delhi: Oxford University Press.

Shah, G. 1991. 'Grassroots mobilisation in Indian politics', in A. Kohli (ed.) *India's Democracy: Analysis of Changing State–Society Relations*. Hyderabad: Orient Longman Ltd, pp. 262–304.

Shiri, G. 1977. *Karnataka Christians and Politics*. Madras: Christian Literature Society.

Sheth, D.L. 1984. 'Grass-roots initiatives in India', *Economic and Political Weekly* 11 February 19 (6): 259–62.

Stein, B. 1968. 'Social mobility and medieval south Indian Hindu sects', in J. Silverberg (ed.) *Social Mobility in the Caste System in India*. The Hague: Mouton, pp. 78–94.

Stephen, F. 1990. *NGOs: hope of the last decade of this century*. Bangalore: SEARCH.

Unia, P. 1991. 'Social action group strategies in the Indian subcontinent', *Development in Practice* 1 (2): 84–96.

Warren, M.A.C. 1967. *Social History and Christian Mission*. London: SCM Press.

Washbrook, D. 1993. 'Land and labour in late eighteenth-century south India: the golden age of the Pariah?', in P. Robb (ed.) *Dalit Movements and the Meanings of Labour in India*. New Delhi: Oxford University Press, pp. 68–86.

Wiebe, P.C. 1970. 'Protestant missions in India, a sociological review', *Journal of Asian and African Studies* 5: 293–301.

Zelliott, E. 1966. 'Buddhism and politics in Maharashtra', in D.E. Smith (ed.) *South Asian Politics and Religion*. Princeton, NJ: Princeton University Press.

4 FEASTING FRIENDS, EATING ENEMIES: AMITY AND ENMITY IN KALAUNA

Michael W. Young

In this chapter I return to the inexhaustible topic of feasting in the Austronesian-speaking community of Kalauna, a village-based society in the foothills of Goodenough Island, in the Massim region of eastern Papua New Guinea. While contrasting two radically different customary feasts in Kalauna I shall also be concerned with the affects and sentiments which motivate, imbue and sustain them. In acknowledgement of Bill Epstein's scrupulous handling of my own ethnographic material from Kalauna – which he has cited extensively in his work on the anthropology of affect in Melanesia (Epstein 1984 and 1992) – I shall address some of the interpretive questions he has posed.

The literature on the anthropology of the emotions is now dauntingly large and offers a variety of theoretical perspectives (for an already somewhat outdated review see Lutz and White 1986). Suffice to say that in the present chapter I adopt a position which might seem rather closer to that of the cultural-constructionist than the psycho-social perspective. This is in part an artifact of the status of my data and my mode of ethnographic presentation, for I fully agree with Epstein that ethno-psychologists are theoretically disposed – by their view of emotion as a cultural rather than a natural category – to attend to 'emotion talk' to the neglect of emotional expressions and the psychological and physiological processes which underlie them (1992: 251–7).

My earlier depictions of Kalauna's ethos have tended to concentrate on its fractious, shame-ridden and resentful aspects (see Young 1971, 1974, 1983a, 1985, 1986b, 1987). In this chapter I restore some balance by dwelling first on an unequivocally positive sentiment and emotion.

105

NUAKABUBU: AN AXIOM OF AMITY

Nuakabubu is a concept of great cultural salience and moral import in Kalauna. Referring to a social sentiment as well as an individual affect, nuakabubu is a hardworking term that embraces compassion, sympathy, amity, kindness, generosity, charity, pity, tenderness and kindred warm feelings associated with 'love'. In recent generations it has become encrusted with Christian sentiments, emphasising 'loving one's neighbour', mutual help and disinterested giving.

I failed to elicit a satisfactory folk etymology for the word, though *nua*- refers to mind, heart or feeling (*nuaku*, my mind, heart or feeling), while *kabubu* is a leaf used to cover food while it is cooking in a pot. The reduplicated form *nuanua* means thought, desire, wish, intention (*yaku nuanua*, my thought). Accordingly, many terms for sentiments, affects and mental states are prefixed by *nua*-.

The semantic field of nuakabubu is impressively wide. It overlaps but is not concordant with the range of meanings of the English word 'love', though most notably it excludes the erotic, sexual or romantic connotations of 'love' in English. The Ancient Greeks might well have translated nuakabubu as *agape*, to be clearly distinguished from *eros*. The common term *nuanua*- for 'wanting' or 'desiring' may be used for urgent sexual desire or erotic longing, whereas being romantically obsessed or in the somewhat more settled condition of 'being in love', one would say *nua'udu*, meaning literally 'to remember', implying that one cannot get the beloved's image out of one's head (or heart). Nua'udu is also used when mourning the dead: one remembers them with love; hence a general term for the memorial feast held about year after death is *nua'udu'udu*.

As we shall see, there is another kind of commemorative feast of 'love' called *nuakabukabubu* which, among other things, celebrates the identity and solidarity of a descent group. Interestingly, the Greek term *agape* also came to refer to a 'love feast' of the early Christians at which the rich fed the poor. Nuakabubu likewise received an ideological boost from Wesleyan Mission Christianity, which has promoted nuakabubu as charity and brotherly love. It is pertinent to note that Jenness and Ballantyne, the earliest linguistic authorities on Bwaidoga (the island's lingua franca), glossed nuakabubu simply as 'good will displayed by some action' (1928: 253). This might well have been an adequate translation in 1912, the year of Jenness' fieldwork, when Bwaidogans had experienced only a decade of mission teaching. But nowadays demonstrable 'good will' is a woefully weak gloss for one of the richest words in the language, one that evokes an entire moral ethos.

Nevertheless, the notion that one should 'display' or behaviourally manifest the sentiment of nuakabubu 'by some action' is accurate and revealing, for with their characteristic Melanesian pragmatism Goodenough islanders place a good deal more faith in what people do than in what they say they think or feel. Nuakabubu was one of the very first words I learned on Goodenough and I interpreted it initially in the limited sense indicated by Jenness and Ballantyne. As people shook my hand they would shyly mutter 'Nuakabubu'; and when people brought me small gifts of bananas, pawpaws, coconuts or other foodstuffs, they would say 'Nuakabubu', conveying by this act their 'goodwill'. If I offered to pay for such gifts, the word would be repeated more emphatically, with a gesture of refusal: one should not pay for nuakabubu.

Nuakabubu, then, is both the name of a sentiment or emotional disposition and also the name of the customary gift which expresses it. Such gifts are supposedly made without expectation of return, though as we might expect (following Mauss), disinterestedness is largely 'social pretence'. In the large periodic feasts or festivals that culminate in magnanimous distributions of pork and raw vegetable food (see Young 1971: ch. 11), nuakabubu is the most benign of the three categories of prestation. Those designated nuakabubu are 'friendly' gifts of amity and goodwill to visitors to whom the sponsors are neither indebted nor hostile. Nuakabubu is appropriate to the social domain of 'generalised' reciprocity at the altruistic end of the morality spectrum (Sahlins 1965).

Needless to say, to refuse to accept (and in some circumstances to refuse to give) a nuakabubu gift is to announce a state of animosity. To refuse or reject in Kalauna is *atuluva*, 'to push away'. In gross terms it is tantamount, as Mauss wrote, to 'a declaration of war ... a refusal of friendship and intercourse' (1954: 11). Refusals were linked in sequence over a period of several months and were politically consequential; indeed their political ramifications showed that refusals were not simply the 'opposite' of acceptances (cf. Young 1985).

In yet other contexts nuakabubu connotes consideration, caring and the 'feeling-with' of the English terms compassion and sympathy. Similar concepts to nuakabubu are found throughout the Pacific.[1] For a Melanesian example we need look no further than the Tolai, among whom the concept of *varmari* is also sometimes glossed as 'love', though Epstein (1992: 123) also points out that it does not refer to erotic love (which is expressed by *mamainga*, to want or desire). At the heart of varmari, Epstein writes, 'lie the notions of compassion and concern ... used not simply as an indication of spontaneous feeling but also as standing for amity and harmony in social relationships and at its widest reaches a symbol of human solidarity itself' (1992: 149). In Kalauna, likewise, kinship norms and values are evoked by the term nuakabubu. It is redolent of what Meyer Fortes called the 'axiom of amity' among kin. The extension of this axiom to strangers in Christian brotherhood and humankind more generally, while an impossible ideal, is indicative of the altruistic and moral components of nuakabubu.

ANCESTRAL SPIRITS

In Kalauna people are expected to feel and express nuakabubu towards their ancestral spirits, who in turn are assumed to feel nuakabubu for their descendants. Before I turn to the description of a nuakabubu feast something needs to be said about the place of the ancestors in Kalauna society. Although the religious ideology has been modified by almost 80 years' exposure to Christian ideas, people still firmly believe in a traditional pantheon of demi-gods, mythical heroes, demons and spirits. Today, as before, spirits of the ancestors, *inainala*, are believed to inhabit and 'look after' the hamlet's stone sitting circles and people's houses; simultaneously they occupy the garden lands they cleared and planted in the distant past, whence they are addressed and exhorted by magical spells sung by their descendants (spells, of course, which exist by courtesy of the ancestors).

Ancestral spirits may punish breaches of privilege or copyright, since ultimately the 'customs' (*dewa*) which distinguish one descent group from another were 'invented' and patented by them. The most important dewa (particularly myths and magical systems) are said to 'come from the ground', referring to the master myth of Kalauna origins, in which the clan ancestors emerged in a specified order from a hole at the top of a sacred hill, bringing with them the unique dewa which were to become the emblems and ritual competences of the groups they founded.

Any emic definition of a Kalauna descent group, then, must acknowledge its deceased members, guardians of custom, property and propriety. Ancestors are part and parcel of its identity vis-a-vis other such groups. Over time, of course, the memory of particular named ancestors is gradually erased and they join a shadowy pool of ancestral spirits, though in incantations they are rhetorically differentiated according to generation. This imaginary group of dead kin appear to have few expectations of the living: Kalauna people make only the most perfunctory gestures of 'sacrifice' to them, though their presence is acknowledged in many other ways.

The affective consequences of a belief in ancestral spirits are significant, and few Kalauna people live their lives ignorant of or indifferent to inainala. They behave as if they were a constant presence, though in a casual and taken-for-granted way. One man whose house I shared told me he 'felt good' when enacting certain customary routines about the house. The observance of traditional dewa can be its own reward. But since the ancestors make few daily demands on the living, people are not compelled to remember them. Exceptions arise when misfortune occurs, for inainala can be punitive when their prohibitions are breached, their property misused or their special places trespassed upon. In some instances their incantations can backfire and inflict harm on the magician who recites them incorrectly. But sickness attributed to ancestral displeasure is rare compared to that attributed to the malicious sorcery of the living.

In any event, fear and anxiety are not emotions generally associated with ancestral spirits. Ghostly vengeance of the newly dead may certainly be feared for a time, particularly of those who died violent deaths, and people may be acutely anxious for several nights if the spirit is thought to be resentful and vindictive. But such anxieties following a death more usually focus on the living relatives, whose vengeful anger is far more greatly feared. The mundane feelings most commonly expressed towards ancestors, however, are quiet respect and a casual reverence. Piety, too, the sentiment of dutifulness, is an affective category of sorts (the transmuted love of a child for a long dead parent) which motivates Kalauna people at certain times.

FEASTING 'THE ANCESTORS' HANDPRINTS'

I now describe a particular instance of the ceremonialised expression of nuakabubu: a feast in which the human participants simultaneously express amity and 'sympathy' towards their fellows and their ancestors. Significantly, the pretext for the feast as I observed it involved land. Needless to say, land is of immense importance in maintaining group identity in Kalauna: indeed, it is a constitutive element, for a group without land is inconceivable, almost a contradiction in terms (just as a Kalauna individual without land would be deemed a virtual non-person). There is an affective, ancestor-mediated relationship between land and descent group identity, expressed in nuakabubu-inspired commemorative feasts. What follows is a concrete instance I observed in 1989.

In that year the senior patrilineage (*unuma*) of Anuana 1 (a subclan hamlet of Lulauvile) consisted of four adult men. Kiyodi was the nominal leader, principal heir of the master-sorcerer Kimaola, who was banished from the village in 1976 (Young 1983a: Epilogue). In recent years Kiyodi and another senior member of this unuma named Siyoka had taken turns to inaugurate the yam planting in Kalauna (see Young 1971: 149–50). The food and sex taboos associated with this role are onerous. The yam magician cannot eat any yams at all during the year in which he performs the rites; nor should he sleep with his wife at any time between the first planting and the final harvest, a matter of eight or nine months.

Kiyodi's patrilineage owns a large block of land named Hahulu on the fertile slopes below the village. It had not been used for a generation or more, since the death of Kiyodi's grandfather Ewahaluna. In 1989 the men of this group decided to hold a memorial feast in order to 're-open' the land and make new yam gardens on Hahulu. They invited their *tubuya* ('sister's children') to join them: that is, men born of women belonging to Anuana 1 subclan.

This kind of memorial feast is called *nimakabukabubu*. Etymologically, it is related to *nuakabubu*, though *nima-* ('hand') replaces *nua-* ('mind/heart') and *kabubu* is reduplicated. In describing it, some men referred to nimakabukabubu by circumlocution as *nimakali kana ana*. *Nimakali* means the handprint, 'for which we eat' (*kana ana*); that is, 'feasting in memory of the ancestor's handprint'. But its more correct name of nimakabukabubu emphasises 'feeling compassion' for the hand (*nimana*) of the ancestor, the instrument by which he had worked the land and secured it for his descendants by metaphorically putting his mark on it. The iconic image of handprint, of course, is wholly apt for commemorating a man's association with a particular piece of ground. More so than a footprint, a handprint betokens an intimate working relationship to the soil that all subsistence gardeners enjoy.

It wasn't only Ewahaluna's handprint that was being commemorated; it was also those of all the deceased owners of that land, in effect the handprints of the collectivity of the subclan's ancestors. Although they did not make the analytical distinction themselves, this aspect might be seen to express two separate themes or functions, so to speak, one for internal or private consumption and the other for external or public consumption. First, the commemoration of ancestors and the self-satisfying due of filial piety ('but for those men we wouldn't be here') is the unuma's private affirmation and celebration of its own identity. But no less important is the commemoration of a man–land bond (symbolised by the image of possessive imprints of hands in the soil) which might be said – rather grandly – to be a premium paid to public 'memory' to ensure the economic and political survival of the owning unuma as a social entity. That is to say, it is by means of such feasts that groups advertise to the wider community their stewardship of a particular piece of garden land and publicly announce their intention of keeping it.

There is an equally important, though less obvious, aspect to the nimakabukabubu: its inaugurative role in ceremonially 're-opening' the land for horticultural use. It is common practice throughout the Massim on the occasion of death to place interdictions or prohibitions on productive resources associated with the deceased: notably, garden or hunting lands, fruit trees, fishing reefs or rivers. In Kalauna these prohibitions are called *kwala* and are said to 'close' the land, grove, reef or river. The deceased's hamlet may be 'closed' in a similar way by placing the prohibition on the circular stone platform, the *atuaha*, of the owning subclan. The penalty for breaching these mortuary prohibitions is a shaming gift of food, designed to instigate a competitive food exchange (*abutu*) which would also serve as a memorial feast to the dead person. Whether or not abutu occurs, the prohibitions on land, sea, river or atuaha are normally lifted after one year; the resources are then regarded as accessible or 'open' for normal use. (Hahulu, interdicted for Kiyodi's grandfather many years ago, was somewhat unusual in being 'closed' for so long.)

Nimakabukabubu, then, conjoins commemoration and prohibition-lifting, though it appears that the memorial aspect (the 'handprint') can be focused on other kinds of resources or artifacts and need not be associated only with land.[2]

The date for Kiyodi's feast was set about two weeks in advance, and people spent some of this period fishing. They smoke-dried the fish and later added it to the pots of tubers they cooked for the feast. During the afternoon of the feast-day Kiyodi killed and butchered a pig donated by a 'sister's son' who wanted to garden at Hahulu. In its social composition, the group participating in the feast consisted of the wider clan segment to which Anuana belongs, namely Lulauvile II, plus tubuya ('sister's children') and a few other cognates. About 25 families were represented.

Each family cooked a dish in a clay pot or aluminium saucepan. Some cooked taro, others yams, still others bananas. The yam and taro tubers were as large as possible and, in feasting mode, not sliced but boiled whole. Most pots were flavoured with coconut cream, and some were garnished with smoked fish. There were also smaller pots of greens such as cabbage and pumpkin shoots.

The man who acted as Kiyodi's master of ceremonies summoned people to bring their pots to the principal atuaha of Anuana I, an imposing stone structure which is the ancestral focus of the hamlet. When all had placed their pots on it, the master of ceremonies began to redistribute them according to two rules of thumb: each family should receive a different pot to the one it provided; and each family should receive a pot equal in size in exchange for the pot it donated. As in all such distributions, women carry the pots away for their families to eat in the privacy of their own houses. Before they did so Kiyodi made a short speech, the main message of which was: 'We make this feast only to remember those of our group who have died. There is nothing to worry about. When we plant at Hahulu nothing will happen.'

By this he meant to reassure everyone that no one (of his own group at any rate) would magically despoil or 'chase away' the yams, so they could plant without undue concern for the bounty of the harvest. Kiyodi also announced that, as planned, Siyoka would be ritual guardian of the yams that year. The very next week (the first week in August) he would go to his garden plot at Hahula and 'stir the soil' with his be-spelled digging stick; then he would plant a single, exemplary yam, and sing his incantation to call the inainala from far and wide. Kiyodi warned the people to stay away from their new gardens for a few days (to give enough time for the ancestral spirits to visit), then they could all 'stir the soil' and plant their own seeds in their own time with their own special, be-spelled digging sticks. This injunction applied to the entire community, not simply to those 40-odd men and women who were intending to plant at Hahulu.

And so the nimakabukabubu concluded. Like any such feast it 'made people happy', but there was the additional joyful prospect that the rich land thus inaugurated, so fertile after its long fallow, would yield an abundant harvest. But thanks were also given to the ancestors' spirits who would be summoned to inspire the yams to grow, most importantly those ancestors of Anuana who had been remembered in this feast for their 'handprint' traces on the land. The indivisible links between land, yams, the living and their ancestors were instantiated during a feast which brought together an extended and residentially dispersed group of kinsmen and bound them for a season in the common pursuit of prosperity.

MIWA: THE CANNIBAL FEAST

In stark contrast to nimakabukabubu feasts of amity were the cannibal feasts of a century ago. These may aptly be counterpoised as feasts of enmity. My data are deficient, of course, being based entirely on a selectively remembered oral tradition, but some suggestive themes emerge.

Cannibalism on Goodenough Island was practised in two principal modes: the indiscriminate, hunger-driven cannibalism that occurred in periods of famine, and the revenge cannibalism (*miwa*) that consummated blood feud. The latter was understandably more selective and ceremonialised and it is that which I describe briefly here.

On the basis of information collected in 1911–12 in the Bwaidoga district of southeast Goodenough (about a decade after the suppression of cannibalism in that area), Jenness and Ballantyne wrote:

The cannibal feast was always considered an act of revenge. Sometimes the prisoner was dismembered and disembowelled on the stone platform while still alive, sometimes he was despatched beforehand with a club. Rarely the women were allowed to torture him ... As a rule the body was cut into segments and laid upon a mat; nothing, not even a drop of blood, was allowed to escape, lest the victors be cheated of part of their revenge. Each family received a portion, which it cooked like ordinary meat, and everyone down to the smallest child shared in the feast. Where only one prisoner had been taken, his head and hands were given to the wife or nearest kinsman of the man for whom the prisoner was the atonement. (1920: 88)

Two generations later, in both Bwaidoga and Kalauna, I was able to confirm and amplify this broad picture. In Kalauna at least, bodies were sometimes kept overnight in a stream, weighted by stones. Then members of the killer's group, accompanied by sisters' husbands, would fetch the body to the killer's hamlet, carrying it on their shoulders as pigs are carried, strung by the wrists and ankles over a long pole. The victim was referred to as *ama kaliva* ('our man'), *ama kevakeva* ('our meat') or *ama daiyaya* ('our blood'), the form of the possessive denoting that the speakers themselves will eat the body. A *pandanus* mat was placed on the stone sitting circle and the body laid upon it, where it was butchered with bamboo knives. The blood that flowed from the body during the butchering was carefully collected in coconut-shell cups or wooden bowls lined with cooked cabbage, and it was drunk by female relatives of the person for whom the present victim was miwa (revenge). The flesh was cut into small pieces which were then skewered on the tough dried spines of coconut leaves – presumably like kebabs. Thus secured, the pieces of meat were boiled in pots together with vegetable foods such as yams, taro and bananas. The body's extremities and genitals were cooked whole, and seem to have been among the choicest morsels. Women are said to have been particularly partial to male genitalia, and men to the vulvas of female victims. The elderly of both sexes relished the palms of the hands and soles of the feet. Other prerogatives of the elderly were the tongue and brain, also valued for their flavour. Unlike pork and fish, human flesh was never smoke-dried; it was said to putrefy quickly and stink.

Concerning distribution the accounts are inconsistent. Some say that children below the age of puberty did not partake, others that even the youngest were encouraged to eat the victim's flesh. There was even disagreement as to whether the captor or killer was allowed to eat his victim, though according to the principle of *niune* (which prohibits the direct recipient of a gift to consume it) he would certainly have been forbidden to do so (see Young 1971: 69–70, 1983b: 395). It seems to have been the practice for every clan or every hamlet which constituted the community to receive a share of the victim, and not simply those who were claiming miwa blood revenge. So far as Kalauna is concerned, however, it is unclear whether the cooking and feasting were done entirely in the hamlet of the avengers (such that members of other groups were invited to come and select their morsels of flesh from the cooking pots), or whether a distribution of limbs and morsels took place immediately after the butchering, to be taken severally to hearths in other hamlets (as is the case for the majority of village-wide pig distributions today). In view of the excitement of the occasion, however, it would not be surprising if miwa cannibal feasts were communal and even orgiastic affairs. (One old man told me that people did not sit down while eating the flesh of their miwa victim but ran around whooping; their repast concluded with dancing and singing insulting songs about their enemies.)[3]

Most interesting of all in this respect were the extreme measures taken by avenging kin in extracting, as it were, their pound of flesh. In Bwaidoga, at least, there seems to have been an imperative to consume a miwa victim down to the very last morsel. I was told the bones and teeth would be pounded to dust, the nails and hair shredded, and everything blended with the vegetable food cooked with the flesh. All the internal organs were eaten, including the intestines. One old man of Bwaidoga was remembered for having strung up over his fire the intestines of his miwa victim (one who had purportedly killed and eaten his son); for months afterwards the old man sprinkled powdered excrement onto his food ('like salt') and when it was quite finished he chewed the dried intestines. Kalauna informants denied that they went as far as to eat the excrement of their victims, though they were not disgusted at the prospect so long as it was done in the spirit of revenge. Kalauna's revenge speciality was to break open the victims' bones and suck the marrow. Significantly, the phrase *luluna ya kudana* ('his bone I suck') refers to competitive food exchange with one's traditional enemy. The coconut cups which had been used to drink the meat-broth of the victim were used until all traces of his or her 'grease' had disappeared. It is conceivable that this total assimilation of the victim was intended to absorb or erase his or her identity. At any rate, such dedicated revenge was literally all-consuming, and seems sometimes to have been conducted obsessively and with deep satisfaction.[4]

The emotional aspects of cannibal feasting are impossible to reconstruct with any certainty. Even the oldest of my informants had long since been weaned off human flesh and could suggest only standard affective responses: principally 'anger' followed by 'happiness' at achieving revenge. It is difficult to believe (even by anthropologists practised in empathy) that some fear, revulsion and disgust were not evoked during cannibal feasts. A tinge of fascinated horror, too, probably, if not the 'unspeakable horror' reported by missionaries of their own reactions to instances of cannibalism. The late nineteenth-century war-leader and tyrant-hero of Kalauna, Malaveyoyo, instructed his warriors to eat their captives raw on a prominent rock within clear sight of their relatives – an act surely intended to increase their humiliation and horror. Eating the uncooked flesh was said to cause *meadoba*, blood lust, which induced a fighting frenzy in his warriors (Young 1983a: 105).

Interestingly, some informants expressed 'pity' or 'sympathy' (nuakabubu) for youthful victims. Such 'pity' was considered a legitimate motive for the occasional 'salvation' (*yave*) of captives, and there was an institutionalised practice for its expression. Whether instigated by one of her menfolk or acting on her own accord, a woman could take off her leaf skirt and throw it over a captive before he or she could be killed.[5] This act of compassion saved the captive's life, and he or she might then be either adopted, married or released. Thereafter, the kin and descendants of the rescued captive and his or her saviour acknowledged a special relationship called *solama* or *tolama*. Today, people sharing this bond still offer one another protection and hospitality when visiting (see Young 1971: 49–50, 1977b).

The spirit or ghost (*alualua*) of the cannibal victim presented a minor problem since it tended to remain with the bones. (I neglected to inquire whether this might have been a reason for crushing and eating the bones in Bwaidoga; if so, it would indicate a deliberate attempt to obliterate the spirit along with its mortal remains, perhaps as a means of annihilating the person's identity.) The ghost was understandably vengeful and likely to haunt those who had killed and eaten its body. Like the troublesome ghost of any manner of violent death, it could be driven away by a ritual of banishment involving conjurations and a cacophony of loud noise. But the interesting notion that the spirit lingers wherever the bones remain meant that exiled spirits could not become inainala, ancestors. Partly for this reason, a convention was observed by Kalauna and neighbouring villages, according to which they exchanged the bones of their victims for burial on their own territories. This might have been motivated by compassion (for their own spirits rather than for those of their enemies), but judging by the imprecations that were hurled at enemies when they were summoned to collect their bones it was the opportunity to insult them that Kalauna men most enjoyed:

> Hey! Hey!
> Your skulls will break!
> You will eat our shit!
> Come and fetch your brothers' bones!

This taunt was remembered from the time of Malaveyoyo. But cannibal monster that he was, Malaveyoyo is credited with inventing competitive food exchange (abutu) to end the cannibal era. He substituted the bloodless 'fighting with food' of abutu for eating enemies.

TRADITIONAL ENEMIES, ABUTU, FOOD AND FAECES

There is a category of persons in Kalauna who lie outside the ambit of everyday amity and goodwill, and to whom one neither expresses *nuakabubu* nor offers gifts in this compassionate mode. Such persons are designated *nibai-* 'enemies', and the noun inflects to indicate personal possession as in kinship terms and body parts. Linguistically, Kalauna people are thus 'inseparable' from their enemies. Nibai- are hereditary and institutionalised, however, so one neither chooses one's enemies nor necessarily hates them. They are ascribed on a group basis, like the *fofofo* (exchange partners) whom they complement (see Young 1971: 69-74). Structurally defined, nibai- are paired descent groups (at unuma or subclan level, within Kalauna itself as well as in neighbouring villages), whose ancestors are believed to have cannibalised one another in the past. An opposing category of descent group is tolama, mentioned above, defined as those who 'saved' one's ancestors from being killed and eaten by compassionate acts of nuakabubu.

Thus the relationship of nibai- is predicated on particular historical incidents of homicide and cannibalism. As we have seen, vengeance or revenge (miwa) generated reciprocal acts of oral aggression. In this light it is obvious why the nibai- relationship is integral to the ideology of competitive food exchange in Goodenough communities. As a symbolic expression of blood-feud based on cannibalism, 'fighting with food' (abutu) is an apt vehicle for oral aggression, one that harnesses many of the dominant values and 'affect-ridden' concepts of the culture (Epstein 1984: 44, 1992: 276; Panoff 1970).

I have described abutu and the configuration of values in which it is embedded in considerable detail elsewhere (1971, 1986b, 1987), and Epstein has summarised some of these ethnographic materials in his essay on the experience of shame in Melanesia (1984) as well as on Tolai affect and ideation (1992).

It will be helpful to cite here in full a paragraph from the latter source:

The central feature of *abutu* is to put one's opponent, one's *nibai*, or 'enemy,' to shame by presenting him with food in such quantity that he cannot possibly make immediate return. Now this statement at once discloses a seeming ambiguity in Kalauna attitudes toward food. For the people of Kalauna food is the supreme symbol of love and amity, and the giving of food is the chief expression of solidary social relations. Yet in the context of *abutu* it serves primarily as an instrument of aggression. How is this apparent contradiction to be explained? Translated into psychological terms I believe that what the situation implies is a profound ambivalence toward the giver of food, proto-typically the mother, a loving and nurturant figure who has also in some way provoked the hostility of the child. But this hostility cannot be allowed overt expression; it can only be discharged in disguised form in some ritualized context such as *abutu*, where the aggression can be redirected against 'real' enemies. But I consider that the data also allow us to make the further inference that this discharge of hostility takes an anal form, that is to say, the food that is cast at one's opponents in a competitive exchange takes on the symbolic guise of an anal product. (Epstein 1992: 277)

Epstein then nominates the yam as the ideal symbolic object, both as a focus of male pride (and therefore appropriate for competitive exchange) and as an 'anal product'. Hence, he writes, 'it is as though, on the level of the unconscious, the measure of a man was to be able to display his prowess and humiliate his rivals by producing bigger turds than they did' (1992: 277–8).

There are at least three issues here which invite comment and require substantiation: first, ambivalence towards food; second, yams as faeces; and third, maternal frustration, infant hostility and oral–anal aggression. Although I cannot address these issues with anything like the detailed consideration they deserve, I can offer some additional ethnographic commentary.

Epstein asks how food, the 'supreme symbol of love and amity' in Kalauna, can be used as an instrument of aggression. Since the full data were not available to him when he wrote, a brief digression on Kalauna food categories is helpful.

In addition to several pigs, the centrepiece of any abutu consists of one or more platforms of the large, hard, dry yams which have been secretly preserved for up to a year by the practice of *lokona* – magically aided conservation by abstention. Such yams, of the class called *kuvi* (botanically *Dioscorea alata*), are presented with war-like displays of *sefaiya*: prancing and yelling. They are 'feared' for their size and quality (even when on the point of rotting and virtually inedible) for they are notoriously difficult to repay by matched equivalence. Outstanding debts of lokona yams are a cause of considerable unease and anxiety, for the debtor is notionally the status inferior of the donor, who retains the moral ascendancy until the yams are repaid. Thus the prize lokona yams which all self-respecting Kalauna men hoard against the day when they can give them aggressively to their enemies are said to be a source of 'fear' (*matauta*). Moreover, they are not food like other foods. Such yams belong to a category of food called *valaiya*: hard, dry and 'juiceless' yams, taro, or bananas. People sometimes refer to it as 'bad food', for valaiya lacks *huyona*, the 'juice' or 'essence' which (in local ethnophysiology) is vital to growth, bodily strength and good health. This life-enhancing 'juice', the irreducible nutritive component of most food, is found in a complementary and opposite category called *lakwada*, soft, moist and 'crumbly' foods. In brief, the values associated with these two kinds of food are context-bound. The soft 'juicy' staples are associated with the domestic sphere of nurture; they are redolent of hearth, home and motherhood. The hard, 'juiceless' valaiya food smacks of the political arena of abutu, of tough and disciplined manhood (Young 1986a: 117–18).

In giving 'juiceless' lokona yams to one's enemy, one is not 'feeding' him in the sense of contributing to his health and nurture; rather one is presenting him with a 'poisoned' gift that might be deemed a denial of nurture. (Such yams are in fact very infrequently eaten, for people suspect them to have been 'spoiled' by their owner's lokona magic, which is believed, at the very least, to stunt growth.) The ambivalence concerning food in Kalauna, then, is epitomised by a categorical distinction between what might be crudely characterised as 'good food of love' and 'bad food of hate'.

These facts support Epstein's proposition that (some) yams may be unconsciously equated with faeces. In particular, valaiya yams of the kuvi class – non-nutritive, 'poisoned', 'bad', 'feared', coercive and shame-inducing as they are – could well be symbolic of the 'bad body contents' of psychoanalytical theory. When Kalauna men present their enemies with lokona yams it is at least plausible that they are, in effect, saying to them 'Eat my shit!' In Epstein's terms, '... *abutu*, a projection on the symbolic plane of infantile intra-psychic conflicts, combines both oral and anal elements; its central impulse is reflected in the means it offers of exacting revenge by forcing enemies to eat excrement' (1992: 278).

I have some reservations, however, for a great deal more is going on during abutu than this simple model suggests. To begin with, scatological jokes and anal-fixated badinage notwithstanding (see Young 1977a and Epstein 1992: 278), Kalauna people do not make any conscious equation of valaiya yams with turds; but then, we would not expect them to if the associative processes involved are unconscious. What can be stated with more assurance is that Kalauna people deem it a mythological truth that kuvi yams are 'born of women' (Young 1983a: 228ff.). Accordingly, as in many parts of Melanesia, they are attributed with certain human faculties, such as hearing and the capacity for emotion. If yams are 'people', their aggressive exchange in abutu symbolically enacts the exchange of cannibal victims, as Malaveyoyo's innovative substitution intended.[6] But we should note that only a relatively small proportion (between 5 per cent and 10 per cent) of the total number of kuvi yams exchanged in abutu qualify as valaiya or 'bad food'. The great majority of yams are eaten by their recipients with evident enjoyment, and any association with faeces – even an unconscious one – seems implausible.

It might also be objected that the ethnographic facts undermine any categorical symbolic distinction – whether moral, political or gustatory – between eating an enemy's excrement and giving one's own excrement to the enemy to eat. If Kalauna people found it acceptable to eat the faeces of a miwa cannibal victim, why taunt their enemies with 'You will eat *our* shit!'? The taunt must surely be interpreted as an aggressive challenge of the kind: 'We are so powerful that we have eaten you completely, even your shit! See if you can do the same to us!'

A comparable objection concerning abutu is less easily countered. The intra-psychic model of abutu based on oral-anal aggression might be phrased as follows: one gives 'bad food' (= excrement) to nibai-, those who cannibalised one's ancestors; they pay back with similar food, measure for measure, so there is an exchange of 'bad body contents' (mutual gifts of 'poison', if you will). Appropriately, the 'victors' are those who give the most 'excrement', thereby humiliating their rivals. But note that a displacement occurs, for the exchanging enemies pass the food on to their respective fofofo partners, since the rule of niune forbids antagonists to eat their own enemy's 'excrement'. In these terms, the displacement might seem to make little sense, unless as another form of 'discharge' of the hostility and aggression associated with abutu.

THE ORAL-ANAL FOUNDATIONS OF KALAUNA'S ETHOS?

Writing of Duau people of Normanby Island in the southern D'Entrecasteaux, Geza Roheim saw 'oral sadism as the key to their character' (1950: 241). This was evident, for instance, in their practice of cannibalism, their modes of betel chewing and their sexual play (characterised by biting and scratching). In Kalauna there is a similarly suggestive configuration of verbal idioms, behavioural traits and customs indicative of oral aggression if not sadism: in addition to abutu and cannibalism one might adduce *tufo'a* hunger-inducing sorcery, gifts that idiomatically 'bite', and the immobilised 'masters of the feast', *kaiwabu*, who epitomise the values of containment and restraint.

Roheim asserts that the oral sadism of Duau people is caused by 'bad mothers' who typically tease their infants at the breast and wean them abruptly. The infant trauma induced by ambivalent love and feeding frustration gives rise to body destruction fantasies and oral sadism; these are repressed and redirected into attempts to be 'good mothers', given cultural expression by hoarding food, restraining appetite and feasting one another with conspicuous generosity (1950: ch. 3, passim).[7]

I doubt that Epstein would go as far as Roheim in claiming that all such cultural forms are behavioural manifestations of an oral-anal sadism induced by maternal frustration. Still, Epstein has postulated 'a profound ambivalence' of the Kalauna child towards the giver of food, 'prototypically the mother' (1992: 277); and elsewhere, too, he has wondered how 'Goodenough infants experience the relationship with the parents, especially the mother' (1986: 48).[8] This is not the place to pursue this difficult issue in any detail, but I offer the following salient facts. As will be seen, infancy in Kalauna appears to be far less traumatic than Roheim argues for Duau.

Kalauna infants are breast-fed for two years or longer, until a subsequent child is born or until it has more or less weaned itself off the breast. During this period there is a post–partum taboo on sexual intercourse which is rationalised by the harm coitus may cause the infant. A woman's milk is believed to be 'spoiled' by her husband's semen and the child would become puny and sickly if it continued to suckle. The food taboos observed by nursing mothers are also explained by the need to maintain 'good', 'pure' milk for the health and well-being of the child. Like male semen, meat of any kind is thought to pollute breast-milk; while 'red' foodstuffs are forbidden owing to their symbolic association with blood. The ideal foods for a nursing mother are white, 'clean' yams (classed as lakwada, soft and moist), which ideally is also the first solid food to be fed infants at about five months. Some cases of abrupt weaning did come to my notice, but they seem to have been dictated by necessity. There is certainly no assumption that a child must be weaned suddenly or after a set period. Babies sleep with their mothers and suck on demand. Babies who bite the nipple are discouraged by gentle taps and withdrawal of the nipple. Weaning can be achieved quickly by rubbing the nipples with ginger. Alternatively, a mother can absent herself in her garden hut for several days, leaving the child in the care of grandparents.

Kalauna people say breast milk is 'sweet' (*diyadiyana*) and ginger 'bitter' (*wolana*). Although I have no observational data to confirm the reactions of Kalauna children weaned in this fashion, one might well suppose that they suffer some trauma. From being a source of comforting sweetness, the mother's breast turns suddenly into an object of discomforting bitterness. I should note that although ginger is cultivated it is not used for culinary purposes in Kalauna (as it is in some other Massim societies). Its sole use is 'magical': for curing and as a prophylactic against harmful spirits and human enemies in wartime. In all its uses, therefore, including to deter a child from suckling, ginger is a *repellent*. It may be significant, then, that the *sisikwana* magic adults use to quell their appetite is said to make food 'bitter' (Young 1983a: 180).

Yet I remain sceptical that an infantile experience which affects only *some* children can somehow give rise to a generalised and unconscious 'hostility to the mother' sufficient to create a distinctive cultural ethos characterised by – among other things – attitudes indicative of oral-anal aggression. The generally benign picture I have drawn of infant suckling and weaning in Kalauna contrasts with the starkly malign one presented by Roheim for the Duau. If he was correct in placing so much explanatory weight on the infant's early experiences, one would expect the adult personality structures (not to mention the cultures) of Duau and Goodenough peoples to differ markedly. Yet I would defy anyone to distinguish them by their behaviour, demeanour, disposition or character. Culturally, too, despite the fact that Goodenough society is anomalous in being organised patrilineally, D'Entrecasteaux peoples share a very close family resemblance.

NIMAKABUKABUBU AND ABUTU: A COMPARISON

Let us return to the Kalauna feasts and conclude on a more festive note. How best might we conceptualise the essential differences between feasts of amity and feasts of enmity? According to a useful analytical dichotomy proposed by Robert Paine, exchanges can be characterised by two dominant 'modalities': the 'incorporative' and the 'transactional' (Paine 1976; see also Young 1985). An exchange in the incorporative mode is based on notions of identity, mutuality and sharing; value is sought jointly by the parties to it, and symbolic communications concerning the objects of exchange are generally uncontested. An exchange in the transactional mode, on the other hand, is based on notions of opposition or complementarity; each party seeks its own value, according to which there is some advantage to be won, and symbolic communications are therefore more elaborate and open to contestation.

I shall compare the two types of feast I have described in terms of group identities and sentiments involved, the types of food eaten or exchanged, the role of the ancestors, and the respective feasts' ostensible purposes and affective consequences.

Nimakabukabubu is an incorporative feast, stressing identity by involving only clansmen and the tubuya category of sister's children. The cooked food that characterises the feast is pooled and redistributed equally; it consists entirely of lakwada: 'soft', 'moist' foodstuffs which are nurturant through the bodily production of huyona, the 'juice' essential to growth and good health. The dominant ethos of nimakabukabubu is the amity of nuakabubu, evoking contentment and happiness. The sponsors' ancestors are commemorated through their works, their 'handprints'. The stated purpose of nimakabukabubu is benign. It is to make accessible or available for human use something that had been prohibited following a death. The affective consequences of nimakabukabubu are positive, if relatively short term; no debts are incurred and (if it proceeds according to plan) no ill-feeling results. Above all, this feast exemplifies and expresses the axiom of amity which defines the solidary sentiment of nuakabubu.

In contrast, abutu is a competitive, transactional feast which highlights the complementary identities of opposing 'enemies'. Each side comprises the sponsoring clan (and its tubuya), insulated from their 'enemy' by exchange partners (fofofo). The raw food that characterises the exchange is ideally (though not predominantly) valaiya: 'hard', 'dry' tubers on the verge of rotting, non-nutritive food which does not produce the 'juice' of growth. The dominant ethos of abutu is the enmity of rivals, evocative of pride and shame, anger and spite (*veumaiyiyi*; see Young 1974; Epstein 1992: 272). The sponsors' ancestors are commemorated only in so far as they are conjured by various spells, recruited to the cause of their descendants' battle. The purpose of abutu is agonistic, even malign: it is to humiliate enemies, avenge insults, assert dominance. The political consequences of abutu can reverberate for a long time, so its affective consequences are as enduring as the food debts it incurs. Grudges may persist for years. This kind of feast might be said to exemplify and express an axiom of enmity.

The dominant affects of abutu are anger, pride, shame, humiliation and the masochistic self-pity of veumaiyiyi, for one must 'give until it hurts'. Passions are engaged by abutu in a way quite foreign to incorporative feasts like nimakabukabubu. Everything would seem to depend upon the social identity of the group(s) taking part. In the case of abutu, contention is generated and even celebrated: traditional enemies evidently *enjoy* engaging one another by fighting with food. In these fractious contests (enlivened by conventional displays of aggression called *sefaiya*) group identities are affirmed by opposition and hardened by rhetorical assertions of difference. Distinguishing customs, dewa, come into their own on these occasions, and all the speeches made amid the clamour of the actual prestations stress such inborn, dewa-based differences between contesting clans. In abutu one can witness group identity at its most fervent and iconoclastic. The affect that does most to carry these assertions of identity is a kind of stewing, simmering anger. One sees it in the jerky haste of the men as they fetch their yams and wave them, jutting-jawed and teeth-clenched, under the noses of their rivals; one hears it in the taut voices of the orators; one detects it in the bulging eyes of spectators chomping furiously on their betel nut; one sees it even in the way women's leaf skirts swish aggressively to and fro as they carry yams away on their heads.

So far as the nimakabukabubu feast is concerned, it is evident from the complex entailments of what is ostensibly a fairly simple commemorative feast that group identity is being publicly restated and reaffirmed through explicit connections between ancestral land and descent group membership. The group identity (notionally defined by ancestors) is affirmed by ceremonial feasting with its underpinnings of affective states associated with nuakabubu. The memorial feast in a Melanesian community is invariably more than it seems and – as here – one glimpses a religious aspect of ostensibly practical activities. The spiritual concern runs like a luminous thread through the mundane fabric of a secular event.

NOTES

1. For example, *alofa* in Samoa (Gerber 1985: 145–6), the Tongan cognate is *ofa* (Kavaliku 1977; quoted in Kavapalu 1991: 122); and in Polynesia *arofa* in Tikopia and Tahiti, while the Hawaiian cognate is *aloha* (Pukui and Elbert 1957; cited by Levy 1973: 342).
2. To use a personal example, an Anuana man told me:

> We could do nimakabukabubu for your book *Fighting with Food*. Suppose you die; we in Kalauna hear the news and we are very sorry. We Lulauvile men forbid people to look at your book; it is a kwala. Then one day we want to remember you, so we open the way for people to read your book again. We make a nimakabukabubu for it and remove that kwala. Lulauvile people eat, and they are happy. Or perhaps, because your book is about abutu, we could decide to make abutu for your memory!

In other words, in what is ostensibly a monograph about Kalauna, I myself as author am indelibly inscribed. This book was my 'handprint' in the collective memory of Kalauna. It was reassuring to know that whatever its merits as a commemoration of Kalauna 'customs' circa 1968, *Fighting with Food* was also a memorial to my personhood as Kalauna people might wish to remember it. (Very occasionally in the field is one granted these happy moments of vindication!)

3. I was puzzled at being unable to elicit more 'rules' of exchange concerning cannibalism; it was the gruesome details of culinary practice that older people best remembered.

4. For an oral account of the circumstances of the last cannibal feast in Bwaidoga, see Young (1977b). My main informant concluded his lengthy narrative by describing how the *miwa* victim, Kavolei of Kukuya on Fergusson Island, was killed by a blow to the throat delivered by the capturing hamlet's headman. The account then continued:

> They brought firewood and chopped it up small, then they lit a fire and placed Kavolei upon it. They singed and roasted him and cut him into tiny pieces. And bit by bit they ate him. For their revenge they ate his shit also. Not a drop of blood remained. This was the end of our war with Lavega. (1997b: 139)

The only living eye-witness to the event told me:

> I saw Kavolei die myself ... They carried him to the sitting circle in Wifala [in Bwaidoga]. The one that is still there today. They sat him down on it, but they didn't roast him immediately. They cut him up first, and plucked out his vitals while he was still alive. They started to cut him up, then he died. They roasted taro and soaked it in his blood and ate it. And some old women took his penis and cut it down the middle. They rubbed it in sand to clean it, and ate it. (1977b: 140)

Contrast these accounts (collected in 1973) with Jenness and Ballantyne's, which describes Kavolei's end in more heroic (and emotive) terms:

> [Kavolei] was trussed with ropes and bound with torches. He knew that he was to be burnt alive, so he began to count all the enemies he had slain. Not a groan escaped him in his agony, though he wriggled once or twice, and even his inhuman torturers could not but admire his courage. (1920: 88)

5. This gesture of mercy was honoured also in the southern Massim (see Seligman 1910: 546–7).

6. Harrison (1982: 159) cites an Avatip (Sepik) expression: 'When we eat yams we are eating the flesh and blood of men.' Although I cannot recall hearing it stated so graphically, Kalauna people would concur (adding, no doubt, ' ... and women').

7. While many of Roheim's writings on Duau are pertinent to the present discussion, I cannot examine them here. Suffice to say that I am uncomfortable with the extravagance of his reductively 'global' psychoanalytical interpretation which makes so many inferences based on a cavalier assemblage of 'evidence'.

8. Elsewhere (1983a: 88–91) I have observed that it is father–son hostility which is more pronounced in Kalauna, and in so far as this might be explained in Freudian terms, I did so by accounting the father's role in shaping the son's ambivalent attitude toward food: as something good and nurturing *and* as something bad and shaming.

REFERENCES

Epstein, A.L. 1984. *The Experience of Shame in Melanesia: An Essay in the Anthropology of Affect*. Occasional Paper no. 40, Royal Anthropological Institute of Great Britain and Ireland.

—— 1992. *In the Midst of Life: Affect and Ideation in the World of the Tolai*. Berkeley: University of California Press.

Gerber, E.R. 1985. 'Rage and obligation: Samoan emotion in conflict', in G.M. White and J. Kirkpatrick (eds) *Person, Self, and Experience: Exploring Pacific Ethnopsychologies*. Berkeley: University of California Press, pp. 121–67.

Harrison, S. 1982. 'Yams and the symbolic representation of time in a Sepik River village', *Oceania* 53 (2): 141–62.

Jenness, D. and A. Ballantyne 1920. *The Northern D'Entrecasteaux*. Oxford: Clarendon Press.

—— 1928. *Language, Mythology and Songs of Bwaidoga*. New Plymouth (New Zealand): Avery and Sons Ltd.

Kavaliku, S. 1977. '*Ofa!* The Treasure of Tonga', *Pacific Perspective* 6 (2): 47–67.

Kavapalu, H. 1991. 'Becoming Tongan: an ethnography of childhood in the Kingdom of Tonga', PhD thesis, Australian National University, Canberra.

Levy, R.I. 1973. *Tahitians: Mind and Experience in the Society Islands*. Chicago, IL: University of Chicago Press.

Lutz, C. and G.M. White. 1986. 'The anthropology of emotions', *Annual Review of Anthropology* 15: 405–36.

Mauss, M. 1954. *The Gift*, trans. I. Cunnison. London: Cohen and West.

Paine, R. 1976. 'Two modes of exchange and mediation', in B. Kapferer (ed.) *Transaction and Meaning*. Philadelphia, PA: Institute for the Study of Human Issues, pp. 63–86.

Panoff, F. 1970. 'Food and faeces: a Melanesian rite', *Man* 5: 237–52.

Pukui, M.K. and S. Elbert. 1957. *Hawaiian–English Dictionary*. Honolulu: University of Hawaii Press.

Roheim, G. 1950. *Psychoanalysis and Anthropology*. New York: International Universities Press.

Sahlins, M.D. 1965. 'On the sociology of primitive exchange', in M. Banton (ed.) *The Relevance of Models for Social Anthropology*, ASA Monographs no. 1. London: Tavistock, pp. 139–236.

Seligman, C.G. 1910. *The Melanesians of British New Guinea*. Cambridge: Cambridge University Press.

Young, M.W. 1971. *Fighting with Food: Leadership, Values and Social Control in a Massim Society*. Cambridge: Cambridge University Press.

—— 'Private sanctions and public ideology: some aspects of self-help in Kalauna, Goodenough Island', in A.L. Epstein (ed.) *Contention and Dispute*. Canberra: Australian National University Press, pp. 40–66.

—— 1977a. 'Bursting with laughter: obscenity, values and sexual control in a Massim society', *Canberra Anthropology* 1: 75–87.

—— 1977b. 'Doctor Bromilow and the Bwaidoga wars,' *The Journal of Pacific History* 12 (3–4): 130–53.

—— 1983a. *Magicians of Manumanua: Living Myth in Kalauna*. Berkeley: University of California Press.

—— 1983b. 'Ceremonial visiting in Goodenough Island', in J.W. Leach and E.R. Leach (eds) *The Kula: New Perspectives on Massim Exchange*. Cambridge: Cambridge University Press, pp. 395–410.

—— 1985. 'On refusing gifts: aspects of ceremonial exchange in Kalauna', in D. Barwick, J. Beckett and M. Reay (eds) *Metaphors of Interpretation: Essays in Honour of W.E.H. Stanner*. Canberra: Australian National University Press, pp. 95–110.

—— 1986a. '"The worst disease": the cultural definition of hunger in Kalauna', in L. Manderson (ed.) *Shared Wealth and Symbol: Food, Culture and Society in Oceania and Southeast Asia*. Cambridge: Cambridge University Press, pp. 111–26.

—— 1986b. 'Abutu in Kalauna: a retrospect', *Mankind* 15: 184–97.

—— 1987. 'Skirts, yams and sexual pollution: the politics of adultery in Kalauna', *Journal de las Société des Océanistes* 84 (1): 61–71.

5 STATES OF ANXIETY: CULTURAL IDENTITIES AND DEVELOPMENT MANAGEMENT IN EAST NEW BRITAIN

Alan Rew

It is a feature of a therapeutic study of this kind that much of the most significant research material emerges in its later stages, when the emphasis of the work shifts from diagnosis to therapy. (Isobel Menzies Lyth, 1988: 82)

This account – based on applied fieldwork in New Britain – was initially intended as a footnote to questions that A.L. Epstein (1992b: 247) raises about the future of Tolai identity and the role of Papua New Guinea's towns. For the people of Matupit Island that Epstein studied, nearby Rabaul Town (over the causeway on the 'mainland' of East New Britain) was another social world, despite the small distances involved. But, especially for the elite, these specific spatial identities are superseded as the Tolai increasingly participate in the social and economic life of Papua New Guinea's towns and cities (Salisbury 1976). The future for the Tolai does, in part, lie in Rabaul and other towns where many Tolai live, work, trade or vote. The questions about cultural identity raised in this chapter do not depend on urban juxtaposition, however, but on pre-colonial and colonial history and in the varying fortunes within contemporary Papua New Guinea of decentralisation and micronationalism. Seen in the context of the Independent State of Papua New Guinea, the relations between the Tolai urban and peri–urban provincial elite and the largely rural non-Tolai populations of the Province – the villagers of Pomio District and the two Bainings census divisions – are at least as salient for Tolai cultural identity as are specifically urban–located social relations.

The occasion for my fieldwork was a multi-discipline consultancy commissioned by the Papua New Guinea National Planning Office as part of its 'Least Developed Areas Programme'. Lack of economic and social progress in the Pomio District of East New Britain had led to demands in the National Parliament for the division of the province into two, and the separation of Tolai and Pomio peoples. The Prime Minister of Papua New Guinea had intervened and promised a study of the economic, social and institutional feasibility of a separate administrative status for the District. This was subsequently widened to include an area study and regional planning analysis of Pomio District and the two Bainings census divisions. A team from W.S. Atkins International – a major consultancy with worldwide experience in planning, financial and technology management – on which I was the social planner, was appointed in 1984. The fieldwork on which my account is based was short by conventional anthropological standards. Fieldwork was limited to three months and so my ability to check and cross-check all details at village level was restricted (although it should be noted that not all the ethnographers of East New Britain have taken a full year for their studies). Nonetheless, I had access to much political and statistical information and to a range of elite and ordinary village contacts that would be difficult for an ethnographer working in the conventional research mode to replicate. Furthermore, my investigations were designed in such a way that the planning and management framework of the province itself became an 'analysand', the subject of appreciative inquiry about its organisational health and impairment, rather than the passive object of distant academic scrutiny. The Tolai are now dependent upon a larger state and planning system in which they are admittedly an elite but are also subject to the discerning tactics, emotional challenges and mounting anxieties of an increasingly vociferous, erstwhile subject population. The political and planning framework within which Tolai and non-Tolai work is thus a crucial part of the analysis of current identities.

Responsible for the social analysis of the regional planning studies, I was able to address a theme of crucial importance in A.L. Epstein's work – the relationship between 'continuity and change'. As one would expect, this relationship in his work has also changed, not only because of the circumstances of fieldwork but also because of paradigm shifts and personal research priorities. Epstein's early work in the Copperbelt of Zambia (especially his 1958 monograph) highlighted relationships of political sociology and political economy, albeit with a continuing concern for meaning and its construction. His more recent research has emphasised cultural identity and perception of the self and emotions among the Tolai, albeit within the context of change and urban development. One purpose of my chapter is to show that the reproduction of cultural identities must consider both these elements in counterpoint to each other.

THE EAST NEW BRITAIN PROVINCE AND ITS RESOURCES

New Britain is the second largest island within the independent state of Papua New Guinea. The island's main town, Rabaul, was the centre of the administration and commerce for the former German New Guinea. The island includes the territories of two of Papua New Guinea's 18 provinces – East and West New Britain. The constitution of Papua New Guinea allows for considerable decentralisation from the central government to provincial administrations and assemblies. Pressure from the Tolai of East New Britain was an important factor in ensuring that the new multi-nation state took a decentralised form in the discussions that led to independence from Australia.

For administrative purposes, East New Britain is divided into three districts – Rabaul District, Kokopo District and Pomio District. The province is further divided into 20 community governments, of which seven made up the Pomio-Bainings area. Community Government boundaries coincide with those of census divisions and provincial electorates (see map).

In terms of each of climatic, topographical, population, ethnological, geological and transport features, the Gazelle Peninsula at the north-east extremity of New Britain differs sharply from the rest of the island. The Tolai settlements are on the Gazelle Peninsula and are flanked by natural borders. To the north and east is the sea and relative ease of contact with the offshore islands of Watom, the Duke of York Islands – both the Duke of Yorks and Watom are Tolai settled – and southern New Ireland. To the south and west of the Tolai area of settlement, there is a broad valley which separates it from the rugged Bainings mountains. The whole southern half of the province suffers from very high rainfall – more than 6000 mm each year on the extreme south coast – and this constrains day-to-day life and economic development. Development prospects are further constrained by steep slopes and

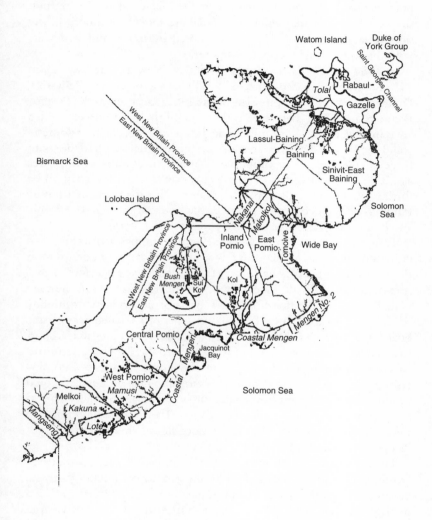

East New Britain Province, showing Pomio-Bainings community governments and ethnic and linguistic groups in 1993. KOL – Non-Austronesian languages/major dialect; *Mamusi* – Other languages/major dialect.

generally low agricultural potential but with specific areas of higher-potential land scattered on the coast and in inland valleys. In contrast, the Gazelle Peninsula, where the Tolai are settled, has more gently sloping land, much of which is occupied by free-draining, fertile, volcanic soils of high agricultural potential.

In 1984 the human population of East New Britain was about 145,000. More than two-thirds of these lived on the Gazelle Peninsula, Duke of Yorks and Watom Islands; and less than a third in the Pomio-Bainings area. The Tolai area is thus one of the most densely settled areas in Melanesia – with more than 100 people per square kilometre – and the Pomio-Bainings area among the least densely settled – with three people per square kilometre. Within the Pomio-Bainings area about 45 per cent of the people live on or close to the coast and a further 40 per cent live in hill villages. The majority of Pomio-Bainings peoples continue to live in their area of birth and so ethnic and linguistic distinctions are easily mapped (see map).

Transport infrastructure within Pomio-Bainings is minimal and communications are difficult. A few sections of road exist but, for most Pomio-Bainings people, the primary means of transport is by foot. Travel is exceedingly difficult, especially in the inland areas and in the high rainfall zones where flooding rivers, poor or no bridges and muddy roads isolate particular areas for prolonged periods. Coastal people have boat access to each other and to Rabaul. The difficulties in transport to and from the major market of Rabaul undoubtedly play a dominant role in constraining the development of the cash economy of Pomio-Bainings at present. Many of the area's smallholders produce, or could produce, saleable crops but in quantities too small to attract regular visits from the coastal shipping companies. The Gazelle Peninsula, on the other hand, has a complex network of all-weather roads to service its dense rural and urban population.

The principal occupation for Pomio-Bainings villagers is subsistence farming. The important food crops are taro, sweet potato, yam and bananas. A significant but small number of households are involved in the cash economy. Many inland villages in the Pomio District grow tobacco, some of which may be sold for cash where a market outlet exists. The principal product of the whole area, however, is copra produced from household coconut plots along the coast line. Cocoa is grown widely by villagers in the northern parts of the two Baining areas neighbouring the Tolai Gazelle, but smallholder cocoa is rare elsewhere because of very high rainfall. Cardamom production by villagers has expanded rapidly in recent years in the hill villages of Lassul-Baining.

The balance between village subsistence and cash crop production shows an abrupt change near the boundary with the main Tolai settlement on the Gazelle. Subsistence crops dominate in Pomio-Bainings, and cash crops dominate on the Gazelle. There are few plantations in Pomio District and many of these are presently run down or abandoned. Other types of economic activity include some plantation cultivation of coconuts and cocoa but more than half of these are in the two Bainings community government areas. Forestry and timber logging are significant, because the area contains large areas of primary forest. Fishing is practised in the villages along the coastline but is especially important on the north Bainings coast, in East Pomio and in Melkoi. The catch is used mainly for home consumption, although some is used to trade for vegetables and tobacco with nearly inland hill villages. Other sources of cash for Pomio-Bainings people include royalties paid for bait-fish used by pole-and-line tuna boats, wages from plantation employment both in the area and on the Gazelle, and remittance of earnings by family members working elsewhere in Papua New Guinea.

THE SOCIAL AND CULTURAL CONTEXT

The Tolai

The density of population in the Tolai area is matched by a concentration of social science resources. The Tolai have attracted four major anthropological inquiries in recent decades – those by Bill Epstein (1969), Scarlett Epstein (1968), Richard Salisbury (1970) and Frederick Errington (1974). Peter Sack (1974) has undertaken studies in legal anthropology and law among the Tolai; Ian Grosart (1982) has examined political relations and the rise of nationalism; Polansky (1966) has studied Rabaul Town; and Bradley (1982) has researched Tolai women and development.

Despite this concentration of anthropological and related social science analysis on the Gazelle Peninsula, there is remarkably little comment on the relationship between the Tolai and their neighbouring peoples. They are not mentioned in Epstein's (1992b) recent analysis of affect and the anthropology of Tolai emotions; nor are they significant in his initial monograph (1969) on Matupit village and island. There is a clear but brief statement of the relationships[1] in his study of *Ethos and Identity*:

> relations between Tolai groups were qualitatively different from those that obtained between Tolai and a number of other peoples who were autochthonous to the area: the Bainings, the Taulil, the Sulka and Butum. Warfare among Tolai was governed by convention, and the transfer of *tambu* provided a customarily recognised way of making peace. The Tolai raided the other groups for slaves, and had gradually pushed them from their areas of settlement further and further inland. (1978: 44)

There is further comment in a footnote to this statement. The word 'Baining' appears to mean slave and even today little is known ethnographically about the Bainings 'who have tucked themselves away in the fastnesses of the Baining mountains' (1978: 44). The absence of any reference to the Pomio-Bainings throughout Epstein's *In the Midst of Life* is, at first glance, surprising in view of the book's rather full account of Tolai ethnicity.

Fuller explanations of Tolai relations with the neighbouring autochthonous people are given in T.S. Epstein (1968). She writes of sporadic contacts with groups such as the Bainings, Butums and Taulils who lived on the fringes of the Tolai area. She makes the point that, apart from these contacts, the Tolai were effectively isolated from contact by land with the rest of East New Britain. Her studies were of an inland Tolai parish, Rapitok, some 60 miles south of Rabaul on a mountain ridge at the fringe of Tolai settlement. She writes that it 'borders the Taulil, another linguistic group with whom the inhabitants were engaged in continuous warfare during pre-contact days'. Some Rapitok men were known to be descendants of captured Taulil women and their Tolai 'masters'. The children of these relationships were regarded as belonging 'for all practical purposes' to their fathers' matrilineages. Conquest and the patrifiliation of the children of Taulil slaves may have been the normal sequence of events, since Epstein notes that 'men, rather than lands, were scarce' and that leaders tried to raise their status through gathering a following of neighbouring peoples by conquest. At the same time, a Tolai victory in war could mean a cannibalised death for members of the conquered groups (Epstein 1968: 55). The importance of physical accessibility is underscored by her observation that, in German times, Rapitok was seen as extremely distant and that this could be gauged by the fact that a report on native taxation had stated that the two Taulil parishes – only some three miles further inland than Rapitok – could not be considered for tax collection because of their isolated position.

Salisbury, in his study of Vunamami, refers to the plans of the Roman Catholic mission and its boarding schools for the conversion of local people to Christianity. He notes that 'slaves captured by the Tolai from the Bainings were bought for 20 fathoms of shell money and given their freedom; the orphans were adopted by the mission' (1970: 30). In these early years, there was evidence of trade because Salisbury mentions Tolai men's interest in the less obvious commodities that were brought to market from time to time, including 'feather head-dresses and stone clubs originally obtained from the Bainings' (1970: 177). Otherwise, the Tolai were involved with the Bainings as mission teachers (1970: 324).

Another account is given in Sack (1974: 78). He writes that, unlike the usual situation in Melanesia, the Tolai were not a part of any extensive inter-tribal trading networks:

Trade with their neighbours in the south and south-west (Sulka, South Baining, Butum, Taulil) was negligible or non-existent. There was some trading going on between the North Baining and the inland Tolai but, at the beginning of European settlement, the relations with these neighbours were dominated by the coastal north-west Tolai and were feudal or colonial, rather than comparable to the trade partnerships in other parts of Melanesia.

The terms 'feudal' or 'colonial', and 'slave' used by T.S. Epstein and Salisbury, indicate a very different relationship than those which apply in the trade partnerships in other parts of Melanesia, where equivalence and suspicion are overlaid with the amity necessary to ensure peace within the trade. Sack writes, for example, that Tolai relations with the people on the New Ireland coast facing the Duke of Yorks were different. 'The people living there were not regarded as foreigners but as relatives; they formed an outlying province of the Tolai "common market".' This trading entity also covered an area in Nakanai 100 miles along the north coast in now Western New Britain. The northwest Tolai undertook regular trips to this area to obtain shells for the manufacture of *tambu* shell money. Sack continues as follows:

although individual trade friendships had probably already been established, it appears that contact with the Nakanai was generally kept to a minimum. These contacts were not a purpose of the trip but merely a necessary evil, a process that the Tolai went through in order to obtain the shells they needed, but which they avoided if they could. In contrast to this limited external trade, internal trade [among the Tolai] was highly developed ... the driving force behind the regular, public markets of the Tolai was not so much mutual economic dependency due to ecological factors but voluntary specialisation in order to acquire shell money. The Tolai bartered only with friends, otherwise traded strictly on cash terms. (1974: 76)

This Tolai-centric view of the world has been carried forward to the contemporary East New Britain provincial government constitution. The constitution lists and provides policies about 'the five distinct and separate geographical areas within the province' which are given as: Bainings; Duke of York Islands; Gazelle Peninsula; Pomio; and Watom Island. The Duke of York and Watom Islands, however, are only distinct as geographical entities because they are separated from the Gazelle Peninsula by water. Otherwise, they are an integral part of the Tolai world and are only separated in terms of specifically Tolai perceptions of spatial identity and contrast. All of the Tolai habitations – the Gazelle, Watom and the Duke of Yorks together – occupy only 10 per cent of the province's area. The constitution does not draw attention to the considerable variation in human and physical geography in the remaining 90 per cent of the province, occupied by the many language and cultural groups of the Bainings mountains and the Pomio District.

THE MAENGE PEOPLE OF POMIO DISTRICT

All the anthropological sources point to a very selective and inward-looking Tolai world until the time of colonial administration and, in the case of their own province and island, in very recent history as well. The sources available for the Bainings (for example, Fajans 1985 and Whitehouse 1995: 89ff.) and for Pomio District (Panoff 1969a, 1969b) show, however, a much more dynamic recent history with the increasing enculturation of the numerically smaller culture groups by the largest one, together with the growth of a single 'proto-nationalist' movement of brotherhood (and sisterhood) based on new spatial interactions, cargo-cult thinking and organisation, modern politics, and the potential in traditional clan structures for pan-island solidarity.

This overall picture emerges from my own fieldwork and the prior, and longer fieldwork of M. and F. Panoff. They studied the Maenge or Mengen people living along, and in the hinterland of, the coast from Wide Bay to Jacquinot Bay. (The hinterland is considerable, even reaching the other coast at Nakanai at one point – see map). M. Panoff (1969a) shows that, although the Maenge did not play any notable part in traditional trade and warfare, their geographical situation on the coast was sufficient to give them, from the outset of colonial administration, a key position as intermediaries between the white missionaries, government officers, plantation managers and recruiters and the other coastal and inland tribes of Kol, Tomoive, Bushmengen or Longueinga, Sulka and Sao. The Maenge's numbers were higher than all those other tribes considered together and perhaps sheer numbers and their colonial role as intermediaries led to the gradual extension of their language within the area to the detriment of the Sao and Longueinga languages which were formerly distinct.

Three very important further factors have assisted this Mengen-isation and realignment of the Pomio peoples. The first is close spatial juxtaposition through officially sponsored and voluntarily adopted rural resettlement. The second has been through the potential for inter-tribal movement and identification using traditional clan linkages. The third has been the district-wide importance of the Pomio *Kivung* movement – a political and religious movement with roots in both recognisably Melanesian cargo-cult thinking and in modern national politics.

Resettlement was important at the time of the Panoff's fieldwork and a cause of 'Mengen-isation'. By settling down on the coast, inland or bush people lent themselves more easily to administration control, and the extension of cash cropping, in return for which they were exempted from working as carriers for both the government and mission. Rural resettlement was a major policy priority in the 1960s but had ceased to be important in the early 1980s at the time of my fieldwork. Panoff records, however, that new residence arrangements following resettlement has led to novel marriage patterns, especially among Tomoive women who have married Maenge and Kol men (1969a: 48). Further evidence of increased inter-tribal social interaction in Pomio is provided by increased bilingualism among Kol and Maenge speakers (1969a: 49) and the acquisition of techniques, such as swimming and canoe making, which were previously unknown to the inland dwellers (1969a: 49).

There is one article of Pomio and Maenge faith that might suggest that the openness to inter-ethnic contact and cultural assimilation found in the case of resettlement is the norm rather than the exception. Panoff (1969a: 22) writes that:

when asked to describe differences between the Maenge and their neighbours, most informants will claim that all the peoples of New Britain are organised along the very same lines and that, as individuals, they would not therefore find it difficult to fit into the social grouping of the Tolai or the Arawe.

He goes on to show that this happy optimism rests on false premises, since even so physically and socially close a people as the Bushmengen or the Kol recognise different principles of clan and tribal organisation from those of the coast dwellers. Yet the belief in a single pattern obtaining throughout the island is in fact of major importance to the understanding of inter-tribal relations. 'When a Maenge claims that he will be able to find clan mates in any linguistic community whatsoever, the exaggeration of his statement illuminates his [largely positive?] psychological attitude to tribes living on the borders of his territory' (Panoff 1969a: 23).

In broad structural terms, the Maenge as well as their immediate neighbours are distributed into roughly similar kin groups and the vernacular names of these groups are easily translated from one language to another. These two features of kin organisation could suggest cultural homogeneity. The trouble is that the membership rules and functions of these groups differ considerably from one tribe to another. For example, the rule of descent differs; whereas the Maenge, Mamusi, Sao and Sulka have matri-clans, among the Tomoive and Kol patrifiliation is more significant. Kol clans are known as 'vines' and are able to recruit their members through either line, although membership through patrifiliation is by far the most frequent. This leads to some incompatibility in kin organisation in the area: the Kol, for example, ascribe the creation of the original 'vines' to ten mythical persons of whom three were male, a possibility thoroughly inconceivable to Maenge. Furthermore, although the clans of most peoples of the Pomio area are exogamous, in the case of the Kol 'vines' they are not.

Panoff concludes that, despite many formal equivalences, the Maenge and their neighbours are anything but homogeneous. Why, then, do they state that the similarities are more important than the differences? He finds the solution in the use of clan names and moieties as 'totems' when Maenge travel. The Maenge and their neighbours boast of their ability to guess the moiety of any stranger irrespective of his tribe through looking at the palm of his hand. So not only do the Maenge know in what villages of their own linguistic community they can find clan or moiety mates, but they also have a very good idea of the geographical distribution of people recognising the same 'totems' as themselves among the neighbouring tribes. This knowledge will be more valuable and treasured when one's 'totem' is known to have its origins outside the present Maenge area, or when its name is duplicated or approximated in non–Maenge languages, and these are both frequently occurring phenomena.

'CARGO'-THINKING AMD MICRONATIONALISM

The relative ease and dynamism of Pomio's inter-tribal relations certainly assisted the development of the ideology of pan-Pomio brotherhood cultivated by the long-standing district-wide social movement led (in different ways) by two, successive, elected representatives for Pomio in the (now) National Parliament – Michael Koriam Urekit and Alois Koki. This movement has been variously referred to as 'the Pomio cargo-cult', '*ol Komiti bilong Koriam*' (Koriam's disciples) and 'the Pomio *Kivung*' (the Pomio Association). For ease and to reflect the predominant circumstances of 1984, I shall refer to it simply as 'the Pomio Kivung'.

The movement is discussed as a predictable, and largely appropriate, Melanesian response to major religious, political and economic changes and to the need for social order by Bailoenakia and Koimanrea (1983). The movement is also treated as a classic and outdated cargo cult in a far less sympathetic light by Tovalele (1977). The historical background and cluster of cults preceding Kivung's emergence is reviewed by Trompf (1990). Whitehouse (1995) adds further depth using data gained from some 18 months in the Bainings area between 1987 and 1989. Each of these authors discusses the main observances of the Kivung – the specially dedicated food gardens, the first offering of the food's essence to the ancestors, the emphasis on the Ten Commandments as contemporary laws and so on. The interpretation each gives is, however, different. To Tovalele, these observances are part of a delusion; to Bailoenakia and Koimanrea, they are a religious and political response to change that is totally understandable in a Melanesian context, with its heavy charge of millenarian thinking yet also pragmatic, while culturally grounded, political organisation. Walter (1981) shows how determined rural leadership can radically alter the circumstances of Papua New Guinea rural life even if for short periods. In his eyes, the Pomio Kivung and similar micronationalist movements are the outcome of new rural leadership patterns. Trompf (1994: 264–5) highlights two religious reciprocation principles: 'blessings would not flow unless the new rules were obeyed ... [nor without] the efficacy of positive reciprocity with the dead'. A highly sympathetic view of its religious, organisational and national political achievements is given from 'inside the cult' by Whitehouse (1995).

Trompf (1990) dates the Kivung from 1963. Panoff (1969a) dates its beginning to the late 1950s but recognises that it may have gone through various transformations and had already known dormant or more limited forms prior to those years. He describes, for example, the important role played by the paramount *luluai* (headman) of the Pomio area, Golpaik, immediately after the Second World War. He promised the inland Kol that the Agricultural Department would create cocoa and coffee plantations if only they would live on sites specially prepared for them on the coast. Second, he spread a terrifying rumour that an earthquake would shortly destroy the whole of the interior of East New Britain and that only those on the coast would be safe. He had very good connections with the Kol people since he had fled there during the war and from there had assisted the coast-watchers and the Allied forces. After the war, what he had promised appeared to materialise in a way that outshone even the most optimistic 'cargo' expectations. The Australian administration sent a ship full of food to the Pomio area to be distributed free among the population as a means of regaining control. The Kol received a large share of the unexpected cargo of rice and canned meat and were able to live from it for two months without caring for their food gardens. The event added considerably to the credibility of subsequent cargo-cult activities.

The Pomio Kivung displayed, from the early 1960s to the time of my visit, most of the characteristics recorded by Lawrence (1964) in his classic study of the cargo movement of the Southern Madang district. In Pomio, cargo ritual was practised in cemeteries and an emphasis was laid on the Ten Commandments as the laws of the movement and the means of securing material goods and improvement. The days of the week had been re-named and special prominence given to Thursday, while Friday was devoted to collective work in the 'cargo' or movement gardens set aside in each village. Moreover, there has been an extensive and well organised collection of 'voluntary contributions'. Most villages are controlled by Kivung male triads (or three-man committees). Panoff (1969a) notes that these '*komiti*' resembled the boss boys appointed by Yali in the Southern Madang, except that they appeared to be more efficient. Whitehouse (1995) distinguishes their roles as orators.

Flourishing first in the Maenge country, the movement began to exert its influence over the Mamusi, the Kol, the Tomoive and many of the other villages on Wide Bay. It remained faithful to its origins, however, and the Maenge leaders were asked for guidance on many matters of importance. This continued to the present (Whitehouse 1995). In 1984 there were Kivung elements in, for example, Sinivit-East Baining villages in continued contact with visiting Maenge spokesmen. I did not observe any ritual expression of Kivung in the Baining areas comparable to the public posts outside villages marked with the Ten Commandments and collective garden observances found throughout Pomio: rather, traditional Bainings ceremonies of the snake and fire dance were used to mark overt signs of political opposition such as continuing to fly the Australian flag and the use of leadership titles – *luluai* and *tultul* (appointed village headman and assistant to the headman) – from the era before independence and even before self-managing local government. Despite these possible differences in expression, the Pomio and Baining movements shared contacts and a sense of opposition to what they perceived as the Tolai political and administrative hegemony of Rabaul. Kivung is, in fact, a Tolai word meaning 'meeting or association'; but, as a result of colonial political history, with the added sense of an association in opposition to the government of the time. Throughout Salisbury's monograph on the Tolai village of Vunamami, 'kivung' is simply referred to as 'an association'. In the Tolai areas around Rabaul in the 1950s, however, 'Kivung' became the common name for the Tolai social movement opposed to the introduction of local government.

Emissaries have continued throughout the 20 to 30 years of the movement to rekindle the faith of certain villages, to enlist support from new areas, and to get in touch with other 'cargo' or 'kivung' movements which have developed independently of the Maenge organisation. For example, Maenge liaison officers maintained contact with the cargo movement of the Nakanai (see Counts 1971). These missions are given a proxy official character by the host villages and are called 'patrols'. Whereas local government and community government taxes are unpopular, there is considerable pride in the system of contributions to the movement inspired over a long period by the various movement leaders. There is also a widespread feeling that members are right to set up institutions of their own, along the same lines as European ones as they see it, but which are not Tolai or provincial in their referents.

This suggests that Kivung has been successful in furthering extensive inter-tribal cooperation as a proto-nationalist or micronationalist movement that transcends existing linguistic and ethnic boundaries. For example, members call one another 'sibling', always using the pidgin word *brata,* even when within the same linguistic community. Panoff (1969a) records that the Maenge, Kol and Mamusi all identified closely with Koriam Urekit, the leader of the movement at that time, calling him their 'king', so that a wider-than-language group integration was achieved through his name.

What has been especially distinctive in the case of the Pomio Kivung is that *two* of its acknowledged leaders have been the elected representatives for the area in the National Parliament or Assembly in Port Moresby. At the time of the Panoffs' study, the undisputed single leader was Koriam who was not a local, Pomio man but who came from Ablingi Island near Arawe in West New Britain, had worked in Rabaul and met Paliau the leader of the renowned Manus Island movement. Koriam campaigned for the House of Assembly, for a constituency of which Maenge and their neighbours were only a part, as an indigenous Melanesian able to oppose and beat white expatriate candidates. In 1979, at a by-election, Alois Koki was returned as the Member of Parliament for the now separate constituency of Pomio. He had been a notable mission teacher working throughout the Kandrian-Pomio area and was closely related to Bernard, a relative or associate of Kolman, Koriam's right-hand man. The position of these two parliamentarians has been, quite understandably, far from clear –

they were part heroes, part messiahs and prophets, and part mediators with government. Panoff (1969a: 54) captured the essence of this difficult balancing act in the case of Koriam as follows:

he has succeeded in instilling much wisdom into the beliefs and actions of his Maenge supporters and in preventing them from surrendering to unreason, as evidenced by the part he played in deprecating money collection and in making a sensible allotment of those funds already collected. In actual fact, he had been so successful that in 1968 the local leaders of the movement withdrew their support.

Despite periodic reverses, the strength and determination of movement leadership has been most notable. The movement's leadership and organisation and the belief in, and use of, a single pattern of social structure throughout the island have led, in turn, to a strong micronationalist sentiment overriding local language and cultural boundaries. It is remarkable therefore that Kivung's binding of Maenge, Kol and Tomoive and even Baining as brothers and sisters in the movement is in sharp contrast to these same people's reaction to New Guinea Highland labourers, despite – or perhaps because of – the high incidence of labour in-migration into Pomio. In the 1960s some 90 per cent of Maenge men had worked under contract on European plantations for between two and twelve years. Labour migration was also very prevalent in the mid-1980s. Their frequency of contact with expatriate managed plantation compounds in the Pomio area and elsewhere in New Britain – such as at Cape Hoskins, Nakanai and on the Gazelle – does not seem to have made them more charitable to Highlander 'foreigners'. Although locals and Highlander in-migrants are isolated together in plantation compounds, Panoff is emphatic that no invitations are extended to Highlanders to participate in Kivung activities. Moreover, since many of the Highlanders' fellow tribesmen serve in the police, they are all refused the appellation 'brothers'. They are regarded as so culturally and socially distant that it is sometimes denied that they are subject to the same colonial rule or can be culturally akin to the New Britain population (1969b).

OIL AND WATER

Just as there was an aggregation of New Guinea Highland workers on the plantations as 'Chimbu' foreigners, so too all Tolai, Maenge,

other Pomio, Bainings, Kaliai, Nakanai and other parts of East New
Britain would be designed as 'Rabaul' if they were working in the
capital city, Port Moresby. Ethnic identities in the major cities worked,
at least in folk theory, to group together *wantok*. The literal translation
of this pidgin word is 'one talk (language)'. It was often used by
individuals from a given area to indicate amity that could not be
precisely defined. People from the same sub-district, for example, might
regard themselves as wantoks, even though they knew no one in
common and their vernacular languages were different. They could
discuss the same events and had visited the same towns and markets
and could, therefore, regard themselves as sharing a common experience.
The attribution of ethnic identities by fellow workers or other relative
strangers would usually ignore these issues of detailed common
experience underlying the concept of wantok either because of
indifference or lack of knowledge. The external attribution relied, rather,
on the use of administrative boundaries. People were assumed to be
fellow countrymen or *Landsmannschaften* merely because they came
from the same province or district. The use of administrative
categorisation to provide external definitions of identity and the
assessment of common experience to provide subjective definitions
are not just urban phenomenon in Melanesia but can also be found
at provincial capital and sub-district (now district) levels (Rew 1975
for Port Moresby, and Rew 1980: 54 for rural Milne Bay).

Although, when viewed from outside the province, the Pomio tribes,
the Bainings and the Tolai could all be categorised as 'Rabaul' people,
there is no common experience on which to base the identification
when seen from the perspectives of the East New Britain peoples
themselves.[2] Indeed, the reason for my work in the province had been
part of a response to the demand from Pomio leaders for the creation
of a separate province in the south of the island and their secession
from East New Britain. Trompf (1994: 263) notes an early demand
for a separate local council in 1964. Demands for autonomy continued
until, in the face of sustained protests, a study of the feasibility of a
'Special Area Authority' for Pomio and the Bainings was agreed; and
I was responsible for the social analysis and the compilation of social
indicators for this.

It became obvious during the consultancy studies that there was
considerable anxiety and resentment about Tolai people and their
domination of provincial affairs. In most of the Pomio and Bainings

villages there was abundant evidence of this gulf and the tensions between them and the Tolai. One very vivid illustration of the underlying social relation was given to me, in pidgin, in the form of a *tokpiksa* (image) by a leader from the Sinivit-East Baining area:

If you put kerosene in a Coleman Lamp and put a match to the wick, you will have a powerful light. If, however, you put kerosene in the lamp's tank and then add water, when you come to put the match to the wick, you will be disappointed. On its own, kerosene is a good thing and, when you use it properly, the house will be lit brightly. Now water is something to drink and, if it is clean and pure, you will be happy at being refreshed. This *tokpiksa* I am giving you is about the Tolai and the Bainings. They are the kerosene and the water.

The Uramit Baining leader's vivid image neatly summarises the argument so far in the chapter – oil and water do not mix.[3] The chapter also provides a corrective to the Tolai view of island history, Salisbury (1970) having already provided the indigenous Tolai corrective to the history written from only colonial sources. The argument in the rest of the chapter is that the pre-contact structure of Tolai and non-Tolai relations, which were based on domination and fear, was then overlaid by structural mimesis, in which the Pomio and Bainings responded to conflict within the island by echoing the politics of the governing group, first Australian and then Tolai. This structural relation was not, however, static: the period before and after independence led to the expansion of political arenas and to increased political resources for well-placed individuals and groups. Finally, at the time of my own studies, the symmetries of structural mimesis were being progressively challenged by development-induced anxiety and its need for management. Each of these four explanations for the Tolai 'oil' and the Pomio-Baining 'water' – they may be phases – is dealt with in turn.

Domination and fear

The key events in that total 'Tolai-Pomio-Bainings' history lie in the movement of shells for *tambu* and in slaves for sexual, workforce and nutritional purposes, thus echoing Lombard's argument that the shift in the hegemony of the old world from the Middle East to the

Mediterranean could be traced in the movement of precious metals and slaves (Friedman 1994: 40). These movements indeed do indicate one major reason for the 'oil-and-water' view of Tolai and non-Tolai identities. There could only be enmity, fear and retreat from interaction when the only categorisations allowed to Bainings people in Tolai ideation were 'labourer', 'slave', 'pupil' or 'cannibal food'.

Structural mimesis

Another explanation for the chasm is also possible, one that recognises this background of animosity and deep-seated historical distrust but also examines the politics of the immediately pre-independence and modern state. In this view it was the very coherence of the Tolai people as a colonial, and then post-colonial elite, with their domination of Rabaul and its hinterland, together with their useful role as intermediaries in the colonial administration, that has led to a countervailing reaction and opposition from the peoples excluded from power. This analysis in fact echoes one advanced by Epstein (1958) in his account of *Politics in an Urban African Community*. There he argues that the industrial organisation of a mine on the Zambian Copperbelt in colonial times stimulated a similar, unitary response from the mine workers in the form of a single trade union. The politics of one echoed the politics of the other. A similar model could be used to analyse Pomio-Bainings and Tolai relations. The very fact of domination by the Tolai necessitated a *similar* organisation of forces by the autochthonous peoples in order to oppose them. The use of a Tolai word (Kivung) to describe the Pomio social movement of opposition and the fact that it is the *same* word that expressed the Tolai's own opposition to colonial rule is, in terms of this model, doubly appropriate. In other words, the Tolai's opposition to the Australian colonial regime has been echoed by Pomio people's association in order to oppose the Tolai. Increasingly, the Bainings have been forced to align themselves with the movement of opposition, as unity of purpose on the Tolai side demanded a similar unity of non-Tolai response. The final demand of the Pomio-Bainings Kivung has been similar to the demand of the Tolai *Mataungan* Association – 'give us political independence' or, at least, Special Area status.

The expansion of political resources

It would be true to the oil-and-water analogy for Pomio-Bainings relations with the Tolai if the account ended here. But their recent political experience has only in part shown a clear symmetry of opposition, or the presence of uncomplicated political fault lines, in their relations with the people who live around their island capital. The transition to political independence and the construction of a national development strategy for Papua New Guinea (Allan and Hinchliffe 1982) has challenged those previously highly separated Pomio-Bainings and Tolai identities because of the priority given in post-independence arrangements to political and administrative decentralisation (Axline 1986). In the pre-independence period, cultural, political and economic diversity could be accepted as a 'natural' condition of colonial politics and administration. The Tolai were important, educated intermediaries and acknowledged as dynamic farmers and businessmen. The Bainings and Pomio groups could be treated as separate, forgettable, mysterious and awkward entities. The demands of potentially secessionist movements groups such as the Tolai Mataungun Association, however, ensured that the Independent State of Papua New Guinea accepted a large measure of provincial and local level decentralisation. The consequences of decentralisation could sometimes be eccentric – as we saw in the designation of Watom and the Duke of York Islands as special areas in the constitution of East New Britain. Despite this oddity, however, both the provincial constitution and the National Development Strategy give a similar priority to the reduction of social and economic disparities.

A key document in the institutionalisation of the strategy for decentralisation and equity was the Faber Report, produced by the Overseas Development Group, University of East Anglia (see Allan and Hinchliffe 1982). Increasingly, as this report was accepted as the basis of the National Development Strategy, the aims and the machinery of government at both national and provincial levels had placed a priority on the reduction of disparity through spending on basic services and the encouragement of community-level representation and administration. As these developments proceeded, Pomio and Bainings leaders entered the sphere of knowledge of development policy and management, within which the full terms of their engagement are largely unknown and highly contingent, and in which there is always the prospect of both immediate and longer-term benefit and the threat of wider interactions and integration. Contemporary Pomio-Bainings leaders enter a world in which, increasingly, it is Tolai decision-makers and 'foreigner' Papua New Guinean decision-makers in Port Moresby who provide a structure of rules, regulations and resources that determine whether or not particular roads are built and who decides the nature and distribution of the improved services that are essential in grassroots priorities for improvement.

The attempts of Pomio-Bainings leaders to direct and control planning outcomes and to secure social and infrastructural services for their area took place against a backdrop of considerable instability in the first years of the East New Britain provincial government. The provincial government's first term (1976–81) was dominated by a succession of votes of no confidence against the faction and leaders currently in power. As vote followed vote, power and leadership fluctuated. Although the decentralised public service continued to function, the leadership and faction changes did little to help establish a stable, provincial planning framework. Provincial government's second term introduced four orientation seminars for the re-elected and newly elected provincial politicians to explain the implications of their voting and the distinction between their functions and those of the public servants. This appears to have made some impression and, in 1984, planning officials stated that a better working relationship between politicians and public servants had been established.

Within the province, the basic unit for administrative and political purposes is the community government, the boundaries of which coincided with each of the Provincial Assembly electorates. They had been introduced in 1977 to replace the local government councils of pre- and immediately post-independence days. There are twenty community governments, each consisting of a council of elected members, chaired by a president and assisted, administratively, by a council clerk or executive officer, who is given some secretarial help. The provincial government also provides an assistant coordinator for each community government to monitor its performance and to act as the means of communication between the two governmental levels. Within the Pomio-Bainings area there are, officially, seven community governments. In West Pomio, however, local opposition to the concept has prevented the community government's actual formation and an executive area management team has been appointed instead. There are also major defections from local government, especially in Sinivit-East Baining, with various villages refusing to endorse community government or to pay its taxes. Despite defections in some areas, however, local leaders recognised that community government offered new sources of employment and funds for its establishment, and for business development and capital works.

Papua New Guinea's independence, then, brought in its wake a variety of new political interactions and activities that very quickly became conduits and resources for the transmission, maintenance and amendment of identities. In some cases the extra resources have given further causes for Kivung activity, including campaigns of rejection. In other cases, challenges to its hegemony have been encouraged by community government formation; this culminated, in the Melkoi area, in a strong challenge to Kivung at the national political level.

The containment of anxiety

In his research and consulting, Jaques (1955) uses the idea of social systems as defences against intolerable individual anxiety. He writes that 'effective social change is likely to require analysis of the common anxieties and unconscious collusions underlying the social defences determining phantasy social relationships'. Menzies Lyth (1988) further develops the perspective, which owes much to Melanie Klein's theories, in a case study of nurses at work. She shows how the nursing service set up social defences that facilitated the *evasion* of the anxiety that arises from the workplace but that contributed little to its *modification or reduction*. This leads her to suggest that the success and viability of a social institution is intimately connected with the techniques it uses to contain anxiety and that an understanding of this aspect of the functioning of a social institution is a critical diagnostic and therapeutic tool when facilitating social change. She recognises that plans for change that are rational when seen in economic or other terms are often ignored or fail in practice. One difficulty is that rational plans do not take into account the anxieties and social defences in the institution concerned, nor provide for a therapeutic handling of the situation as change takes place.

The anxieties and social defences created by the pressures towards 'development' in newly independent states are rarely considered by planners and policy theorists. As Epstein (1969) shows, change often involves considerable cultural continuity. Although this perspective is necessary to counter the attribution of social change to external factors it may also understate the sources of major dislocation, conflict and uncertainty. The creation of provincial and community governments in East New Britain, for example, generates leadership contests that are, at first glance, readily assimilated into a conventional style of Melanesian 'big-man' politics. The pursuit of reputation and followership by local and provincial leaders does in many ways follow time-honoured patterns – the premium placed on powerful oration and the mobilisation of many followers to ensure a humbling display of goods that will signify the leader's power and organisational skills. The context may have changed – the orations now take place on the floor of the Provincial Assembly and community government halls and for the traditional exchange of food tubers and the killing and distribution of pig meat (or, in the case of the Bainings, pythons on the occasion of their fire/snake dances) is substituted the power of office and its spoils – but, it can be argued, there is continuity in the cultural principles.

In addition to this style of provincial and local politics, which can be discussed within the terms of conventional social anthropology, there were also many *development-induced anxieties* that had contributed additional emotional energy to the long history of fear, disappointment, opposition and grievance that marked inter-ethnic relations. The anxieties arose because people and politicians wanted 'development' but did not want it on terms that were mediated through Rabaul and what were thought of as Tolai institutions. Furthermore, the rules of the game for the planning and administration of development projects and programmes within the province or elsewhere in Papua New Guinea were barely articulated. Many people desired 'projects', which they saw as achievable and able to improve their lives; but simultaneously they doubted the capacity of their provincial and community institutions to plan and implement them. In these circumstances, the officials charged with implementing programmes within the study area were anxious because their responsibilities were diffuse and unclear and were not localised. Similarly, villagers were anxious lest, in trying to achieve development, they also brought with it feared Tolai institutions and people.

In this situation, the stakes at local level often appeared so high and the overall political and planning context so unspecific and poorly sanctioned that expectations and concrete possibilities would rarely match. Any individual official or leader would only very rarely have the means to plan or complete even the smallest extension or capital works project. In this context planners and local officials found it difficult to organise their work. When projects were attempted, they had to be both simple in design and single-minded in terms of the chain of direction and command if they were to have any chance of success. For example, Melkoi – in the extreme south of the Pomio district – was a prime fishing area but very far from Rabaul; a cold storage freezer was clearly needed there in order to increase the trade in fish and thus increase the incomes of Melkoi fishermen. Despite no shortage of funds and complete agreement about the economic need for cold storage at Melkoi, no equipment could be supplied or construction undertaken because at least three departments were involved and their work could not be coordinated, work needed to be undertaken simultaneously at Melkoi and Rabaul and this could not be planned, and there was no local precedent to follow. At the same time, there were many newly constructed community schools in the district because their construction involved the use of a simple, acknowledged design, on a single rural site, had high political visibility, there was only one department responsible, and – after the first was built – there was a local planning precedent to follow.

In the southern parts of the Pomio-Bainings area, the anxieties induced by development were largely generalised and focused on frustrations about the planning and the administration system, known ultimately to be run at the behest and under the control of the Tolai majority, that prevented them from receiving 'development'. But in the north of the Province, in the Baining areas, there was much ambivalence about road development; these were welcome if they provided a road out of the mountains for the Bainings' profitable cardamom crop and unwelcome if they led to pressures on Baining land from the land-hungry Tolai.

The planning studies undertaken by East New Britain provincial government, and continued by the consultancy team of which I was a part, must be seen in this light. The anxieties were many and often very specific – about land, transport and social services – but all of them were seen through the prism of the underlying conflicts, alignments and perceptions of identity. The consultancy thus had the potential to bridge the political divide, partly by providing a conduit of information across the divide and partly by helping to mediate the setting of priorities.

KEY SOCIAL INDICATORS

The terms of reference required, among other analyses, the development of a set of social indicators for the area and province to capture grassroots perspectives and for use in the development of plans and budgets. The intense debate over 'equity' in economic development chances did, in part, reflect real discrepancies in access to education, health, business support and transport and communication services. The social indicators work (Rew 1985b) was therefore thought necessary in order to correct specific imbalances in access and welfare. In part, the concentrated interest in equity also arose from an increasing emphasis on distributional issues within the discourse of development itself at that period. In Papua New Guinea, this discourse had been transmitted by means of the watershed 'Faber' Report (Overseas Development Group 1973). The almost segmentary character of the Papua New Guinea state further contributed to a wariness about the honour of any territorial segment and of its leaders at each of region, province, district, sub-district and community government levels and as measured in actual and potentially available indicators of disparity.[4] Indicators were intended to highlight the need for improvement and to bring rationality to decision-making about service provision; they also served to highlight segmentary conflict and anxiety about past and future allocations.

One major anxiety concerned land and Tolai aspirations to acquire the lands of the Pomio-Bainings area. At the time of our study, the only national government power which was left to be transferred to East New Britain Province concerned land administration. Uncertainties about its transfer left many village spokesmen and area leaders very apprehensive. They reported that the methods of land control and administration were very much a black box to them and that the impact of land scarcities in, and population movements from, the Tolai areas were largely unknown. Much of the anxiety of the Uramit Bainings people about forms of government and their membership or not of the Sinivit-East Baining community government in fact centred around land. They were adamant that their own land laws and those of the Tolai were radically different. They were, for example, a patrilineal people, whereas the Tolai were matrilineal. They reported no tradition of land alienation and felt on the whole that their institutions could cope with contemporary pressures from the Tolai to acquire more land; but worried how the Tolai might use provincial priorities and mechanisms. My compilation of quantitative land and labour scarcity and use indices, and the creation of a qualitative indicator for 'land anxiety', proved very useful in the subsequent debates with planning officials, who were inclined to treat agricultural and other production as prior and land as a secondary, downstream consideration.

There was also considerable ambivalence and anxiety about transport developments. As a whole, East New Britain Province is relatively well provided with provincial roads when compared with other provinces. Within the study area there were marked differences between the community governments – West Pomio and Central Pomio, for example are very poorly served by East New Britain standards. At the same time, even these local areas had a similar provision – in terms of kilometres of road – to the provincial average for, say, Chimbu and Gulf Provinces. Another measure which comes closest to the villagers' understanding of road access can be taken from the Provincial Data System (PDS) where the thresholds for service provision are stated in journey times – for example, more than 15 minutes distant, more than one hour away, or more than two hours away. On the basis of these social indicators of accessibility, Pomio District is not particularly favoured, nor particularly disadvantaged in relation to the other eight districts of the New Guinea Islands region. However, a second reading of the data suggests that Pomio District could be far more disadvantaged than at first appears. Of the five most disadvantaged districts of the New Guinea Islands region, Pomio and nearby Kandrian District in West New Britain Province are almost equally, and very significantly, disadvantaged in terms of access to roads. In 1979, Kandrian District had an estimated 54 per cent of its population, and Pomio District an estimated 53 per cent of its population, more than one hour's journey from a road used at least once a week by a vehicle. The next most disadvantaged district in these terms – Talasea District – had only 29 per cent of its population more one hour's journey away from a road in similar use. This indicator, therefore, suggests that both Kandrian and Pomio Districts have had historically very low levels of capital expenditure in relation to their land mass, the number of inland peoples and the difficulties of sea transport.

Seen in the context of these levels of disadvantage, it might be thought that Pomio-Bainings leaders would welcome further transport development. This was not the case. The attempt by provincial government to develop roads which linked their areas to the Tolai areas was bitterly resented and the cause of much suspicion. Yet, paradoxically, another cause for fierce resentment was the failure of provincial government to fund, or even maintain on a voluntary labour basis, the Malasait to Raunsepna road that was essential for Bainings people to carry out their highly profitable and increasingly important crops of cardamon. The institutional protections needed to resolve the paradox and the governmental resistances involved could only be assessed in the later stages of the study when we moved from diagnosis to suggestions and recommendations.

The greatest frustration at local levels concerns villagers' access to basic services. In Pomio-Bainings, 28 per cent of villagers and their children are further than one hour's journey away from a community school, 44 per cent of villagers are further than one hour away from a road in use, and 40 per cent of villagers are more than 15 minutes away from an all-year-round source of drinking water. Pomio and Bainings are, in that order, the *most* disadvantaged of all five recognised geographic areas of the province when assessed in terms of these three basic services. Fifteen villages – some 8 per cent of the total and with a population of nearly 4000 people – were experiencing severe difficulty in access to services, lacking all or five of the six most basic services in water, education, health and transport. There was only one other village, of less than 100 people, in the whole of the province with this degree of difficulty, and that was in the Duke of York Islands.

The control and direction of capital works funding in the study area was suspect since community governments' priorities differ, at times, from the general findings from the Provincial Data System and from my fieldwork. For example, in East Pomio, where education and water supply account for 38 per cent and 3 per cent of the works budget respectively, my findings suggested that access to community schooling was relatively easy whereas access to water supply was a major problem. Similarly, in Central Pomio, social indicators suggested that no one in the area is more than two hours journey from an aid post and that only a relatively small proportion of the population is disadvantaged with respect to health centre access. The community government has, however, allocated 41 per cent of its works grant in the health sector. Again, Central Pomio appears to have water supply problems but only 4 per cent of the grant is geared to alleviating them. This mismatch between need and expenditure reflects the fact that, where you already have basic facilities in the area, it is easier to find advocates for further expenditure and further justification to develop add-on facilities. Where there is no strong advocacy or tradition of implementation – as in the case of water supply – despite demand for improvement from villagers very little is done to service it. The same is true of transport. There is an urgent need for footpath development and repair in West and Inland Pomio and Melkoi, in particular to develop and repair bridges washed away in floods and so on. Yet, footpath establishment and maintenance receives almost no allocation by the community governments, whereas they will spend money on small amounts of road near the station headquarters.

It should be emphasised that I could not find any instance of some provincial or local group rationally serving its own interest by pre-empting rational decision-making and denying services to Pomio-Bainings. Rather, it is the lack of planning and coordination services and technical coordinating capability that makes the planning of service and infrastructural questions so fraught and uncertain. Their planning and allocation brings new sets of people more closely into discussion, but these discussions centre on problems that are impossible to solve given existing capabilities and knowledge and the complex governmental machinery which must be motivated into action. The frustrations in following the 'road belong development' exacerbate tensions and anxieties.

SOCIAL THERAPY

The Tolai also have their anxieties.[5] Epstein's account of Tolai affect (1992b: 162, 196) describes their fear of *tabaran* (malevolent spirits that inhabit both the wild 'bush' areas beyond human settlement and their dreams), sorcery and of human separation and death. Death emerged as a frequent theme. Yet *burut* (fear) is not, apparently, a frequent personal emotional experience and is of only moderate importance to the Tolai as a whole (1992b: 78). It is significant that, with some difficulty (1992b: 66), Epstein found a Tolai word for 'disgust' or 'contempt', this emotion (*milikuan*) does not figure at all in the table rating emotions in terms of their importance and frequency.

I mention these aspects of Tolai emotion since in almost all of my discussions with Bainings and Pomio people the discussions turned very quickly to their fears about Tolai aggrandisement and their hurt at Tolai contempt. In the words of one Pomio villager who erupted angrily in a general discussion about his district's development, 'The Tolai always denigrate us [*daunim mipela*]. For them we are just dogs, pigs and rubbish.' In the present account of Pomio and Bainings development we see the reverse and less positive side of the coin of Tolai ambition and self-assertiveness. The desire for achievement had led Tolai communities to compete with one another in accepting innovation from the onset of the colonial period to the present (Epstein 1992b: 266). Salisbury (1976) documents the increasing individuation in the life-chances of the Tolai elite as they respond to political and economic development in the independent state. This successful pursuit of material progress and recognition by colonial and post-colonial regimes has brought the Tolai many benefits; but it appears to have a cost in the envy of the 'bush-people' of their own hinterland and intense resentment at what is seen as Tolai indifference and contempt towards near neighbours.

It is as if the Tolai and the Pomio and Bainings people have interpreted the sets of moral choices and anxieties arising from economic and social change in contrasted ways. More seems at issue than the near universal knowledge gap between 'haves' and 'have-nots' but it is difficult to describe and analyse the moral and emotional dimensions involved because of the close interrelationship of structure, culture and affect. Heald (1994: 3–5) illustrates something of the problem when arguing that different national traditions have interpreted the psychoanalytic corpus in remarkably different ways. American Freudians have emphasised the conscious, self-directing aspects of the personality and its possibilities for adaptation, while British psychoanalysis of the Kleinian persuasion stresses the projection and introjection of the conflictual and contradictory images and feelings which arise in interactional settings. I am correspondingly intrigued by what seem to me as separate Tolai and Pomio interpretations of the morality of provincial development and by apparent similarities in national traditions of psychoanalytic interpretation. Is the Tolai vision close to that of the optimistic (American) Freudian; does the Pomio perspective at all resemble that of the more pessimistic (British) Kleinian?

In an evaluation of the performance of the Less Developed Areas Programme and of Province-wide Integrated Rural Development Projects (IRDPs in Papua New Guinea, Crittenden and Lea (1989: 114) claim that

the effectiveness of programmes and projects is related to the appreciation of planners and managers for the socio-political context and their understanding of the physical and cultural environment in which programmes take place. It also depends upon the establishment of close ties between all those involved in the planning and implementation of projects, including the beneficiaries. Strengthening existing institutions and working through them is essential.

Judged by those criteria, the Pomio-Bainings area planning study and my consultancy was a success.[6] Our proposals, for a development strategy assisting the existing social responses to change rather than *a priori* sectoral growth schemes, and for the strengthening of Pomio-based planning capabilities, were accepted by all of the key parties. On 4 December 1987, the national government and the East New Britain provincial government signed a development agreement for the Pomio-Bainings. Under the agreement, the national government agreed to finance, without external aid funding, a package of investments in the Pomio-Bainings areas, with a total projected cost in excess of Kina 5 million (approximately £3.4 million). The agreement and the strategy on which it was based were generated from our study, without the need for a separate design process or detailed implementation plan. Crittenden and Lea (1989) seem to disapprove somewhat of this shortcut and argue that the legal status of the development agreement is unclear. They note that funds are transferred from the Department of Provincial Affairs to the East New Britain Province by cash fund certificate. This may be an achievement rather than a necessary weakness because, by disbursing funds through the provincial government rather than bypassing it, provincial government could be an active stakeholder in the sub-provincial programme rather than a powerful and resentful onlooker.

It is difficult to judge the importance of one's own work in the set of negotiations that followed between the National Planning Office, provincial government and the Pomio–Baining leadership and in the circumstances of major political upheaval in Papua New Guinea that finally led to a change in the national administration and in prime ministers. I was told, however, in Papua New Guinea on subsequent field missions, that the planning studies had been especially appreciated and had provided a way forward for all parties. First, in the social indicators work I had emphasised the process of consultation and fieldwork with key stakeholders before the design of any set of indicators, rather than specific statistical outputs. I had tried to put in place a system of statistical monitoring and social reporting that could be kept in place by community government and provincial planners. There is no evidence that this system long survived my departure but it did give rise to a set of information on services and quality of life that was accepted for at least the medium term. Second, the bottom-up approach taken in the social indicators work led directly to agreement on a development programme based on small-scale, service-based community development (Rew 1985a). This was agreed, by all parties, as the only feasible way forward for the Pomio–Bainings area, both in terms of its internal diversities and because of the highly charged questions of cultural identity that were involved in relations between Pomio–Baining and Tolai people and between Kivung adherents and Kivung opponents. One measure of acceptance is that demands for an alternative form of government have quietened.[7]

This chapter started with phrases and footnotes on neighbouring peoples found in the Tolai ethnographies. Another footnote, from Epstein's account of Tolai identity (1992b: 286, fn. 17), points to one extremely interesting dynamic within the projections and introjections of Tolai–non-Tolai interactions. Epstein records how the kivung of younger Tolai men active in the Anti-Council movement of the early 1950s 'probably originated on Matupit Island and *then spread inland*' (my emphasis). It is ironic that Pomio and Bainings people so actively resent Tolai disdain and so angrily reject Tolai institutions but have turned, nonetheless, to a Tolai political innovation to state their micronationalism; and, moreover, to an innovation whose origins appear to be on Matupit Island, the field site of the ethnographer of Tolai identity.

NOTES

1. Baining people were rarely mentioned among Tolai on the Matupit side; contact with the Bainings' on the Kokopo side was probably more frequent (A.L. Epstein, personal communication).

2. In earlier years, Tolai asserted their own identity as Tolai when they contrasted themselves with *vok*, mainland labourers from mainland New Guinea. The term 'Tolai' is a designation of quite recent vintage – from the goldmining days in places like Bulolo when other workers heard Tolai greet each other with a term that meant 'friend' or 'mate' (A.L. Epstein, personal communication).

3. Either in general or, in the *tokpiksa*, in a Coleman lamp. It is significant that Koriam's close associate was Kolman (or Coleman) described as 'the ultra-secretive "religious frontman" of the movement' (Trompf 1994: 263). Kerosene is – appropriately in the New Britain context and to describe the Tolai – imported, 'modern' energy; water is – equally appropriately for the conception the Pomio and Bainings peoples have of themselves within New Britain – a god-given and uncontaminated source of enduring human life.

4. A fuller listing of the key social indicators studies and sources I used in my analysis is given in (Rew 1996: 32–6).

5. The Tolai word for anxiety is *nginarau*; but this word can also mean eagerness or impatience (Epstein 1992b: 74–5).

6. Crittenden and Lea argue in their review of the main IRDPs that these undoubtedly had some successes which are often lost in the largely anecdotal informal evaluations made by their critics. Roads, schools, health centres and agricultural extension centres were built and the benefits of other programmes will continue to accrue for many years. They bear evidence that the national government did make a valiant effort to decentralise economic and social development to isolated and neglected areas and that, despite some hand-over problems, the projects and programmes initiated by autonomous or semi-autonomous programmes were then integrated into the operations of line departments and provincial divisions. Many staff trained in the programmes moved on to senior positions elsewhere.

7. The Kivung, claiming to govern its affairs better than other parts
   of the country, is increasingly led by younger men who distance
   themselves from the 'cargo' history and conduct political campaigns
   for Pomio's rectitude and development. Their moral crusade and
   ethnic particularism is captured in their (pidgin) name *Pomio Tru
   Grup*. One of their number was elected to the 1992 Parliament
   and there was further success in conventional political terms when
   he subsequently became national minister of health (cf. Trompf
   1994: 264).

REFERENCES

Allan, R. and Keith Hinchliffe. 1982. *Planning, Policy Analysis and Public
Spending: Theory and the Papua New Guinea Practice*. Aldershot:
Gower.

Axline, W.A. 1986. *Decentralisation and Development Policy: Provincial
Government and the Planning Process in Papua New Guinea*, PNG
Institute of Applied Social and Economic Research Monographs
26. Port Moresby: IASER.

Bailoenakia, P. and F. Koimanrea. 1983. *The Pomio Kivung Movement*,
Point series 2, Goroka: Melanesian Institute.

Bradley, S.C. 1982. 'Tolai Women and Development', unpublished
PhD thesis. London: University College.

Counts, D.E. 1971. 'Cargo or Council? Two approaches to
development in Northwest New Britain', *Oceania* 41: 287–97.

—— 1972. 'The Kaliai and the story: development and frustration in
New Britain', *Human Organisation* 31 (4): 373–83.

Crittenden, Robert and David A.W. Lea. 1989. *Integrated Rural
Development Programmes in Papua New Guinea*, PNG Institute of
Applied Social and Economic Research Monographs 28. Port
Moresby: IASER.

Epstein, A.L. 1958. *Politics in an Urban African Community*. Manchester:
Manchester University Press.

—— 1969. *Matupit: Land, Politics and Change among the Tolai of New
Britain*. Canberra: Australian National University Press.

—— (ed.). 1974. *Contention and Dispute*. Canberra: Australian National
University Press.

—— 1978. *Ethos and Identity: Three Studies in Ethnicity*. London: Tavistock.

—— 1992a. *Scenes from African Urban Life: Collected Copperbelt Essays*. Edinburgh: Edinburgh University Press.

—— 1992b. *In the Midst of Life: Affect and Ideation in the World of the Tolai*. Berkeley: University of California Press.

Epstein, T.S. 1968. *Capitalism, Primitive and Modern: Some Aspects of Tolai Economic Growth*. Canberra: Australian National University Press.

Errington, F. 1974. *Karavara: Masks and Power in a Melanesian Ritual*. Ithaca, NY: Cornell University Press.

Fajans, Jane. 1985. 'The person in social context: the social character of Baining "psychology"', in G. White and J. Kirkpatrick (eds) *Person, Self and Experience: Exploring Pacific Ethnopsychologies*. Berkeley: University of California Press.

Friedman, Jonathan. 1994. *Cultural Identity and Global Process*. London: Sage.

Gerritson, Ralph, Ron May and M.A.H.B. Walter. 1981. 'Road belong development – cargo cults, community groups and self-help movements in Papua New Guinea', *Working Papers of the Department of Political and Social Change* 3. Canberra: Australian National University.

Grosart, Ian. 1982. 'Nationalism and micronationalism: the Tolai case', in Ron May (ed.) *Micronationalist Movements in Papua New Guinea*. Canberra: Australian National University Press.

Heald, Suzette. 1994. 'Introduction', in Suzette Heald and Ariane Deluz (eds) *Anthropology and Psychoanalysis: An Encounter through Culture*. London: Routledge.

Jaques, E. 1955. 'Social systems as defence against persecutory and depressive anxiety: a contribution to the psycho-analytical study of social processes', in Melanie Klein, Paul Heimann and Roger Money-Kyrle (eds) *New Directions in Psycho-Analysis*. London: Tavistock.

Koimanrea, F. 1984. *Report of the Political Conflict between the Pomio Kivung Group Movement, non-Kivung Groups and the East New Britain Provincial Government*. Rabaul: mimeo.

Lawrence, Peter. 1964. *Road Belong Cargo*. Manchester: Manchester University Press.

Menzies Lyth, Isabel. 1988. *Containing Anxiety in Institutions*. London: Free Association Books. (Orig. 1959.)

Overseas Development Group (1973) *A Report on Development Strategies for Papua New Guinea*. Port Moresby: University of East Anglia.

Panoff, Michel. 1969a. 'Inter-tribal relations of the Maenge people of New Britain', *New Guinea Research Bulletin* 30 (Australian National University, Canberra).

—— 1969b. 'An experiment in inter-tribal contacts: the Maenge labourers on European plantations', *Journal of Pacific History* 4: 111–27.

Polansky, E. 1966. 'Rabaul', *South Pacific Bulletin* second quarter: 3–7.

Rew, Alan. 1975. *Social Images and Process in Urban New Guinea*, American Ethnological Society Monograph no. 57. St Paul, MN: West Publishing.

—— 1980. *A Ranch for Cape Vogel: Failure and Promise in Regional Development*, PNG Institute of Applied Social and Economic Research Monographs 14. Port Moresby: IASER.

—— 1985a. 'A development strategy for Pomio-Bainings', in *Pomio-Bainings Area Study: East New Britain Province* (4 vols). Port Moresby: W.S. Atkins and Touche Ross, vol. 1, pp. 1–15.

—— 1985b. 'Social services and social indicators', in *Pomio-Bainings Area Study: East New Britain Province* (4 vols). Port Moresby: W.S. Atkins and Touche Ross, vol. 2, pp. 1–112.

—— 1996. 'Development management and ethnic identity in New Britain, Papua New Guinea', *Papers in International Development* 18: 1–36 (Swansea: University of Wales).

Sack, Peter. 1974. 'The range of traditional Tolai remedies', in A.L. Epstein (ed.) *Contention and Dispute*. Canberra: Australian National University Press.

Salisbury, Richard. 1970. *Vunamami: Economic Transformation of a Traditional Society*. Melbourne: Melbourne University Press.

—— 1976. 'Language and politics in an elite group', in W.M. O'Barr and J.F. O'Barr (eds) *Language and Politics*. The Hague: Mouton.

Tovalele, P. 1977. 'The Pomio cargo cult, East New Britain', in R. Adams (ed.) *Socio-economic change*. Lae: Institute of Papua New Guinea Studies, pp. 123–39.

Trompf, G.W. 1990. 'Keeping the *Lo* under a Melanesian Messiah: an analysis of the Pomio *Kivung,* East New Britain', in J. Barker (ed.) *Christianity in Oceania: Ethnographic Perspectives*. Association of Social Anthropologists of Oceania, Monograph 12. Lanham, MD: ASAO.

—— 1994. *Payback: The Logic of Retribution in Melanesian Religions*. Cambridge: Cambridge University Press.

Walter, M.A.H.B. 1981. 'Cult movements and community development associations: revolution and evolution in the Papua New Guinea countryside', *IASER Discussion Papers* 36. Port Moresby: IASER.

Whitehouse, Harvey. 1995. *Inside the Cult: Religious Innovation and Transmission in Papua New Guinea*. Oxford: Clarendon Press.

PART II   'BELONGING ...'

Part II explores the experience of belonging to a cultural diaspora, both from the point of view of the individual and the social collectivity in which a person's fundamental social worth finds it meaning. In these chapters self-consciousness is explored through evolving narratives which members of the diaspora devise and tell about themselves, their origins and so on, and about how they are linked to global 'cultural streams' (religion, nationality, ethnicity) and to local communities which are simultaneously home and a place of exile, a physical place and a node in a transnational network defined by the continual movement of ideas, capital, people and materiel.

The defining experience of these diaspora is that of participating in the traditions and values of a homeland and, because they live outside that homeland, they also possess a strong sense of displacement and loss because of the entanglements and tensions that come with 'minority' status in a host country. The threat of immersion is particularly relevant for three reasons. First, the history and demographics of immigration meant that the small numbers of males who formed the core of early settlement could not create or sustain a cultural presence until they were joined by women from the diaspora who, via morally sanctioned marital unions, allowed a measure of social closure. Second, these communities re-created core religious institutions to serve the needs of members. Finally, the sense of displacement reinforced with the local quotidian experience of being 'different' – essentialised in terms of race, nationality, ethnicity, religion and so on – sustained the use of narratives to generalise/normalise individual experience as the experience of the 'community'. This continuous recasting and retelling of the past becomes, at a certain point, the dominant narrative used to organise and communicate the experience of social identity.

6 CULTURE, SOCIAL ORGANISATION AND ASIAN IDENTITY: DIFFERENCE IN URBAN EAST AFRICA[1]

John R. Campbell

Contemporary work on ethnicity often takes as its starting point an emphasis on the social mechanisms of ascription and categorisation through which individuals define commonality and 'difference' from others. In the context of urban complex societies anthropologists are increasingly running up against the limits of the discipline's structural-functionalist premises of holism and integration which creates problems in conceptualising 'society' and 'culture' (Barth 1989, 1992). In contemporary urban East Africa we find a complex society composed of individuals and groups with varying forms of linkages to and participation in African, European and Indian cultural traditions.[2] In such societies any assumption concerning the logical coherence or shared nature of culture presents obvious methodological and epistemological problems regarding its conceptualisation and study.

In this chapter, I provide an account of the development of ethnicity among immigrant East Indians in urban, mainland Tanganyika (now Tanzania). Following Barth, my goal is to understand the development of the Asian cultural tradition – embracing Hindus, Shia Muslims and Sikhs[3] – in urban Tanzania by examining its historical development and present configuration. This involves the recognition that each tradition or cultural stream coheres through time and is faced with a problem of reproducing itself as a distinctive set of ideas, knowledge, customs and values. Analysis of a tradition must necessarily examine its coherence and contents by describing its social organisation, distribution in space, history and prospects (Barth 1984: 82). This requires that: (1) we acknowledge that such traditions are weakly bounded and therefore require an examination of the entire context within which they are realised; (2) we provide an account of their history

169

as a means of understanding the traditions' continuity; finally (3) that we identify the main endogenous and exogenous processes which affect cultural transmission and change (Barth 1984: 85–6).

The focus on the Indian/Asian cultural stream in East Africa represents an attempt to explore the development of contemporary Asian ethnicity and social identity both within its specifically local/urban context and as part of a wider tradition with important links to the Indian sub-continent. It should be clear from the outset that other races, cultures and 'traditions' in East Africa have also played a prominent role in the shaping of urban society and culture, however, at least partially for reasons of space these latter cultures and traditions cannot be adequately addressed in this chapter.

Knowledgeable observers of, as well as participants in, contemporary Asian life in urban East Africa find it relatively easy to identify its key characteristics: namely the significance of religion/sect, of family and community, and of the economic role(s) played by community members. The specific institutions and roles are widely assumed – by social scientists (many of whom are Asian) and by East African Asians – to have developed out of 'traditional' Indian institutional practices.

Despite the ease with which formal institutions are identified as central to Asian social life, major differences of emphasis and meaning emerge from within the respective communities themselves and from those who have sought to compare these communities to their parent communities on the sub-continent. Within communities we would expect members to distance themselves from other groups in such a way as to draw attention to gross difference, namely of religion and/or sect and secondarily in terms of the organisation of family and community life. What is much less clear is the extent to which individuals within a community differ over the meaning, role and so on of their own institutions and practices on the basis of differences in gender, age and social position.

Anthropological accounts, most of which directly or indirectly compared parent and diasporic communities, report a number of socio-cultural anomalies. For example, Pocock was the first to point out the shift in East Africa to an idiosyncratic ranking of individual Hindu castes in the absence of a caste system, and of a disjuncture between the occupation of individuals and the occupation traditionally associated with their caste (1957). Subsequently, Bharati concluded that the social structure of caste no longer functioned in East Africa except as an 'ideology'; though Bharati's informants denied that caste had any social significance, he clearly saw its relevance to continued endogamy (1967).

Writing about Tanzanian Sikhs, Fleuret argued that, with the exception of endogamy, caste was 'defunct'; she attributed this to the character of Indian immigration (passenger or free as opposed to indentured) and continued social interaction with Hindus and the caste system (1975). Finally, the East African Shia Muslims – Ismaili Khojas, Ismaili Bohoras and Khoja Ithna'asheris – who had converted to Islam from Hinduism, were said to combine caste beliefs, values and practices with Shiism (Amiji 1969; Kjellberg 1967).

In their own way and for different reasons, community members and anthropologists have reified aspects of Asian culture – that is, caste, sect, family and community – emphasising only a part of the experience of Asian social life in an effort to differentiate between the different communities in East Africa *and* to distinguish the diaspora from parent community. Both accounts are ahistorical – ignoring the piecemeal and indeterminate beginnings of Asian settlement – and overemphasise the importance of formal institutions (which were not fully developed until relatively recently) at the expense of social behaviour and the experience of individual community members. An emphasis on formal institutions also ignores the manner in which the various traditions and social identities have been reproduced, particularly the struggles which individuals engaged in to ensure personal survival and cultural continuity.

To deal with these problems this chapter traces the development of Asian social organisation – along a continuum from casual to corporate forms – within the different 'communities' as a means of understanding the nature and extent to which ethnic identity was and is socially expressed, reproduced, reinforced and transmitted (Handleman 1977; Barth 1989).

INDIAN MIGRATION AND SETTLEMENT TO 1885: PATRONS AND 'DUKAWALLAHS'

During the 1830s the Sultan of Oman moved his palace to the island of Zanzibar bringing with him a retinue of Omani Arab officials – as landlords and plantation owners – and Indian merchants and financiers who managed the Sultan's tax and revenue collection, served as money lenders and financed trade between the African mainland and India, Europe and the Americas (Sheriff 1987). The economic influence of the big Indian merchants was considerable and was exercised in part through daily *baraza* or public meetings at which merchants met with the Sultan to discuss business; an individual's financial standing reflected directly upon that of his community (*Samachar* 1929: 39).

Though Indian settlement was initially restricted to Zanzibar town and Indians were prohibited from trading directly with the mainland, a small community of traders began to form as early as 1811 and by the 1870s the Indian population was large and permanently settled. Motivated by opportunities in trade and recurrent famine in western India, the number of Indians living in Zanzibar town rose from 214 in 1819 to 5406 in 1879 (vastly outnumbering the 139 resident Europeans). Residing predominantly in the 'Indian Bazaar', the majority of the population were Gujarati-speaking Muslim Khojas and Bohoras (converted Hindus from Cutch and Kathiawar in western India), followed by a much smaller Hindu population, and even smaller numbers of Goans, Singhalese, Memons, Baluchis and Parsees (Gregory 1971: 31–7; Sheriff 1987: 146–7).

The size of the Hindu population was small due to caste restrictions which prevented wives and families from being brought to Zanzibar. Hindus or *Banyans* were predominantly low-caste individuals who dominated the wholesale trade and were involved in money lending. Muslims, on the other hand, faced no restrictions against bringing families and, though immigration from India continued, many Ismaili Khojas were born and permanently settled in Zanzibar and were fluent in Ki-swahili, the lingua franca of the coast.

The Ismaili Khojas are a Shia sect organised under the authority of the Aga Khan, their *Imam* or spiritual head. Growing sectarianism within the Ismaili community in western India reached Zanzibar in the 1860s and led to increasing dissension amongst members (Amiji 1971, 1975). Local dissenters sought to preserve a tradition of local control and initiative and resisted the Imam's growing authority. However, increased pressure forced dissenters to leave the Ismaili *jamat khana* (congregation or community) under the threat of excommunication which involved expulsion, the stopping of an individual's commercial credit and social ostracism. Many dissenters joined the Ithna'asheri Shia sect and, by 1905, the split between the two had become complete with each establishing separate *jamat khana*, mosques and cemeteries, bringing to an end social intercourse and inter-community marriage (Rizvi and King 1973: 16). Sectarianism, therefore, became an important factor shaping relations among Shia Indians at a time when many were moving to the mainland.

Beginning in the 1880s British and German colonisation on the mainland – which established the Kenya Protectorate and German East Africa (GEA), respectively – consciously sought to build on Indian coastal settlement to expand trade into the interior and, in Kenya, to provide labour to construct the railway. Prior to this date a small number of Indians resided on the Tanzania coast – in Kilwa, Lindi, Bagamoyo and Tanga – as agents for large Zanzibar-based Indian trading houses, though numbers began to grow significantly in the 1880s (Mangat 1969: 9; Gregory 1971: 37). First settled in 1856, Dar es Salaam's growth was uneven: in 1874, 21 Indians resided there (1 Wannia, 13 Bhattia, 1 Mooltani, 3 Bohoras and 3 Khojas with their families); while in 1886 the community was composed of 45 Bohora, 14 Hindus and 47 Khojas (Gray 1952: 10, 18).

Typically the traders who owned the Zanzibar-based merchant houses drew upon cultural and social links with co-religionists to recruit assistants to work in their shops. Some of the larger trading 'houses' – for instance those of Alidina Visram (Ismaili), Sir Tarya Topan (Ismaili), Sewa Haji (an Ismaili), A.A. Jevanjee (Bohora) and Jairam Sewji (Hindu Bhattia) – might stretch from Zanzibar west to the Congo, south to Mozambique and north to Ethiopia, and employ 500 agents. After a period of apprenticeship, patrons (*sethnokar* or *brahmania*) provided assistants with credit to establish their own shops on the understanding that the latter would provide political support within the community and operate as their creditor (Amiji 1971: 606–7; Mangat 1969: 14ff., 77–83). Prior to the First World War many of these petty traders or *dukawallahs* settled in small mainland villages.

Until 1910 these mainland Indian communities were uniquely constituted. In the first place, traders from different ethnic backgrounds served as agents of the trading 'houses'. Second, all Muslims – and coastal African society was itself predominantly (Sunni) Muslim – regardless of sect worshipped in a common mosque. At the same time these relatively isolated communities of traders established liaisons with African women with whom they had children. It was only after 1910 that Indian women began to arrive in sufficient numbers that it became possible to establish endogamous, arranged marriage (Bharati 1965: 133; Amiji 1975: 37, 1971: 606). In short, small numbers and diverse origins favoured the formation of coastal communities based on shared social practice and values, communities in which, on the one hand, Asian males were integrated into local African society and, on the other, were also vertically linked through a patron and Shiism to Zanzibar and the world of Islam.

Despite official encouragement for Indian settlement in GEA, settler hostility to Indians resulted in controls over their immigration, settlement and commerce (Honey 1982). Notably, Indians were prevented from acquiring urban land, new forms of tax were imposed on their businesses, and monopoly control of overseas shipping and inland transport was transferred to German firms, in the process restricting Indians to wholesale/retail trade.

British occupation of the German capital Dar es Salaam in 1917 was followed by a devastating guerrilla war in the interior which set back commerce and economic development for many years. At the same time, British policy restricted Indian settlement to specified towns contributing decisively to the dramatic growth of Dar es Salaam's Indian population and to the city's role as the territorial hub of Indian society and politics.

Table 1 Indian Population in Dar es Salaam and Tanganyika Territory by Year

	1887	1901	1913	1921	1931	1948
Dar es Salaam	107	1,064	2,874	3,163	8,475	15,203
Territory	1,751	3,681	9,645	10,299	25,144	46,254

Source: Honey (1982: Table 4, p. 122 and Table 12, p. 296).

DAR ES SALAAM AND THE FOUNDATION OF THE INDIAN COMMUNITY: 1917–39

The movement of the dispersed rural network of Indian traders into Dar es Salaam and other towns decisively broke their social isolation – organised around dyadic social ties between a trader and his patron

– and laid the basis for individual integration into nascent urban associations that were to become increasingly sectarian in character. The context within which this occurred was one of continued colonial control over Indian settlement – restricted not only to towns but to particular parts of towns – and Indian commerce, and of rising nationalism in India which provided an impetus for local political organisation.

Reputedly the first Indian to settle in Dar es Salaam was a Daudi Bohora trader, Amiji Musaji, in 1856.[4] Musaji's trading enterprise allowed him to accumulate considerable wealth, part of which he bequeathed to his community in the form of a mosque built during German occupation. For his beneficence, the Bombay–based *Da'i-al-Mutlaq* or spiritual head of all Bohora, bestowed the title of *Sheikh* upon him prior to 1900, in which *ex officio* capacity he acted as the community religious leader until shortly before his death in 1917 when the *Da'i* sent an official emissary to oversee the community.

The Ithna'asheri reached Dar es Salaam in 1875, and the community mosque was completed in 1908 (Rizvi and King 1973: 19). The Ismaili Khoja must have arrived about the same time for in 1921 they petitioned the British for additional land near their mosque to accommodate a three-fold increase in numbers.[5] The Hindu population grew slowly and fragmented over differences in caste and temple (Morris 1956; Pocock 1957). In part because only the poorest had migrated to East Africa, and then only from certain castes in western India, no all–inclusive caste system existed. For this reason and because of the initial shortage of Indian women, the local Hindu community attempted to consolidate itself through endogamy – arranged marriages with suitable women from India – rather than in terms of ritual purity. Similarly, in 1915 a small Sikh community was established with the arrival of a Sikh regiment of the British Army who built the first *Gurdwara* (temple) in 1925.[6]

The colonial administration spurred Indian self-organisation by dealing only with the 'Indian Community' in the form of a Central Indian Council or Association which purported to speak on behalf of all Indians (Morris 1956: 197). This fiction was administratively convenient so long as the Association spoke with one voice; however, growing immigration and prosperity led to ethnic and social differentiation which was increasingly difficult to organise under the banner of a central association (see Tables 2 and 3).

Sectarian and religious difference aside, in 1914 resident Indians formed an Indian Association (IA) in an attempt to pull together all mainland Indians to lobby Britain and the League of Nations to make Tanganyika an 'Indian colony' (Honey 1982: 293ff.; Mangat 1969: ch. 4). Further impetus for organisation derived from growing nationalism in India and the arrival of politicised Hindu migrants who led local Indian Associations.[7]

Formed in 1918, the Dar es Salaam IA became the headquarters for outlying associations. The principal actors were a group of 'bankers' – in effect the Territory's leading merchants (all Dar es Salaam-based; eight Muslims and one Hindu) – with a membership in the hundreds, and local associations in 46 different areas (Honey 1982: 276–82, 294). Its principal concern was to protect Indian commerce by lobbying government. In 1923, for example, colonial legislation imposed new tax and licensing regulations on Indian business against which the IA called a *hartel*[8] (strike) which closed Indian shops for 54 days. The *hartel* failed to alter legislation and was costly to participating merchants; furthermore, it aroused considerable hostility amongst urban Africans who were dependent on Indian shops (Honey 1982: 338–43).

The period also saw the development of several short-lived religious associations – a Maulid Committee and Id Prayers Committee – which brought together the three Shia sects for common religious observance. With the exception of the Ismailis, all Indian and African Muslims shared a meeting hall, called *Anjumah Islamia*, located in the open area separating Indian and African settlement, to celebrate Id and Id-el-fit.[9] In addition, the Bohoras organised a day of public speeches and worship to commemorate the martyrdom of Imam Hussein which was also attended by Hindus. Once established, this commemoration (*Ashura*) was followed by special prayers in the mosque and conspicuous feasting at which the entire Bohora community gathered (Amiji 1975: 50). Finally, it was common for Indian Muslims to attend the major Hindu festivals, and Hindus to attend public Islamic and Sikh celebrations; in each case, however, participation stopped short of attending each other's mosque/temple.[10]

The British, working under a League of Nations mandate proscribing differential treatment to Indians, implemented a system of racial zoning which segregated the races in townships with Indians required to reside in an intermediate area between Europeans and Africans.[11] This entailed the provision of inequitable levels of infrastructure and service

– shelter, water, electricity and so on – between the races, and led to the creation of a 'neutral zone' or *cordon sanitaire* (later known as '*Mnazi Moja*') physically separating Indian from African residential areas.

The 'neutral zone' or open ground separating Africans and Asians also served as a competitive arena for team sports, though such teams were themselves segregated by race and, increasingly, by community/sect. By 1934, if not earlier, official recognition had been obtained for a number of sports 'clubs' to have their own 'grounds' at *Mnazi Moja* and elsewhere.[12] At this date eleven clubs were organised on the basis of race and ethnicity: two 'native' (African) clubs; two organised by immigrant African groups (Sudanese, Comoros); one 'Turkish' club; and six Indian clubs (including the Bohoras, Sikhs, Goans and Punjabis).[13]

The small European population set the standard of racial segregation by creating separate social institutions: in 1903 the Germans organised the first social *klub* for officers and members of the business community, while the British followed suit with the Gymkhana Club (golf and tennis).

Urban Africans, on the other hand, were also beginning to organise. By 1914 Dar es Salaam residents and up-country immigrants were becoming integrated into one of a set of competitive, urban-based *beni* dance and mutual aid societies modelled on European military brass bands (Ranger 1975). *Beni* societies operated as part of paired oppositional groups which actively competed against one another – in terms of dance, dress, pageant and status – forming the equivalent of a European club. The initial basis of recruitment reflected perceived differences in urban social status – between the educated and wealthy versus poor migrants – who were recruited *without* regard to ethnic origin. Later in the 1930s and 1940s *beni* functioned as a means by which poor migrants built up an urban supra-tribal 'community' which provided members with shelter, work and assistance. Throughout the period migrants were integrated into urban life through the adoption of Ki-swahili and participation in multi-ethnic societies. In short there occurred the development of a new urban-based, multi-ethnic 'African' social identity.[14]

The end of the First World War was followed by economic stagnation and the Great Depression which undermined local livelihoods. However, against a backdrop of continuing civil unrest in the Punjab together with growing Indian nationalism, periodic famine and chronic poverty continued to push migrants out to East Africa. The Tanganyika government auction of confiscated German property saw a substantial transfer of urban real estate into Indian hands (in Dar es Salaam Indians acquired 90 per cent of the freehold; Gregory 1971: 389), marking a turn in economic fortune for the Indian population at a time of rising settler hostility in Kenya and the closure of economic opportunities to Indian capital in Zanzibar (Delf 1963: 28–33).

Table 2 Indian Population by Religion, Tanganyika Territory, 1931

Religion	Number	Per cent
Muslim	14,390	57.2
Hindu	7,762	30.9
Jain	–	1.0
Sikh	768	3.1
Parsee	52	0.2
Goan (Catholic)	1,722	6.8
Christian (non–Goan)	168	0.6
Buddhist	6	–
Not specified	61	0.2
Total	24,929	100

Source: Honey (1982: Table 13, p. 297).

Table 3 The Dar es Salaam Population by Year and Community

	1901	1948	1958
Muslim	631	–	–
Hindu	301	14,295	24,981
Goan	132	908	267
Arab	1,067	1,067	2,545
European	–	1,726	4,479
African	–	50,765	93,363
Total	–	68,761	125,635

Source: Honey 1982 (Table 5, p. 123), Tanganyika (1948: Table 6, p. 9, 1958: Table 2).

Note: The 1948 figures combine Muslims and Hindus into 'Indians'; the 1958 figure includes 'Pakistanis'.

By the outbreak of the Second World War the Indian population had more than doubled and was beginning to prosper. At the same time, colonial racial segregation had solidified into a sharply demarcated, socially and physically bounded urban settlement linked to a rigid form of Indian political organisation. Segregation was contributing to the formation of distinct social worlds in which the majority of Europeans, Indians and Africans scarcely interacted outside of work or trade. Indeed, Indians and Africans scarcely met socially since neither hotel, club nor any other institution existed which might have provided an opportunity or setting for social interaction. It was only at the highest levels – the Legislative Council and Municipal Council, to which individuals were nominated – that meaningful social interaction might occur, and then only among the elite.

The major factor promoting changes in local Indian social organisation were initiated by the Aga Khan – following a 1905 *firman* decreeing a written constitution – who established a dispensary (1929), a development fund (1935) and the beginnings of a secular education programme (Morris 1956: 200; Kjellberg 1967). The other communities haltingly followed the example of the Ismailis in local communal organisation. Even so, for the majority life was becoming increasingly rooted in their physically bounded 'community' and its segregated institutions (schools, clinics and so on)[15] defined increasingly, though not yet exclusively, in terms of ethnicity, religion and sect.

FROM ASSOCIATION TO ETHNIC COMMUNITY: DAR ES SALAAM 1939–61

The war years witnessed rationing, rising urban unemployment and a marked deterioration in the condition and availability of housing for a rapidly growing population of African and Indian migrants. Urban conditions were very bad, in part because urban public expenditure, which had always been inadequate, was severely cut. This gave rise to increasing numbers of Indians renting accommodation from Africans in Kariakoo, the quarter nearest the 'neutral zone'.

Europeans viewed this intermingling with alarm, going so far as to accuse Indians of purposely advancing money to Africans with the intention of foreclosing on the debt to acquire a house. Government used various expedients to control or prevent Africans from letting to

Indians including raising the house tax paid by African landlords and restricting letting to specified areas.[16] The widespread nature of sub-letting, and the various claims made about it, gave rise to misapprehension and tension but, given a rapidly growing urban population and a government rent freeze, sub-letting was an unsurprising outcome. While migrant Africans increasingly resorted to squatting, amongst Asians the situation led to sub-letting either from Africans or from Indian landlords, the latter letting space in severely overcrowded tenements in the bazaar.[17]

Urban wages were low and employment was restricted with the major source of work for Africans being government (for example, the railway) or casual work in the port (Iliffe 1970). This period saw the establishment of a national African labour movement based largely on the efforts of Dar es Salaam dock workers and the effects of the strikes between 1939 and 1947 during which government used Indians in a high-profile manner to maintain essential services.

For Indians, particularly recent migrants and those without capital, reliance on kin and patrons for shelter and shop work was an essential step towards autonomy, accumulating capital and establishing one's own business. While it absorbed many migrants, shop hours were long, conditions poor and incomes – though five to ten times more than for African shop workers – were 'meagre' (Honey 1982: 527ff.). There was considerable tension over wages and work conditions between patron/employers and employees throughout the early 1930s and late 1940s . However, a combination of 'kinship' and wider social obligation undercut the shop workers union since many migrants had been 'called' from India on the understanding that they would 'work for several months without pay, receiving instead food and lodging, [and] often only space on the shop floor' (1982: 545). This period of 'training' was later followed by a small salary and perhaps credit or other assistance to set up a shop.

While the availability of shop labour provided family firms with flexibility in coping with economic hardship, some care needs to be exercised before concluding that it was the 'family' that was the bedrock upon which economic success and social survival was based (Mangat 1969: 137–8). In particular, the composition of these 'families' needs to be carefully considered particularly since we know that it was only *after* 1910 that marriageable Indian women arrived making possible the establishment of 'traditional' households. This would suggest that culturally approved and arranged endogamous marriage would have been the exception until the late 1930s.[18] At the same time extensive immigration from the sub-continent occurred bringing growing numbers of 'relatives'.

A situation of considerable fluidity in family structure is also suggested by census statistics. For instance, 1952 data on the length of residence of immigrants underscore the recency of Indian migration – 35.2 per cent had been resident five years or less, and a further 12.4 per cent resident ten years or less (Tanganyika 1954: Table 26). Throughout this period the age profile of the Indian population indicates a population pyramid typical of a young, rapidly expanding population experiencing high fertility and a declining mortality rate. (Tanganyika 1958: Table 19, p. 16).

Oral accounts suggest that the family unit was not, at least for the majority of the population, the traditional Indian 'joint family' but consisted instead of different types of 'extended households' variously headed by a single parent or grandparent (for example, in 1948, 10 per cent of adult women were widows) and were of varying generations in depth (perhaps because most adults were marrying in their early twenties and establishing separate households). It appears that family size and 'jointness' correlated with relative affluence; greater assets being associated with a larger social unit and greater efforts to keep the business within the family of, for example, siblings and their children. At about this time, however, as ethnic organisation became increasingly corporate in character, each community began to adopt a different stance with regard to the role of the Indian family.

At the instigation of the Aga Khan the Ismailis took the lead in collectively addressing the needs of their members (Amiji 1969). In the 1950s a hierarchy of consultative councils was created to look after the spiritual and economic well-being of members through a system of tribunals, religious associations and 'departments' of health, education, housing, youth, women and welfare, and the promotion of industry and commerce. The family was and is the foundation as spelt out in a unique, written body of personal law – regulating marriage, divorce, conjugal rights, adoption and legitimacy – and in which Ismaili communal institutions were established (Anderson 1964).

The Ismailis' initiative was possible precisely because of the Aga Khan's position as the religious and administrative head of the community. Unique amongst Shia Muslims, he has used his authority to 'modernise' the community, while at the same time maintaining control over the direction and pace of change. The growing institutionalisation of Ismaili life was accomplished through an emphasis on religious practice in conjunction with meeting the secular needs of community members. Communal institutions combine both aspects of Ismaili life and were overseen by older, wealthier individuals, part of 'a small plutocratic elite of wealth, related through inter-dynastic marriages and having a common interest in maintaining and furthering the system' (Amiji 1969: 151).

The Ismailis were viewed somewhat ambivalently by other Indians. On the one hand, they had taken the lead in organising the local community and dealing with its needs; on the other hand traditionalists viewed them as Western-oriented modernisers. Ismaili values concerning the 'family', increasingly defined in Western (that is, nuclear family) terms, and particularly its liberal attitude towards women, female education and a movement away from arranged married created anxiety amongst other Indians (Walji 1974: 222ff.).

Other communities were slower to address the needs of their members perhaps because each sect was establishing a unique link between religious and secular domains which in turn affected its members ability to organise. While undoubtedly a key to Shia local organisation lay in part with the manner in which local autonomy was negotiated with central religious authority, a further factor lay in the social composition and outlook of local communities (that is, the degree to which members were educated and working in diverse occupations, as opposed to continued dependence on commerce).

Amongst the Daudi Bohora a centrally appointed *amil* oversaw local communities until 1926 when a *jamat* council was created (Amiji 1969). In the mid-1950s a written constitution was promulgated creating a secular administrative system in which adult males were elected to a management committee on which the *amil* also sat. The extent of the latter's authority – notionally he is said to exercise little voice in 'material affairs' – has been a continuing source of friction in local communities and led to periodic dissension and the use of excommunication to discipline members.[19]

The Shia Ithna'asheri, whose religious leadership resides in a council of elected *mujtahids* in Iran, also established a secular council system in the late 1950s. This was followed by the provision of: a scholarship fund; financial assistance for cooperatives, industry and business; a dispensary; a home for widows; a nursery, primary and secondary school; and a general welfare fund, including a funeral committee which arranges burial for all members (Amiji 1969: 165–7).[20]

The Sikhs, who numbered perhaps 5000 families in 1948 of whom 1000 resided in Dar es Salaam, also adopted a basic management committee focused on maintaining the Gurdwara, guest house and girls' boarding school. However, unlike other Indians, most Sikhs were skilled artisans in government employment (the PWD, railway and post office), and were also distinguished by dress, diet (vegetarianism) and Sunday religious services.[21] During this period the community operated fairly autonomously of central authority in the Punjab until the first visit from the Head of the community in 1964 which brought growing pressure to conform to orthodox practice.

Similar kinds of processes were at work in the Hindu population which resulted in increasing internal differentiation and social organisation modelled on the structure of caste. Extensive growth in numbers and the lead set by the Ismailis in obtaining recognition for their community contributed to a process of 'communal crystallisation' around separate caste or sect organisations (Morris 1956: 207), which in turn reflected a new and 'systematic recognition of difference' between and among Hindus (Pocock 1957: 298).

Religious and sectarian differences apart, other factors were at work which were to result in further division within the Indian communities. For some years tension between Hindu and Muslim had been simmering, notably over nomination to government political bodies.[22] Partition between Pakistan and India in 1947, and the riots and bloodshed which followed, exacerbated the tension in local Hindu–Muslim relations.

Partition also underlined a fundamental dilemma regarding the identity of East African Indians: should they return 'home' or should they remain in East Africa? And if they remained, should it be as African nationals or as a members of distinct Indian communities? As a result of the above tensions the Indian Association collapsed and was replaced by a short-lived Asian Association 'formed by young men who looked forward to a secular, multi-racial Tanganyikan state' (Iliffe 1979: 478) and by the Dar es Salaam-based (Asian) Merchants Chamber. In 1952 the Aga Khan and the Head of the Ithna'asheri commanded their followers to take up citizenship in East Africa.[23] Partition, followed by the growth of African nationalism, was associated with rising tension and conflicting loyalties for Indians who were now confronted with obligations to community *and* country and the need to come to terms with their ambiguous relationship to Africans.

The end of the Second World War brought economic prosperity and a construction boom in Dar es Salaam: from a 1948 baseline of 72 units worth 4.8 million shillings, a peak was reached and sustained between 1953 and 1958 when 1004 units were constructed per annum worth 143.4 million shillings (Mwita 1978: appendix viii, p. 291). Asians were key actors in this housing market in which Asian contractors built for Asian landlords who rented largely to Asian tenants.

Once again the Ismaili set the lead in 1946 when the Aga Khan established the Diamond Jubilee Trust to provide 'every Ismaili family in Africa' with their own home.[24] By the late 1960s this community-based housing cooperative scheme had resulted in an investment in Dar es Salaam of approximately US $35–41 million, and a further US $2.6 million in up-country towns (Walji 1974: 214–15). While Ismaili cooperative construction contributed to the boom other communities were also rebuilding communal properties, but the bulk of construction in the city centre was undertaken by private landlord/merchants who put up multi-storey buildings with shops and *go-downs* (stores) on the ground floor surmounted by blocks of flats.

By the end of this period 'communal crystallisation' was largely complete with most castes or sects having developed distinct and increasingly corporate organisations: the Shia communities were nearly completely institutionalised as compared to Sikhs and Hindus. At the same time, the recognition of difference – manifested in social interaction, marriage, worship, language and so on – in all the communities was marked. By the end of the 1950s colonial restrictions on trade forced many rural Indian traders into Dar es Salaam where racial segregation and corporate social life reinforced racial and ethnic separation. Migration from India and Pakistan continued throughout this period and Indian livelihoods were increasingly restricted to commerce and the property sector. Despite growing official restrictions, the period was marked by community growth and economic prosperity. However, the prosperity of the 1950s failed to eliminate racial disparities – average wages for Europeans, Asians and Africans in 1961 were £1546, £586 and £106 per annum respectively (Mascarhenas 1966: 55) – a growing awareness of which exacerbated racial tension.

BETWEEN COMMUNITY AND NATION: POST-COLONIAL
POLITICS AND ASIAN IDENTITY, 1961–73

Independence in 1961 brought to power the Tanganyika African
National Union (TANU), an African-based party which had been
supported by a small group of progressive Indians and Europeans.
TANU, and in particular its first Prime Minister Nyerere, faced
pressure from its peasant and trade union membership to 'Africanise'
government and the economy to provide economic opportunities for
Africans.

African popular perception of the difference between themselves
and Indians arose partially through differences in wealth as well as from
fundamentally different cultural practices, namely Indian endogamy,
family and kinship, food consumption and so on. African perception
was of course strongly influenced by their subordinate position in the
colonial racial and occupational hierarchy which focused African
resentment on Indians in commerce and the civil service, rather than
on the system's British architects.

At a time of growing African awareness of and resentment toward
Asians, Indian social life had become increasingly structured around
caste and sect canalising the lives of its members as participants in
communal affairs. The result was growing social distance and restricted
social interaction between Indians, as well as between Indians and
Africans. Though the legal barriers to segregation had fallen, only a
limited number of Africans were living in erstwhile Asian enclaves.
For most, relations were marked by mutual suspicion and tension as
reflected in social stereotypes: Africans perceived all Indians as *banyans*
or *dukawallahs* who were personified as 'an excessively lean or excessively
fat trader who sits in his *duka*', 'as a clannish, greedy, petty businessman',
in a word an 'exploiter' (Bharati 1964: 171). Asian appellations for
Africans mirrored their structural position, fears for their future, and
a very limited knowledge of African society: in short they were
concerned about African intentions towards their property and their
women (including the social consequences of miscegenation).

On the other hand, the consolidation of communal organisation also
increased the social distance between and among Indians as represented
in the mutual appellations and stereotypes each group had for the other.
Gujarati-speaking Hindus and Jains, aware of African attitudes toward

them, saw themselves as 'the bearers of an intense religious tradition' based on a set of immutable differences in the Hindu caste system (Bharati 1965: 136). Sikhs, many of whom originated from the low-caste Ramgarhia and whose work was artisanal, were referred to by Indians, Europeans and Africans by the Swahili term *fundi* (craftsman) or, amongst Indians as *kalasinga* ('the black lion'), a reference to their beards. Among Gujarati-speakers, to be called *Cutchi* was a derogatory synonym for being a 'petty, blood-sucking trader'; while among Gujarati-speaking Muslims social stereotypes abounded concerning, for example, the moral laxity of the Ismailis (focusing on their adoption of Western dress and the education and the apparent freedom of Ismailis women; Bharati 1964, 1965).

It was, therefore, against a backdrop of increasingly distinct and separately organised ethnic communities – mutual appellations reflecting the extent to which individuals had made an extensive personal commitment of time, resources and emotion in their communal organisation – that individuals negotiated their social identity.

Independence left Indians without special call on government and bereft of formal political representation, making it difficult for them to negotiate a national identity and associated rights and obligations at a time when the very symbols of their cultural identity were seen by African nationalists as exclusionary and racialist. Clearly a range of choices were open to them: (1) they could leave Tanganyika; (2) they might refuse Tanganyikan nationality but remain resident; (3) they might accept nationality but remain socially segregated; and, finally, (4) they might integrate and participate fully in national institutions. The option chosen would depend on culture and tradition, on personal circumstance, on migration history, and upon the extent to which their social network was relatively open, allowing participation in African social life and national affairs.

The first option is worth mentioning only to indicate that although individuals left, many did not return to the sub-continent.[25] The cultural diaspora created by a century of migration meant that many families had kin resident throughout East Africa and the Indian Ocean who could be called upon for assistance.

Option two was a logical possibility to the extent that individuals had some kind of niche or resource to maintain in Tanganyika *and* they had somewhere else to go, a place of safety, a homeland. Such persons – predominantly Hindus, Sikhs and Punjabis – took up Indian,

Pakistani or British nationality but remained resident to pursue their livelihoods until a percieved threat to life or livelihood forced them to leave.

Option three confronted the Shia Muslims, many of whom had long since cut their ties to India, and who had been directed to take out Tanganyikan citizenship. The challenge to these individuals was direct and difficult. Here the tendency was to re-invest significance in the symbolic boundaries separating Indian from African in order to maintain community life as much as possible, and to participate in a limited manner in national institutions.

The final option, initially taken up by a small number of individuals, represented a first step towards negotiating and defining a new Tanganyikan Asian identity. It entailed a potentially painful breach of communal norms and values and the development of new relations with Africans. To break communal taboos – the most potent of which was marriage or sexual partnership with someone of another race – threatened the foundation of communal life.

The first decade of independence confronted resident Indians with a series of events beyond their control forcing them to question their identity and loyalty to community *and* country. *Uhuru* or independence constituted a radically different context for Indians, one in which the previously subordinate caste of Africans had overnight become politically dominant and the social equal of Indians. How to cope with this fundamentally changed relation constituted what at the time was called 'the Asian dilemma'. In fact, the dilemma and associated angst existed primarily amongst those who found themselves facing a 1966 deadline to take up national citizenship, thereby dropping claims to British, Indian or Pakistani nationality (Ghai 1965: 11–13).

The context within which Indians considered their options was further politicised by the declaration of a one-party state in 1963, and by the 1964 Zanzibar revolution which heightened Indian insecurity because of its explicit anti-Arab and anti-Asian character. Though Arabs bore the brunt of mob violence, Zanzibari Indians were forced to flee to the mainland and had their property appropriated. Perhaps the most seized upon symbol of the revolution to Indians was not the loss of property – reinforced in Dar es Salaam at this time by attacks on Asian shops – but forced inter-racial marriage to Africans. A retrospective Bohora reaction to the situation was that:

Nobody wanted to have inter-marriage ... the Community ... wanted to stay the way they were. For donkeys years they have been like this, their own community, they knew each other, they wanted to marry people whom they knew, only be associated with people they knew.

In fact by the early 1960s 'less than 1% of the East African Asians, Hindu and Muslim alike ... [had] married across caste lines', which gives some indication of how great their reluctance might be to marrying non-Asians (Bharati 1965: 132). Bharati noted at the time that, particularly among Hindus, there was a small but dwindling number of children from African–Indian unions who were derogatively considered half-caste (*chotara*; Bharati 1965: 131–2, 1964: 174–5). Overall it seems clear that the majority of Indians attempted to hedge their bets, remaining resident but also socially segregated.

A paradox of the consolidation of communal institutions is that while they provided the space in which members might insulate themselves from the wider world, communal provision of secular education provided the mechanism of propelling individuals back into the world.[26] Once again the Ismailis led the way by establishing a network of 50 nursery, primary and secondary schools financed primarily by private donations (Kjellberg 1967: 25). Many schools were taken over by government at independence, though the Ismailis continued to run 41 private non–communal schools (at least 10 other Asian schools were also operating in the mid-1960s; Delf 1963: 51).

Access to secular education was coupled with a move into the professions, in short, with occupational diversification. This led in turn to increased involvement in public institutions: some individuals became involved in national politics; some served on public commissions and the public service; some assumed leadership roles in 'community' bodies such as the Dar es Salaam (Asian) Merchants Chamber; and, of course, certain individuals combined professional with community obligations.

The pace of Africanisation also meant that, rightly or wrongly, Indians perceived the intention of government to mean 'they had no future in the country', that state institutions were 'not for them'. At the same time that Indians were being removed from the civil service and replaced by Africans, further restrictions were placed on rural trade, pushing Indians into Dar es Salaam (Ghai and Ghai 1965: 44). The net effect was a growing Indian presence in Dar es Salaam notable for its absence from national institutions. Indian children were being sent overseas for higher education, in part to avoid national service; there were virtually no Indians in the army or police; and many were the accusations that Asians were illegally exporting foreign exchange.[27]

Finally, in April 1971 the government bowed to nationalist demands and passed 'The Acquisition of Buildings Act, no. 13' authorising the nationalisation of all buildings above a value of 100,000 shillings that were rented for residential, commercial or industrial purposes. The principal target was clearly Indian landlords, and the major area hit by nationalisation was Dar es Salaam.

Notice of acquisition appeared in the local press and was immediately followed by the arrival of the police who took possession of the building and attached assets. Basically individuals were evicted – amidst the scarcely concealed glee of Africans – sometimes without being able to remove personal possessions. In Dar es Salaam approximately 1578 buildings were acquired – fewer than 250 of which were eventually returned – affecting 5300 private tenants (Mwita 1978: 301). In the initial surge of acquisition not only privately owned buildings but also those belonging to communal associations – mosques, guest houses and community halls – were also acquired. While the latter were eventually returned, the entire process of appropriation caused a major panic in the Indian population.

The final spate of acquisitions ended in 1973 by which time 2994 buildings had been acquired worth an estimated 500 million shillings; almost all had belonged to Asians (Mwita 1978: 190).[28] The wealthiest and the poorest suffered equally. The once great Karimjee Jivanjee merchant family, who gave Karimjee Hall to the government for use as Parliament House and whose family head had been the first Speaker of the House at Independence, lost nearly everything: in Dar es Salaam alone 47 properties were acquired worth a minimum of 7 million shillings.[29] At the same time, houses belonging to and occupied by individual families were also nationalised and then rented back to their former owners and sitting tenants. While formally exempted from nationalisation, a large percentage of Ismaili cooperative housing was also acquired because tenant-purchasers had rented units to third parties (Mwita 1978: 214–16).

As Vassanji's (1989) fictionalised account of the period makes clear, the nationalisation was so comprehensive that the only asset remaining to most Asians was their children and family living overseas. Thus began a major exodus emptying mosques and community halls and totally transforming the way of life of those left behind. For example, of the descendants of the Karimjee Jivanjee family which established itself in Zanzibar in 1818, only one individual remained. In the nine months following nationalisation an Ismaili family which had come to Dar es Salaam in 1886 witnessed the departure of eleven of twelve brothers and sisters, as well as their children and associated uncles and aunts. As one Ismaili informant recalled of the period:

The kind of distress, the kind of panic that the people felt ... think of someone like my father [who died in 1972] ... one could probably ... get a feeling that he must have had that ... he worked so hard to make a living and earn money and you know, gradually accumulate that money to own that building. It's not a huge thing, it's [was] just a two-storey property. How he might just sort of felt, you know this is no longer mine. And he was already over fifty and no other means of making a livelihood.[30]

The true scale of this exodus, most of which took place between April 1971 and April 1973, is difficult to imagine. Of all the communities the worst hit was probably the Ismailis who had had 40 to 50 separate *jamat khana* and associated schools, clinics and so on throughout the country. As the largest community, the Ismailis had invested more heavily in urban real estate than others. One consequence of the exodus was to close upwards of one-third of the up-country *jamat khana* together with the services that had been used by local Africans. In Dar es Salaam, which had an Ismaili population of 15,000, fewer than one-third remained by 1973, even though the community continued to maintain all four *jamat khana* and mosques. Some idea of the extent of dislocation experienced at this time is provided by the same Ismaili informant quoted above:

Oh [the mosques are] empty! Real empty. For example, Changombe where I grew up the *jamat khana* has become a [empty] hall ... on days of activities they would have [had] no place to seat them, you'd have to you know extend mats outside in the compound and sit outside. That's how full it used to get. If you go now, you know, you feel like it's a football field with nobody playing.

Or in relation to the Upanga *jamat khana* in Dar es Salaam,

If you go today, you feel a pity that you know, they had to build partitions to make it smaller ... It affected you know quite strongly. And I think most of us have now overcome that period of ... depression and bitterness.

CONCLUSION

The Asian exodus of the early 1970s provides a benchmark to assess the content and trajectory of the Asian cultural tradition in East Africa. Even if we ignore the departure of the Sikhs in the 1960s and of Zanzibari Indians following the 1964 revolution, and if we deliberately circumscribe our inquiry to exclude the subsequent expulsion of Ugandan Asians by Amin, we are still forced to examine the interconnection between regional political events and East African Asian culture and society. What occurred in East Africa that could explain an African nationalism containing such vehement anti-Asian attitudes, attitudes which exist today despite the departure of the majority of Tanzania's Asians?

Part of the answer to this question lies in the legacy of colonialism and British success in putting into place a racially compartmentalised society. Over time it was a short step, in the lives of local people, before a specific link was made between relatively different cultural practices and absolute or categorical ethnic and racial difference. In Dar es Salaam, where urban life and livelihoods brought the majority of individuals into face-to-face contact, 'race' came increasingly to be associated with radically different livelihoods, opportunities and living spaces.

Within the colonial context, and particularly among Indian immigrants, a process of social organising occurred. Initial settlement was by single men, and crucial social relations were dyadic, linking relatively isolated shopkeepers to a Zanzibar-based merchant who was both one's patron and a link to the wider world of religion and India. Colonial policy resulted in the urbanisation and physical segregation of Indians; at the same time lengthening periods of residence, propinquity and shared livelihood provided a foundation upon which Asian community life developed.

Seen from within, the evolution of Indian social organisation – from ethnic category upon which dyadic social links were based, to ethnic networks with a specific interactional content expressing social affinity, to corporate ethnic associations – led to the development of a number of distinct Asian communities with separate corporate assets, membership criteria and so on.

These halting steps toward ethnic consciousness and autonomy, based on social ascription (to caste or sect), were perceived by outsiders –

defined situationally to include Indians belonging to 'other' castes/sects, and Africans – as efforts toward social closure. Thus, Africans (and Europeans) had an undifferentiated view of Indians and were unable or unwilling to recognise internal ethnic difference. Indeed, cultural or ethnic difference was persistently racialised.

Until the early 1950s colonial rule provided stability to race relations which were, however, rapidly rewritten in the period prior to independence when political instability exacerbated racial tensions. Perhaps Indian communalism was perceived by Africans as a threat to their ambitions, or perhaps it was rising African nationalism which sparked off Indian involvement in national politics (Iliffe 1979: 476ff.). In any event, against a backdrop of rising numbers of Indians and their increasingly apparent ethnic organisation, political uncertainty spurred racial misapprehension and contributed to a totalising of cultural difference between Asian and African and a further drawing apart and redefining of the boundaries between the two 'races'.

In short, attempts to create 'ethnic' cultural space developed out of a relation of connection or co-mingling each with the other group – Hindu with Muslim with Sikh, and 'Indian' with 'African'. The politicisation of ethnicity in associations and social relations contributed to its redefinition and articulation as one of separation, detachment and boundedness. In other words, there was a distinct movement from sociability in which cultural difference was a factor, to the creation, in the eyes of the Other, of 'pure' ethnic groups.

NOTES

1. An earlier version of this chapter was given at the British Sociological Association's 1995 annual conference at the University of Leicester. I would like to thank Richard Jenkins and the participants at the 'Identity and Affect' workshop held in Swansea in June 1995 for their comments and suggestions.

2. The concept of tradition or stream is *not* restricted to the so-called Great cultural traditions of Islam, Hinduism, and so on, nor indeed to a narrow conception of 'culture' as inhering in a society's body of custom, values and beliefs. Following Barth, I use tradition to refer to any corpus of ideas which contributes to the 'cultural stock' of a society and which manifests a degree of

internal coherence, has a distinctive organisational network and represents a sufficiently distinct corpus of knowledge and assumptions (Barth 1993: 173 and passim). Thus modern public education, the mass media, participation in the world market and so on also constitute traditions which coexist and compete with cultural traditions in the minds of contemporary East Africans.

3. The Goan community is excluded from consideration here because of the absence of comparable information, though in the past they would have excluded themselves from consideration as Indians/Asians.

4. Cf: 'Indian pioneer: the late Sheikh Amiji Musaji', *Young Tanganyika Salgreh* No. 1936; 'Death of pioneer family member a loss to Dar', *Tanganyika Standard*, 4 March 1962; interview with Sh. Amiji's grandson, Gulam Rajah (16 August 1994). African oral accounts suggest that a *Banyan* was the first Indian resident in 1856 (Gray 1952: 2).

5. Tanzania National Archives (hereafter TNA) Secretariat File no. 2784, 'Ismailia Council'.

6. Interview: M.S. Palray (former chairman of the Gurdwara Management Committee) 29 August 1994; and M.S. Singh, 30 August 1994.

7. Throughout this period the Tanganyika Indian Association, which maintained strong links with the East African Indian National Congress and nationalist organisations in India, demonstrated their support for Gandhi and his struggles for Indian independence by calling public meetings and/or *hartel* (Gregory 1971: ch. 9).

8. Major divisions within the Indian communities were apparent with smaller, up-country shops selling out the back door (to avoid having their credit lines to Dar merchants cut), while Goan shopkeepers – many of whom were civil servants – apparently ignored the *hartel*.

9. Interview: J. Merali, 28 August 1994.

10. The exception would appear to be Hindu attendance at Sikh religious observances in the *Gurdwara*, a practice apparently common in India as well.

11. TNA Secretariat File no. 3152, 'Segregation of Races, 1920', and File no. 1733, 'Annual Report of the District of Dar es Salaam 1919–20'.

12. TNA File no. 61/625, 'Annual Report 1934 Township Authority, Dar es Salaam'.

13. At about this time Dar es Salaam Indian teams were playing each other and community teams from Zanzibar. In the 1940s two Muslim 'all Indian' teams were playing in the second division in Dar es Salaam against African teams (interview: J. Merali, 28 August 1994). With the exception of football, sport – including European sport – was segregated until 1961.

14. Membership in *beni* provided individuals with an urban identity relevant to a range of new urban social situations, but was one of several competing identities which were invoked situationally. For instance, the death of a rural migrant brought into play a system of 'tribal elders' and of *watani* or tribal 'joking relations' who oversaw burial arrangements (TNA microfilm no. 30, 'Funerals'; Iliffe 1979: 389ff.).

15. Merchants provided their communities with mosques, primary schools, clinics and so on, as well as helping the wider urban community. For example the Khoja merchant Sewa Hadji gave Dar es Salaam its first hospital for Africans and Indians (Europeans already had theirs) as well as finances to help lepers (TNA Secretariat File no. 7652, 'Sewa Haji Property of in Tanganyika Territory').

16. European concern dates from the early 1930s (see: 'Leasing of Houses by Natives to Non-natives in Dar es Salaam Township', which also includes a petition from African landlords, TNA File no. 61/410/vols I and II). By 1947, '340 Asian families were accommodated in African dwellings in Kariakoo' (TNA microfilm no. 30, 'African Housing, Dar es Salaam').

17. See: 'Overcrowding in Dwellings in Townships – Control of', TNA File no. 26693; and 'Housing Conditions of Non-European Population of East African ports (Dar es Salaam and Tanga)'.

18. In the mid-1940s some Sikh men in outlying areas were still marrying African women because of a shortage of marriageable women (interview: Palray, see note 6).

19. See Amiji (1969: 157, 1975: 41ff.). Affairs came to a head between local members and the *amil* in the late 1960s when the *Da'i* revoked the old constitution without local consultation and introduced one which centralised and reinforced his authority over the *Jamat Khana*. The ructions this created overlapped with the visit of the *Da'i* to Tanzania in 1968 which was abruptly terminated on charges that he had contravened foreign exchange regulations

(Amiji 1975: 56–8). Excommunication was subsequently employed by the *amil* to quell dissension/discussion over local accountability in both Dar es Salaam and Mombasa (interview: H. Jivanjee, 23 August 1994 and P. Bharmal, 5 September 1994).

20. Interview: J. Merali, 29 August 1994.

21. The ethos of the community is one of egalitarianism – the exception being distinctions based on gender – demonstrated in the organisation of the service and in the Sunday communal meal which all resident Sikhs should attend. However, like other communities, there is a preference for arranged marriage which requires wives to be obtained from Punjab. See Fleuret (1975) and Bhachu (1985: ch. 2).

22. This dated back to 1931 and had it roots in a colonial policy restricting the number of Asians who could be nominated to official bodies, in effect leaving some communities without official representation. See: 'Indian Association: Hindu–Moslem Feeling in Dar es Salaam Town' (TNA Secretariat File no. 19588).

23. See 'Khoja Shia Ithna-Asheri Jamat' (TNA Secretariat File no. 26868) and Kjellberg (1967).

24. 'People who came from India, the first thing that they would want is that there is a roof for you and your children ... It's the most important thing because no matter what happens, you can find money, you can go and work as a labourer and do something, but if there is no roof then how are you going to make your family comfortable?' (Interview: M. Sheriff, 23 August 1994). Equally important, a home of one's own is a pension for old age.

25. The majority of Sikhs left during the mid-1960s as a direct result of Africanisation; Palray interview (see note 6) and Bhachu (1985: ch. 1).

26. Asian attainment of higher education qualifications, at a time of Africanisation of the economy, paradoxically equipped young people for work and residence outside Tanzania rather than for life at 'home'.

27. Rather than follow the Ismaili lead and invest in the country (see, for example, Amiji 1975: 57 fn. 64; Bhachu 1985: 28).

28. Only 97 belonging to Africans had been acquired, at least some of which were returned to their owners for reasons which 'are not clear' (Mwita 1978: 194).

29. The files of Karimjee Properties Ltd were kindly made available to me by Mr H. Karimjee, however, their being incomplete, the true cost of nationalisation was far higher than my estimate indicates. In any event, houses, industry, plantations, offices and so on throughout Tanzania were taken with the exception of two properties.

30. Interview: K. Rattansey, 7 September 1994.

REFERENCES

Amiji, H.M. 1969. 'The Asian communities' in J. Kritzeck and W. Lewis (eds) *Islam in Africa*. New York: van Nostrand-Reinhold, pp. 141–81.

—— 1971. 'Some notes on religious dissent in nineteenth-century East Africa' *African Historical Studies* 4 (3): 603–16.

—— 1975. 'The Bohoras of East Africa', *Journal of Religion in Africa* 2: 27–61.

Anderson, J. 1964. 'The Isma'ili Khojas of East Africa, a new constitution and personal law for the community', *Middle Eastern Studies* 1: 21–39.

Barth, F. 1984. 'Problems in conceptualizing cultural pluralism, with illustrations from Somar, Oman', in D. Maybery-Lewis (ed.) *The Prospects for Plural Societies*, 1982 Proceedings of the AES. Washington, DC: American Ethnological Society, pp. 77–87.

—— 1989. 'The analysis of culture in complex societies', *Ethnos* 54 (3/4): 120–42.

—— 1992. 'Towards greater naturalism in conceptualizing societies', in A. Kuper (ed.) *Conceptualizing Society*. London: Routledge, pp. 17–33.

—— 1993. *Balinese Worlds*. Chicago, IL: University of Chicago Press.

Bhachu, P. 1985. *Twice Migrants*. London: Tavistock.

Bharati, A. 1964. 'The Indians in East Africa: a survey of problems of transition and adaptation', *Sociologus* 2: 169–77.

—— 1965. 'Patterns of identification among East African Asians', *Sociologus* 2: 128–42.

—— 1967. 'Ideology and content of caste among Indians in East Africa' in B. Schwartz (ed.) *Caste in Overseas Indian Communities*. San Francisco: Chandler, pp. 283–320.

Delf, G. 1963. *Asians in East Africa*. Oxford: Oxford University Press.

Fleuret, A.K. 1975. 'Social organization and adaptation among Sikhs in Tanzania', unpublished PhD thesis, Department of Anthropology, University of California, Santa Barbara.

Ghai, P. and Y. Ghai. 1965. 'Asians in East Africa: problems and prospects', *The Journal of Modern African Studies* 3 (1): 35–51.

Ghai, Y. 1965. 'The Asian dilemma in East Africa', *East African Journal* March: 6–21.

Gray, J. 1952. 'Dar es Salaam under the Sultans of Zanzibar', *Tanganyika Notes & Records* 33: 1–21.

Gregory, R.G. 1971. *India and East Africa*. Oxford: Clarendon.

Handelman, D. 1977. 'The organization of ethnicity', *Ethnic Groups* 1: 187–200.

Honey, M. 1982. 'A history of Indian merchant capital and class formation in Tanganyika, c. 1840–1940', Phd thesis, Department of History, University of Dar es Salaam, Tanzania.

Iliffe, J. 1970. 'A history of the dockworkers of Dar es Salaam', *Tanzania Notes & Records* 71: 119–48.

—— 1979. *A Modern History of Tanganyika*. Cambridge: Cambridge University Press.

Kjellberg, E. 1967. *The Ismailis in Tanzania*. University College, Dar es Salaam: Institute of Public Administration.

Mangat, J.S. 1969. *A History of the Asians in East Africa, c. 1886–1945*. Oxford: Clarendon.

Mascarhenas, A. 1966. 'Urban development in Dar es Salaam', MA thesis, Department of Geography, University of California, Los Angeles.

Morris, S. 1956. 'Indians in East Africa: a study in a plural society', *British Journal of Sociology* 7: 194–211.

Mwita, D. 1978. 'Urban landlordism and the Acquisition of Buildings Act', LLM thesis, Faculty of Law, University of Dar es Salaam.

Pocock, D. 1957. '"Difference" in East Africa: a study of caste and religion in modern Indian society', *Southwestern Journal of Anthropology* 13 (4): 289–300.

Ranger, T. 1975. *Dance and Society in Eastern Africa, 1890–1970: The Beni Ngoma*. London: Heinemann.

Rizvi, S. and N. King. 1973. 'Some East African Ithna-Asheri Jamaats (1840–1967)', *Journal of Religion in Africa* 5: 12–22.

Samachar. 1929. 'Silver Jubilee Number'. Zanzibar.

Sheriff, A. 1987. *Slaves, Spices and Ivory in Zanzibar*. London: J. Currey.

Tanganyika. 1948. *Report on the Census of the Non-Native Population taken on the Night of 25 February, 1948.* Dar es Salaam: Government Printer.

—— 1954. *Report on the Census of the Non-African Population, taken February 1952,* East African High Commission, Statistical Office. Dar es Salaam: Government Printer.

—— 1958. *Report on the Census of the Non-African Population, February 1957.* East African High Commission, Statistical Department. Dar es Salaam: Government Printer.

Vassanji, M. 1989. *The Gunny Sack.* London: Heinemann.

Walji, S. 1974. 'A history of the Ismaili community in Tanzania', PhD thesis, Department of History, University of Wisconsin–Madison.

7 HISTORICITY AND COMMUNALITY: NARRATIVES ABOUT THE ORIGINS OF THE ITALIAN 'COMMUNITY' IN BRITAIN

Anne-Marie Fortier

[E]very story that relates what is happening or what has happened constitutes something real to the extent that it pretends to be the representation of a past reality. It takes on authority by passing itself off as the witness of what is or of what has been ... Historiography acquires this power insofar as it presents and interprets the 'facts'. How can readers resist discourse that tells them what is or what has been? (de Certeau 1983: 139–40)

In this chapter, I examine different versions of social histories of Italian immigrants in Britain.[1] I look at specialist and popular histories and unwrap what they say about the origins of the Italian presence in Britain, and how they say it. In other words, this is about historicity and community; that is, about how these narratives make sense of the Italian presence in Britain through the meanings they give it.

I shall explore textual narratives that substantiate the existence of an Italian 'community' in Britain by recovering its origins. Put simply, I start from the premise that the 'community' does not exist prior to these writings, but, rather, that these texts are part of its invention. I will draw out the sets of interests invested into these narrations and will examine not only what the stories say, but how the stories make the 'community', as Michel de Certeau puts it: 'The story does not express a practice. It does not limit itself to telling about a movement. It makes it' (de Certeau 1984: 80).

In other words, these stories *produce* what they claim to be *re-*producing and *re-*covering. The naming of the 'community' is examined here as a 'performative act of organising what it enunciates' (de Certeau 1984: 155). By identifying the common threads running through the historical narratives, I hope to reveal the organising principles of these narratives and of the 'community' they instantiate. In short, I will look at how these narratives invent a 'community' by periodising it, stabilising it and objectifying it. Periodisation is about making sense of the present by dividing the past into significant moments in its construction. Here, the 'foundations' and the 'settlement' are two such moments. Stabilisation is about 'points of suture' that secure the incessant movement of 'community identity': kinship narratives and systems of gender differentiation and generational responsibility constitute such stabilising principles (Cohen 1994; Gilroy 1994). Finally, objectification is about making 'culture' and 'community' into a thing that we can stand back from and look at as an undeniable entity (Handler 1988). These interlocking processes, in short, create a sense of particularity from which terrains of solidarity can emerge. I argue, moreover, that processes of objectification, periodisation and stabilisation are configured around concerns for geography, genealogy and differentiation.

At a time when 'face-to-face communities' of immigrants have now dispersed geographically; a time when cultural habits are diversified generationally; a time when the 'problem' of integration is substituted by the 'menace' of assimilation; a time, finally, when 'new' immigrants threaten the collective image of respectability and stability, how do these narratives construct a sense of coherence and unity for the Italian collective identity? The dissolution of 'pockets of Italianness' into the English social landscape is simultaneously a movement of distancing from Italy. As John Gillis (1994) points out, new forms of 'memory work' appear at times when there is a break with the past. In this respect, the narratives examined here are particular versions of 'memory work'. I focus on how the stories recover the 'origins' of the present-day community at a time when 'origins' have multiplied and faded as a result of the relentless passing of time and inevitable fragmentation of the collectivity.

The literature on Italians in Britain is entangled with broader socio-political discourses of 'community'. For the purposes of this chapter, I consider these texts in relation to the project of communal memory and self-recovery found in two Italian socio-religious centres in London: St Peter's church and social club, and the Centro Scalabrini.[2] More specifically, I examine these narratives in relation to the socio-political context affecting their production and use. What are the historical conditions surrounding their production? What are the issues involved in recovering the story of Italian immigration and settlement in Britain?

The sources I use are of two kinds. First, the 'specialist' literature on Italians in Britain: Sponza (1988), Colpi (1991a), Marin (1975), Bottignolo (1985) and, to a lesser degree, Cavallaro (1981). Although I quote largely from the first three – the only monographs covering the Italian population of Britain – my comments also concern the latter two, which also attempt to establish links of communality within Italian populations living in Bristol and Bedford respectively. Second, I also refer to a 'popular' version of collective recollection: a regular feature on the history of London's former Little Italy, in the monthly magazine *Backhill*, published by St Peter's Italian church in Clerkenwell[3] (approximately 1000 copies sold monthly – the Italian-born population of London was about 65,300 in 1981). In contrast with the specialist literature, this text is about a particular moment of the Italian immigrant history: the settlement. It is a feature that is more part of the daily life of the 'community' and its study provides an interesting insight into how a local Italian institution represents the 'community' to itself. In addition, although it concerns a particular section of London, 'The Hill' is paradigmatic of Italian settlements in Britain. As Lucio Sponza writes:

The history of Italian immigration to Britain is to a great extent the history if the Italians in London – indeed, in a relatively limited area of the metropolis for most of the nineteenth century. This is true both in terms of sheer numbers and, more importantly, in the sense that the occupational structure and living conditions were reproduced in a scattered manner in almost all the Italian settlements around Britain. (1988: 19)

From these readings, I unpack two moments in the periodisation of the 'community': the foundations (configured around the issue of tradition) and the settlement (configured around the issue of continuity).[4] Later, I explore in further detail the relationship between family and continuity, configuring the trope of sacrifice/suffering. But first, I will outline the context surrounding the emergence of the literature on Italians in Britain.

THE PROJECT OF RECOVERY

The first attempt to write a general history of Italians in Britain appeared in 1975.[5] Published by Father Umberto Marin, a Scalabriniani father living in England at the time, *Italiani in Gran Bretagna* was published in the aftermath of the integration of Britain within the EC which, according to Marin, incited politicians and sociologists to turn their attention towards the *invisible immigrants* (Marin 1975: 5).[6] Umberto Marin precisely sets out to recover a positive identity for Italian immigrants, at a time when immigration from Italy had considerably reduced. He does this by tracing the heritage bequeathed by immigrants and sojourners coming to Britain, from the peninsula, at different times since the Roman Empire.[7] His intention is for post-1945 Italian immigrants to redeem themselves from the suffering of immigration 'by recovering this patrimony' (Marin 1975: 7).

In the 1970s, the Italians leaving Britain outnumbered those entering. After the post-1945 waves of immigration from Italy, reaching peaks of 6000 to 11,000 entries per year between 1949 and 1962 (with the exception of 1950 and 1952), Italian immigration to Britain stabilised to 1000 to 2000 annually from 1970 onwards (Bottignolo 1985: 209).

The invisibility of Italians is related to other factors as well. First, it is related to the racialised structure of difference in British politics, where, in the 1950s, 'immigrant' meant 'black' (and subsequently Asian). Today, 'ethnic minorities' are, by definition, 'visible', that is, Afro-Caribbean, Asians, South East Asians, and so on.[8] In this context, along with the 1960s 'ethnic revival', a space for so-called 'invisible' immigrants was created.

Second, the Italian population of 1970s Britain – a population settled here since the late nineteenth century – was increasingly diversified along generational, cultural, residential, class and status lines. Former 'Little Italies' had by then disappeared, their population dispersed in suburban areas. Similarly, Italians in London were by then economically integrated in London's multicultural catering industry; Italian sandwich bars are part of the city's landscape, a situation that led a leader of the Scalabrini Order to conclude, in 1983, that the Italians' economic contribution to Britain can no longer symbolise the present experience of Italian immigrants.[9] At another level, the continuous movement of peoples between Italy and other parts of the world, and the extended family networks that span Europe, America and Australia, challenge the congruence between identity and geography suggested in nationalist conceptions of identities informing ideas of 'ethnic community'.

Last, the Italian population has been witnessing over the last 20 years the arrival of young Italian men and women who come to Britain for temporary work or to study English. These migrants, who do not identify themselves as immigrants (Sodano 1995), appear as a menace to the stability and integrity of the 'community'. In a later section, the idea of 'settlement' is discussed in relations to the presence of these new migrants. My point here, is that the renewed interest with Italian historicity coincides with, and is informed by, the combination of all these changes affecting the Italian population residing in Britain.

Indeed, the question of what the 'community' is, how it can be circumscribed and, moreover, redeemed from its 'foreigner condition' (Marin in Centro Scalabrini di Londra 1993: 6) comes to the fore in the face of what 'community' leaders call 'the devastating process of homogenisation which aspires to a total and global assimilation for all, with no roots nor memory for anyone'.[10] As Umberto Marin wrote, 'emigration is not a problem of landing only, nor only of settlement' (1975: 104). Indeed, these are no longer pressing issues for Italians living in Britain in the 1970s. The question to address had shifted to those of meaning, continuity and political recognition. In this regard, Marin's book induced an interest for the Italian presence in Britain, and paved the way for subsequent publications.

One way of solving the problem of the indeterminacy of the Italian population of Britain is articulated around considerations of personal behaviour or commitments. This is the solution adopted by Terri Colpi, in her book *The Italian Factor*, acclaimed by Italian officials and 'community' representatives.[11] From the outset, Colpi states:

[t]his book is not directly concerned with those who have opted or drifted out of the Community; it is concerned with those who have an Italian way of life, are linked with Italy and who feel at least partly Italian. (Colpi 1991a: 16)

This 'Italian way of life', in Colpi's terms, results from a combination of history, experience, origins, cultural habits and attachments. This, Colpi concludes, constitutes the undeniable existence of an 'Italian Factor' inscribed within British society:

Although only around a quarter of a million people resident in Britain today are either Italian-born or of Italian origin, they are a distinct presence within British society. Their long history in this country, their specialist development of the catering industry, their continued contact with Italy, their ever evolving migration picture and finally their strong Italian 'ethnic memory', which makes them cling even after generations to aspects of their Italianness, all contribute to Community traditions. In this era of closer European integration the

Italians in Britain are probably the most European section of British society – a position which is giving them increasing prominence. The *Italian Factor* in British life has truly come of age. Let us see how this has come about. (1991a: 22, emphasis in original)

Hence the texts examined here produce a historicity for an Italian community in the making. They trace and link up threads of history, constructing a narrative through which a community can emerge. Nobody claims that the community is homogeneous. But by seeing how the Italian presence in Britain 'has come about', they are tracing lines of closure. I now proceed to unpack these lines.

THE FOUNDATIONS

In his book on Italian immigrants in nineteenth-century Britain, Lucio Sponza provides a structural explanation of the forced migration of Italian peasants since the early 1800s. Significantly, Sponza (1988) traces the origins of Italian immigration to Britain back to a 'an old tradition of seasonal and vagrant migration' (p. 24) or to 'an ancient custom' (p. 36) which took Italians within different parts of the Italian peninsula (for summer transhumance, or displacement to plains for intensive cultivation), or to France, Austria and Germany and, little by little, to Britain. Migration, then, appears as a characteristic of traditional Italian ways, tied to agricultural practices.

The shift to forced migration began, according to Sponza, during the Napoleonic wars when agriculture was reorganised along capitalistic lines consequently dispossessing small farmers. This, added to continuous harassment from the French armies, forced many to leave.

The evidence of the worsening conditions of the rural population is continuous from the mid-eighteenth century through the nineteenth century. Migration became vagabondage, as families finally collapsed under the weight of debt, took to the road and became beggars. (E. Sori quoted in Sponza 1988: 26)

Vagrancy and vagabondage are recurring themes of Sponza's account of the origins of the Italian immigration to Britain. It is out of this 'old tradition' of vagrancy that the 'founders of the Italian colony' (Sponza 1988: 24) set foot in Britain in the early 1800s.

Sponza pays particular attention to itinerant street musicians and street traders which he labels the 'traditional sections of the colony' (p.

260), by contrast with the political immigrants who remained isolated from 'the bulk of the Italian immigrants' (1988: 260). The political refugees appear as marginal characters in both Sponza's and Colpi's histories, even if they played an influential leadership role within the 'embryonic Italian Community' (Colpi 1991a: 32). So the story of the present-day community begins with the emigration of poor, unskilled peasants forced into vagabondage. As Umberto Marin puts it, during the nineteenth century

popular emigration was added to the secular emigration of elite Italians; along with the artists and political refugees arrived the first *real* emigrati in Great Britain. (Marin 1975: 27, my emphasis)

This statement begs the question about what makes the authenticity of the 'popular emigration'; what makes it 'real'?

The contrast is sharp between the 'elite' and the *paesani*. The former are isolated, presented as more individualistic, while the latter, more gregarious. The typical opposition between urban and rural, between tradition and modernity, supports the foundations of the present-day Italian 'community'. Only Umberto Marin offers to tell us about the earlier emigration of elite personalities (see above). To paraphrase Michel de Certeau, Marin evokes ghosts of the past to create an habitable (and haunted) space for his contemporaries (de Certeau 1990: 162). But in other narratives (namely Sponza, Colpi or Besagni's [in *Backhill*] popular history), the elite are marginalised and obscured from the history. Similar views were expressed by some active members of St Peter's church or other leading Italian men of London I interviewed in 1992 and 1993. It is agreed that the community is an 'amorphous mass', characterised by an internal diversity along the lines identified above. The boundary is configured around moral terms of 'good' and 'bad' Italians, where the 'good' are those involved in the 'community' or interested minimally in their background, that is in Italian culture. The 'bad' Italians, excluded from the 'community', are the elite and members of the Italian officialdom – said to be out of touch with the grassroots London Italian *immigrants* – and contemporary Italian migrants, mostly young, single, here for an indefinite period of time. The question of time of residence in Britain is another marker of distinction that supports the idea of settlement: elites are usually here temporarily, and thus have no idea of the experience of settlement the immigrants go through, so the argument goes.

Emigration, tied to poverty, is also associated with rupture and discontinuity. Emigration is an event that starts from Italy. It is a move away, a breaking away, a caesura:

Emigration constitutes the great caesura, the parting line which separates the remote past, absolute, closed and compact like a circle where all the points are equally distant from real time, from the near past, relative, tightly linked to the present by uninterrupted passages of time. Emigration is the zero moment (*momento zero*) of social growth, an individual and collective product of time, not always located in a definitive historical process, but always brought into focus by a date which initials (*sigla*) a fundamental moment in the personal, family memory. (Cavallaro 1981: 41)

Hence emigration separates the remote past of a tradition from a nearer past of 'forced' displacement. In this respect, emigration is different from *mi*gration.

Whether in the views of Sponza, Colpi or Marin, migration is represented as an ancient tradition, the character of which changed over time. The discursive strategies of these authors locate their stories in a timeless continuity of an ancient tradition of migration – what Stuart Hall labels the 'foundational myth' in narratives of national culture (Hall 1992: 294) – as well as grounding the community in an original folk/peasant society which arrived 'way back' in the 1800s. *Campanilismo, paesanismo* and *comparaggio* recur in these stories as expressions of such a traditional culture, the custodians of which are the peasants. *Campanilismo* refers to 'bell-tower' mentality; *paesanismo* to a similar system of social relationships between co-villagers. *Comparaggio* is the principle according to which close family friends are honorary members of the family and are *compadre* (godparents) to one of the children. Terri Colpi refers regularly to *campanilismo* conceived as the basis for internal division among Italian 'communities' abroad. Colpi's conception objectifies *campanilismo* as a thing which is active or inactive (one chapter section is entitled '*Campanilismo* in operation' (p. 188)) and she ethnicises it by referring to it only in its Italian version. In this respect, the use of Italian to label social behaviours or to refer to particular trades (for example, Colpi consistently calls *figurinai* the Italian statuettes vendors of the nineteenth century) is part and parcel of the objectification of the Italian 'way of life'.

But emigration constitutes a shift, if not a break, in this timeless tradition. From a 'natural' phenomenon, it became a socio-economic one, which incurred a substantial change of meanings. The 'old tradition ... became for many more people the only option' (Sponza 1988: 24). Emigration is indeed the zero moment of collective social growth, from which the original peasant, vagrant immigrants will move forward[12] towards successful integration. The subtle addition of the prefix indicates a break, a move out of the national borders, a change of location or position.[13] This demarcation is most striking in Cavallaro's analysis, as the quote above illustrates. His contention that emigration is a zero moment in (individual or collective) social growth rests on a linear conception of time and displacement, the initial moment being marked forever in the increasingly remote past. In this respect, emigration is conceived as static, confined to a moment of departure. Hence a distinction between migration as foundational, and emigration as zero moment is significant. Migration as foundational opens a *theatre of action*, that is that it founds a terrain of legitimacy for action (de Certeau 1990: 182–3). The meaning of emigration as breaking point is deployed upon this terrain. It is distinguished from migration in terms of temporality, while both remain spatially located in Italy. In other words, the relationship with Italy and with tradition is configured around stories of migration and emigration. Such stories lie precisely at the basis of the London Centro Scalabrini's politics of identity. The existence of the Centro is unequivocally tied to what it coins the 'drama of emigration', a theme pervading the Centro's narratives. The 'drama' is presented as where Italian immigrants 'come from' and is reclaimed by the Centro leadership as constitutive of the future community. 'One does not know where they are going, if they ignore where they are from', writes Umberto Marin (Centro Scalabrini di Londra 1993: 7). The 'drama of emigration' is the *raison d'être* of this institution established in 1968 by the Scalabriniani missionaries.[14]

The question I now turn to is: if migration and emigration are the linchpins with Italy, how is the relationship with England integrated in Italian community discourses? To put it differently, Italy and tradition are integrated as foundational, that is, as where Italians *come from*, via stories of migration and emigration. How is the space Italians *moved to* and now *live in* integrated in their project of communal memory?

THE SETTLEMENT

It was during the second half of the nineteenth century that important numbers of immigrants from Italy started entering Britain. In 1861, the Italian-born population in Britain was estimated at 4608; it had doubled 30 years later to 10,934 in 1891, and again to 24,383 in 1901 (Colpi 1991a: 48).

The late nineteenth and early twentieth centuries are characterised by a change in the occupational structure of the Italian collectivity. From hawking and street entertaining activities of earlier times, the Italian immigrants turned to catering services (ice-cream traders or chestnut sellers and, later, employees in restaurants, hotels and clubs). In historical accounts of Italian immigration in Britain (Colpi 1991a; Sponza 1988), the late nineteenth century is presented as the moment when Italian immigrants changed from being sojourners to settlers; the period when the community became more internally cohesive, stable and sedentary. It is at this time that the 'early community' is known as a settler community.

Changes in the occupational structure are rightly emphasised by Lucio Sponza as significant in shaping the character of the community of the time. Interestingly, the stabilisation of the founding community is associated with this shift, specifically the first moments of settlement appear when Italians began to occupy less vagrant occupations organised around smaller working-units (some of which were family run). For example, the ice-cream vendors, who were also itinerant, worked in more formalised environments. This shift meant the demise of the *padrone*-run hawking groups, which were less formal and perceived as more exploitative (particularly of children).[15]

But the late 1800s are not only marked by a change in occupations. It is at this time, also, that women are presented as significant members of the immigrant population. In Terri Colpi's *The Italian Factor*, the first chapter about pre-1880s Italian immigration contains seven sections, but only in the last one does she introduce the early 'Community' (always with a capital 'C' in Colpi's version). This section begins as follows:

In the 1830s and 1840s the male–female ratio of the Italian presence in this country was very imbalanced and it was not until the middle of the second half of the century, the 1860s and 1870s, that women began to arrive in sufficient numbers to balance the sex-structure of the Colony in London ... Apart from the three groups of semi-skilled craftsmen described in the previous section, the general immigration of the poor Italians with no trades, training or skills continued to be the largest portion of the flow and in the late 1870s this began to follow a more classical pattern of chain migration where the *padrone* and others began to bring over female members of the family. The Community thus became more sedentary and stable ... (Colpi 1991a: 41)

Colpi's way of introducing the 'early Community' suggests an equation between settlement and the immigration of women. Also, the distinction between sojourners and settlers suggests a masculinist conception of mobility and movement: stability, sedentariness is the doing of women and families (see also Marin 1975: 57) *brought* in by the men who have moved into more fixed occupations. The presence of women and families is incompatible with the earlier community of 'vagrants':

As long as the majority of the Italians were street musicians and statuette vendors (by and large involving temporary migration), it is reasonable to assume that there was not much scope for women to join their men in Britain. Moreover, many Italian vagrants were single men and boys. As the Italians settled down and the number of those engaged in vagrant occupations decreased, however, the family unit would be reconstituted, or formed. (Sponza 1988: 59)

Whether there were women 'vagrants' – even if small in numbers – goes unmentioned,[16] while their arrival is made significant and highlighted as the first moment of the settlement.

The relationship between settlement and gender further unfolds in accounts of the post–1945 Italian immigration. In the 1950s, Italian women entering Britain outnumbered Italian men. According to the 1951 census, there were 62 men for every 100 women (in some places the proportion was 1:3; Marin 1975: 93). Entering under bulk recruitment schemes, these women, the majority of whom were single and in their twenties, were destined primarily for the textile, rubber and ceramic industries. Many women returned to Italy after having completed their contract, but 'hundreds settled' (Colpi 1991a: 146). Many of these 'pioneers' of the 'new' immigration from Italy (1991a: 145) married other 'European volunteer workers' coming from Poland, Ukraine, Latvia and the former Yugoslavia. In the course of my field research, I met a few such couples, and one of my closest acquaintances immigrated on her own in the 1950s and married an Englishman.

How is the migration story of these women told by Marin and Colpi? Umberto Marin was the first to provide a detailed compilation of census and other data on post–1945 immigration from Italy. However, he is quick to trace the 'masculinisation' of the population, which he 'proves' (1975: 93) in a table illustrating how men outnumbered women immigrants from 1962 to 1970 (1975: Table 13, p. 176).

Women migrants are represented as wives and mothers, figures which stand for cultural reproduction and stability. Moreover, while the mother figure is reified as the guardian of the family nucleus and 'the symbol of what is most sacred within a family' (Bottignolo 1985: 59; Colpi 1991a: 216), the 'Italian woman' (Marin 1975: 106), through her participation in the labour market and subsequent integration in English society has considerable merit in the much acclaimed serenity and social promotion of the community.

For Marin, Italian women of Britain have not confined themselves to the household which would have led to their isolation from the surrounding social life incurring, by extension, devastating effects on the household and the community. For the good of the family, according to Marin's logic, women should integrate into the host society, one channel being through the labour market. In so doing, Marin bridges the traditional division between work and family, and positions women as stabilising agents in the promotion of a strong yet serene and successful community. By rehabilitating the 'working woman' and relocating her as a wife and mother, Marin substantiates the figure of women as custodians of culture and social stability.

Hence the association between women and mothers reveals one dimension supporting the equation between settlement and the arrival of women. The first moment of settlement is the one of stabilising the gender ratio in order to found families. What is at stake in the shift from 'founding' to 'settling' the community is the issue of continuity:

Indeed, it was not until this second stage of development [between 1880 and 1918] that the Community was assured of a future: an Italian factor would become an enduring facet of British life. (Colpi 1991a: 47)

The settlement constitutes an important symbolic marker that delineates the Italian immigrant collectivity and roots it, as it were, in English territory. It bears repetition that these narratives appear at a time when the 'community' is attempting to define itself in response to the increased presence of 'new' migrants from Italy. In the last 20 years, young Italian migrants have entered and left Britain in large numbers. These 'new migrants' are problematic for the 'community' leadership. The presence of these youths is further complicated by the active involvement of Padre Carmelo, St Peter's parish priest, with young Italian offenders, drug abusers and/or AIDS victims. The most common complaint is that Father Carmelo spends too much time in prisons and not enough with the 'community'. On one occasion, when he gave a sermon about the plight of these youths, an Italian friend complained: 'I don't wanna know', expressing a view shared by many.

Although large numbers of youth come for a variety of reasons, the popular press (both English and Italian) has focused, in recent years, on young delinquents and drug addicts – the number of which is estimated to be between 1400 and 2800.[17] In December 1992, *Time Out* published an article on young Italians coming to London for work, but who 'sink' into a world of drugs, crime and AIDS.[18] *Backhill* published a series of extracts of a speech given by Sir John Smith, Deputy Commissioner of the Metropolitan Police, about 'Young Criminals'.[19] Finally, *La Voce degli Italiani* recently published a series of articles on drugs and drug-dependent Italian youths coming to London, effecting a shift from its previous silence and indifference on the subject.[20]

The proximity of King's Cross to St Peter's church, the Italian church, adds to the drama and to the menace these youths present to the coherence of the 'community'. Moreover, twice a week, the parish offices of St Peter's are open to young men who find food (served by volunteer workers) and advice dispensed by Padre Carmelo.

With this new Italian presence so close to home (St Peter's is also referred to as *La Casa Nostra*), the 'community' is seeking to define and enclose itself. Unlike their predecessors, these youths are not here to settle. 'We have to face this situation, says Monsignor Giuseppe Blanda of St Patrick's International Centre in central London. Mobility is a new phenomenon everywhere.'[21]

In this context, languages of settlement and of family acquire even greater potency. The settler figure emerges as the symbol marking the boundary between e/immigrants and migrants. Migrancy is yet again marginalised. While the foundations of the community are signified by a break in time through the moment of emigration, the settlement constitutes a point of attachment from which ideas of locality and continuity can emerge. Contemporary vagrants and migrants are not locatable within the settlement matrix.[22]

I now turn to 'popular' stories about the London settlement itself, as an exemplar of how kinship, continuity, gender and migration operate in memories of life in 'The Hill'.

'THE HILL'

Started in November 1992, 'The Hill' is a regular feature of St Peter's monthly publication, *Backhill*. Written by an English–Italian woman, Olive Besagni, it tells the stories of former residents of 'Il Quartiere Italiano'. Its typical pieces are on families or portraits of individuals, all of which emerge from stories told to Besagni by former residents or their descendants. These short biographies are set against the backdrop of the everyday life of Little Italy in the late nineteenth or early twentieth centuries.

One typical trait of Besagni's stories is how she traces the social genealogy of the community. Readers are introduced to the characters of each story through their links with other former residents, some of whose stories could have been told in previous issues. In other cases, the genealogy is more conventional and retraces the family tree of the characters. Such genealogical tracings usually provide a transgenerational backdrop to the main story, linking past to present, linking memories to 'real' people, linking the former Little Italy community to the present-day, geographically dispersed 'community'.

The Nastri sons ... all married to English girls, all had good marriages and as you can imagine there are plenty of young Nastri's growing up in England today. All as a result of that journey made by Trofimena and Alfonso way back in the year 1908.[23]

Regular correspondence between Besagni and some readers further adds to this sense of a *living* community which descends from the first settlers in Il Quartiere. In one instance, she reprints a letter she received, where a reader tracing his 'family tree' in order to find his 'roots' asks for information regarding the Alberici family which once lived in Clerkenwell. He then tells of his journey to Clerkenwell.

[S]o I decided to visit Clerkenwell and discovered St Peter's Italian Church, as it seems to be the heart of the Community, and I felt so close to my ancestors and tried to picture their marriages taking place there. On entering the Church Arcade I noticed to the left a commemorative plaque in honour of Italians who died in the 1st World War, and to my surprise was listed an ancestor Giampietro Alberici. I have twice returned to St Peter's to celebrate the Procession in Honour of Our Lady of Mount Carmel which is held in July. Both occasions have been enjoyable and I have really felt that I am retracing the surroundings and traditions that would have been familiar to my ancestors.[24]

In Besagni's feature, details of street names and addresses, of shop and pub names, photographs and accounts of the street-life, bring Little Italy back to life, drawing it as a 'place of origin' descendants can return to and re-member. Today a desolate area of London, this section of Clerkenwell is an inherent part of British Italian historicity; it's story is emblematic of all Italian (past) settlements of Britain. It is a space where the drama of migration is re-enacted regularly by Italians coming to St Peter's church or social club. On occasions such as weekly masses, weekly weddings, funerals, Sunday lunches, and the yearly Procession of the Madonna, a small section of what used to be Little Italy sporadically comes to life as the air fills with voices of Italian *chiacchiera* (chit–chat) and aromas of the local deli. On these occasions, Italians journey back to St Peter's, *La Casa Nostra*, re-enacting a migration back to and out of (Little) Italy.

Migration and emigration are important features of 'The Hill'. Emigration is the founding event of all the life stories Besagni collects, while migration is a recurring event throughout the lives of these people. Migration and displacement are constitutive of the 'community' daily life.

Paradoxically, the repetitive evocations of migration act upon the delimitation of Clerkenwell as an enclosed space. We rarely go beyond the limits of Il Quartiere in Olive's stories, and when we do, it is represented as a temporary emigration out of the colony's borders or a first stop before the final stage in Clerkenwell.

Il Quartiere Italiano emerges from Olive Besagni's narrative as a space enclosed and distant from the rest of the world. Il Quartiere, in this respect, *is* Italy. Thus,

I asked them if they ever felt threatened outside the confines of 'Il Quartiere Italiano' on account of their obvious Italianness. Pasqua said that he 'did to a degree, but it was worse during the War Years.' Victor volunteers that 'whenever we represented the school in competitive athletics or football, we always felt that we were competing for Italy, rather than the school'.[25]

In addition, this flow of crossings is policed by a gendered system of differentiation. Women, in Besagni's texts, travel between Italy and England. Moreover, they journey between households. In this respect, the image of women as custodians of culture is metaphorically perpetuated in their regular returns to Italy and the 'family' homes, thus enforcing the equation between female immigrants, family and settlement. The men, for their part, migrate not only back to Italy, but also to South Africa or to the West End for temporary work. Their mobility is greater, even if forced. Even narratives about courting are marked by a masculinist representation of mobility. Men emigrate to London and to their loves, or they return to Italy to marry and bring their wife back to London.[26] The passivity of the women is striking in these accounts of courtship, where they occasionally reluctantly agree to marry their admirer, eventually *won* by his love.[27]

FAMILY, CONTINUITY, SACRIFICE

As Besagni's articles accumulate, the complex fabric of community life and membership seems to emerge. In her series, the story of the *comunità* is the story of families where the boundaries between family and *comunità*, between homes and Little Italy, between private and public space, are constantly broken down and blurred.

This is a community born out of the shared experience of emigration, an experience of hardship, hard work and hope: 'These were hard times for the family but their situation wasn't any worse than many of their neighbours and friends ...' [28] The family stories are criss-crossed by themes of sacrifice and suffering. Sacrifices which, however, are not without their just reward:

Over the years [Taddeo] developed a rheumatic condition which plagued him for the rest of his life. He vowed that his children would receive a good education and never have to work in the kind of conditions, detrimental to health and family life, that he had experienced. He clearly steered them in the right direction. Antonio ... went into banking ... he was a greatly respected member of the community. Annie was a brilliant seamstress. She was employed in the finest haute couture fashion houses ... Luisa ... although plagued by poor health, she eventually ... became a linguistic secretary. Damaso was an accountant, he enjoyed life, and he could be found in the 'Coach and Horses' where he was known for his formidable skill as a card player.[29]

Sacrifice/suffering are inextricably linked to the reward found in the successful integration of the children into English society. Descent and continuity are not only underpinned by Besagni's stories, but an image of continuity is created, sustained and consolidated via the articulation of descent with an invented tradition of sacrifice, which constitutes an important signifier of the 'immigrant condition'. Sacrifice becomes the recurring image of the plight of Italian immigrants and, by virtue of its iteration, a constitutive force of a collective referent of identification. Collective suffering is most evocatively remembered in the well known story of the *Arandora Star*, a 1500-ton ship that set sail to Canada on 1 July 1940 transporting 1500 men, including hundreds of Italian internees.[30] The following day it was torpedoed and sunk killing over 700 men, 446 of whom were Italians. This tragedy is repeatedly evoked as a significant moment in defining the Italian community of Britain as a distinct entity.[31]

The sinking of the *Arandora Star* was, and still is, the most tragic event in the history of the Italian Community. It also makes the British Italian Community unique in global terms: no other Italian Community in the world has suffered such a blow. (Colpi 1991a: 115)

Its significance is deemed greater through its relation to suffering and collective grief. A significance that no other event in the life of Italians in Britain conveys as powerfully. 'Suffering in common unifies more than joy does', wrote Renan over a century ago (in Gillis 1994: 50).

The tragedy of the *Arandora Star* will remain for many years like a scar, everlastingly painful and bloody, within the living body of the Italian collectivity. (Marin 1975: 86–7)

Sacrifice and suffering are inserted as inherent components of Italian historicity, and are construed as part of the heritage of the immigrant experience. A heritage symbolically transmitted in wedding ceremonies. In one wedding reception in the summer of 1992 a guest paid tribute to the newlyweds in the following words:

Cavaliere Gino Biasi expressed his congratulations and best wishes to the young couple as well as to all young persons present, so that they appreciate and follow the example and the sacrifices of their parents, who do all that is in their power to support their children throughout their lives and to accompany them to the altar on their wedding day.[32]

In short, the world of the Italian *emigrato* is a world normalised by a system where sacrifice guarantees redemption, embodied in the future generations; it is a teleology which charges parents with the responsibility of transmitting this founding value of the emigrated condition to their offspring. A teleology which imputes the children, in turn, with a responsibility towards their parents, as well as towards the community and to Italy. Sacrifice conveys a sense of timeless continuity of the 'emigrant condition'; a continuity which, in turn, is stabilised by a system of generational responsibility, and, as I now argue, one of gender dif-ferentiation.

Indeed, stories of Italian women immigrants stress their emotional suffering, while those of men emphasise their physical or moral sacrifices; women suffer from 'homesickness and isolation at leaving their family-centred way of life behind' (Colpi 1991a: 146). They were 'disconcertingly alone' and 'their search for spouses led to much inter-marriage' (1991a: 146). The men, for their part, *made* sacrifices related to hard work and family obligations, meanwhile '[t]he women at home too made *sacrifici* since, apart from the struggle to survive, they were bereft, often for many years, of their men folk' (1991a: 154).

The teleology of sacrifice works differently for men and women. Men are valued for their hard work and sense of duty. Women, for their part, are valued as family members and founders. This gendered system of differentiation is perhaps most visibly deployed in war remembrances in which the soldier-hero is honoured, while war brides and mothers are ignored.[33]

Set alongside the sacredness of the mother figure, the victimisation of women acquires all its power of representation. Women/mothers, the custodians of culture, are suffering. By extension, the serenity of the community is at stake. In other words, conditions of existence of the 'community' are epitomised in the experiences of women.[34]

First-generation women of the southern Italian communities are the least contented perhaps of all the Italians in Britain today. They are *the living embodiment of the difficulty and sadness of emigration*. (1991a: 218, my emphasis)

CONCLUDING REMARKS: THREE CONCENTRIC TERRAINS OF COMMUNALITY

To summarise, I have looked at narratives about the 'origins' of the present-day Italian 'community' of Britain. In the face of its increasing indeterminacy, these texts recover the Italian presence in Britain by defining new grounds of communality.

The tradition of migration and the drama of emigration lie at the foundations of the 'community'. These foundations format the largest concentric circle of collective experience, linking the 'community' to Italy. This narrative is about loss and recovery: the disappearance of the tradition of voluntary and 'natural' migration, leaving Italy behind but remembering where 'we' come from by telling the story of the drama of emigration.

The middle terrain is about a second, less distant place of origin: the settlement. Narratives of 'The Hill' confine memories of the first settlement to a particular section of Clerkenwell, transforming it into the community's exclusive turf, it's second place of origin. The settlement is also a moment of beginning; it is not an end in itself, while, at the same time, it establishes a boundary between 'real' immigrants and others.

Third, the smallest circle closes in on norms of personal behaviour: kinship narratives, principles of gender differentiation and generational responsibility. These constitute points of attachment from which ideas of locality and continuity can emerge. In this respect, 'community' histories and recollections are not only (and not always) about cultural reproduction; they are also about producing ideas of specificity deployed through principles which spell out norms of selfhood.

NOTES

1. This chapter was first presented at the annual British Sociological Association conference in Leicester, April 1995. I thank all those present for their useful comments. I am also grateful to all the contributors to this volume, for their questions and comments on this paper during our two-day workshop at the University of Swansea in June 1995. I am particularly grateful to John Campbell for his useful comments leading to the final version of this chapter.

2. These two centres and churches play an important role in the 'community' social life. Most of the activities open to all Italians are organised by these two centres. Moreover, many social events of regional associations (for example, Italians from Sicily, Venezia or other regions) take place on the premises of these clubs.

3. St Peter's church, in Clerkenwell, was founded in 1864. The church and social club are associated with the 'old' community, that is, the descendants of the immigrants of the late nineteenth and early twentieth century. Located in the heart of what used to be Little Italy, St Peter's is *the* Italian church. Its leaders are committed to an a-political approach to 'community' services. For example, the monthly publication of St Peter's, *Backhill*, was

created precisely to fill 'the need for a more family type magazine', as a kind of extended parish bulletin, to counterbalance the political tone of *La Voce degli Italiani*, the other widely read Italian journal (personal interview with the editor of *Backhill* in February 1993). St Peter's turns away from politics, which is deemed uninteresting, and towards a cultural politics revolving around family-based languages of 'community'. Memories of the settlement are part and parcel of this process.

4. There is also a third moment which concerns issues of integration rather than origins; however, it is beyond the scope of the present chapter to discuss this here.

5. There are a large number of articles or small publications about Italians in Britain preceding this date and going back to the early twentieth century. Whether included in journals, books covering a broader range of issues and/or populations, or whether publications on their own, these pieces always concern a specific aspect related to Italian immigrants. For a list of earlier publications (pre-1970) see Marin (1975) or Sponza (1988).

6. This label was first used – in reference to the Italians at least – by J.S. and L.D. MacDonald (1972) in a booklet about Italian, Spanish and Portuguese immigrants to Britain.

7. The act of historical reconstruction is striking in the way that Marin traces the immigration of 'Italians' back to the Roman Empire (see also Palmer 1991). It is worth noting that this kind of linkage was an important feature of Mussolini's nationalist politics.

8. In other words, 'ethnic minorities' are 'non-whites', thus reinforcing the dominant position of 'whites' as the norm. It is beyond the scope of this chapter to examine the interface between the British politics of nationality and Italian immigrant historicity, but it is worth pointing out that local 'community narratives' are produced at a particular time in the history of English grand narratives of culture, identity and nationality. Family and kinship narratives pervading Italian 'community' self-representations were brought into focus in what Martin Barker (1981) labelled the 'new familyism' of the 1960s and 1970s whereby the family was constituted as the cornerstone of national culture. Questions of numbers or social decay underpinning debates over the settlement of thousands of West Indian workers in the 1950s were gradually substituted, from the late 1960s, by issues revolving around

cultural difference. The 'problems' related to the immigration of black people became no longer a matter of quantity but rather of quality, that is, of the compatibility of cultural values with English national culture. From housing conditions and promiscuity, the public gaze turned to family, youth and generational conflict in a complex narrative which gives different accounts of the pathological character of immigration (see Barker 1981; Duffield 1984; Lawrence 1982a, 1982b). The emphasis on family life and moral and civic responsibility found in Italian community narratives seem interpellated – which is not to say determined – by grand narratives in their own attempt to seek recognition.

9. Padre Graziano Tassello, in *La Voce degli Italiani*, no. 831, October 1990: 15. The Scalabrini Order is a missionary order catering to Italian emigrants in different parts of the world. It runs a 'mission' in Brixton, South London. Padre Graziano is the director of the Centro di Studi Emigrazione in Rome, also run by the Scalabrini Fathers.

10. *La Voce degli Italiani*, no. 894 October 1993: 5. My translation.

11. Terri Colpi was recently granted the honorary title of *Cavaliere della Republica Italiana* (the equivalent of a British knighthood) for her contribution in support of the Italian community (*La Voce degli Italiani*, no. 934, July 1995: 6). Colpi's popularised version of the history of Italians in Britain is perhaps the one best known to the general Italian public. It provides an impressionist view of the origins and characteristics of the present-day Italian community. In turn, her book stands out as a highly normative and objectifying representation of the community. The Italian *Comunità* is given as a unified 'thing', the membership of which is policed by the degree of conformity to its cultural contents. See also Colpi (1991b).

12. In this respect, Terri Colpi's chronological, visual history of Italians in Britain is appropriately entitled *Italians Forward* (1991b); a title which finds an eerie echo in Silvio Berlusconi's political party *Forza Italia* ('Come on Italy'). Actually, in an opinion survey conducted before the 1994 elections in Italy, the pollsters slipped in a fictitious party called *Avanti Italia* ('Forward Italy') which secured 4 million votes. *Avanti* was also the title of the socialist party daily newspaper from 1896.

13. The prefix e, from ex, means: out, forth, remove, free from, formerly (OED).

14. Usually associated with the post-1945 immigration, the Centro Scalabrini played a leading role in the development of 'new' clubs, *circoli* and organisations that replaced the clubs or organisations which existed prior to the 1930s in London.

15. The *padrone* figure is a commonly used signifier of nineteenth-century Italian emigration. In England, 'the *padrone* transformed the process of emigration into a business; he offered work contracts to people in Italy, sought volunteers to fulfil them, organised transport and employed people himself once at the destination' (Colpi 1991a: 34).

    This type of *padronismo* differs from its North American counterpart, where the *padrone* acted as sort of a broker by recruiting, hiring and controlling fellow Italians on behalf of an indigenous employer (such as the Canadian National Railway Company), often collecting a fee from the recruits apart from the commission he received from his employer.

16. In a conference on New Perspectives in the History of Italians in Great Britain (May 1995), Lucio Sponza pointed out the need for more research on Italian women, past and present. In this respect, a conference participant mentioned a survey of households in 1880s Edinburgh in which one was inhabited by Italian women only. Moreover, these women appear to have been street musicians.

17. From 'A preliminary survey of Italian intravenous heroin users in London', in *Addiction* 88 (1993): 1562–72; quoted in *La Voce degli Italiani*, no. 935, July 1995: 3.

18. *Time Out*, 2–9 December 1992: 10–11.

19. See *Backhill* issues of December 1994/January 1995 to April 1995.

20. Issues of July, August and September 1995.

21. Personal interview, October 1993. Monsignor Blanda has been lobbying the Italian community for some time for support and recognition of these 'new immigrants'.

22. In relation to 'grand narratives', the marginalisation of these youths from the community is echoed in the present climate of mixed fascination and aversion for travellers, and of fear of opening our national borders. Indeed, immigrants and travellers have been subjected to criminalisation in recent years. On the one hand,

migrancy has become unacceptable and subjected to strict legal control. We only need to think of the Criminal Justice Act, and the less publicised Habitual Residency Test. On the other hand, immigrants are now presented as criminals, as testified by recent debates over EU immigration policies. Right-wing Conservatives such as Nigel Evans and Winston Churchill contend that adopting EU guidelines would lead to a 'tidal wave' of illegal immigrants, 'bogus asylum-seekers', 'terrorists' and 'drug smugglers' (*Daily Express*, 15 February 1995).

23. *Backhill*, March 1993: 30.

24. *Backhill*, June 1993: 10.

25. *Backhill*, March 1993: 12.

26. See the stories of Martino Mora (*Backhill*, February 1993: 10), Alfonso Nastri (*Backhill*, March 1993: 12) and Taddeo Molinari (*Backhill*, December 1992/January 1993: 8).

27. *Backhill*, March 1993: 12.

28. *Backhill*, February 1993: 10.

29. *Backhill*, December 1992/January 1993: 9. This last remark on card games might sound superfluous, but such games constitute significant instances in the construction of gendered ethnicities through identifying players as northern or southern Italian men (cards are played only by males).

30. In the week following Mussolini's declaration of war on the allies (10 June 1940), over 4000 Italian men were arrested and interned as 'enemy aliens'. Among them 300 were British-born (Colpi 1991a: 113; also Marin 1975: 86).

31. A plaque bearing the names of all the victims was erected in the portico of St Peter's church in 1960, and an annual commemorative ceremony has been held since that year. Terri Colpi reproduces the list of victims in an appendix to her book (1991a), and a series of articles appeared in *Backhill* in 1993, tracing the stories of some victims. Finally, an exhibition of the work of a Scottish Italian photographer featured the *Arandora Star* as a pivotal point of the visual narrative (Owen Logan, Bloodlines/*vite allo speechio*, The Photographers Gallery, London. 4 February–19 March, 1994).

32. *La Voce degli Italiani*, no. 869, July 1992: 10. My translation.

33. Each year a commemorative mass is held for Italians soldiers who died in the 1939-45 war in the military cemetery of Brookwood. It is a typical ceremony dedicated to the fallen soldier/war hero.

34. Such discourses pervade notions of 'social progress' where different
     cultures are distinguished as more or less modern in terms of
     Eurocentric conceptions of sex/gender systems of differentiation
     (Carby 1982). In this respect, the question of what *kind* of family
     is created in these stories would be the next issue to address in a
     longer version of this chapter. My point here is merely to emphasise
     how ideas of settlement are configured around gender.

REFERENCES

Barker, M. 1981. *New Racism*. London: Junction.

Bottignolo, B. 1985. *Without a Bell Tower A Study of the Italian
     Immigrants in South-West England*. Rome: Centro Studi Emigrazione.

Carby, H. 1982. 'White woman listen! Black feminism and the
     boundaries of sisterhood', in Centre for Contemporary Cultural
     Studies, *The Empire Strikes Back: Race and Racism in 70s Britain*.
     London: Hutchinson, pp. 212–35.

Cavallaro, R. 1981. *Storie senza storia. Indagine sull' emigrazione calabrese
     in Gran Bretagna*. Roma: Centro Studi Emigrazione.

Centro Scalabrini di Londra. 1993. *Centro Scalabrini di Londra: 25 anni
     di servizio. Inaugurazione della rinnovata Chiesa del Redentore*. London.

de Certeau, M. 1983. 'History, ethics, science and fiction', in N. Haan
     (ed.) *Social Science: A Moral Enquiry*. New York: Columbia University
     Press.

—— 1990. *L'Invention du quotidien. 1. arts de faire*. Paris, Gallimard.

—— 1984. *The Practice of Everyday Life*. Berkeley and London.
     University of California Press.

Cohen, A.P. 1994. *Self Consciousness: An Alternative Anthropology of
     Identity*. London: Routledge.

Colpi, T. 1991a. *The Italian Factor: The Italian Community in Great Britain*.
     London: Mainstream.

—— 1991b. *Italians Forward: A Visual History of the Italian Community
     in Great Britain*. London: Mainstream.

Duffield, M. 1984. 'New racism, new realism', *Radical Philosophy*
     37: 29–34.

Gillis, J.R. 1994. 'Memory and identity: the history of a relationship',
     in J.R. Gillis (ed.) *Commemorations: The Politics of National Identity*.
     Princeton, NJ: Princeton University Press, pp. 3–23.

Gilroy, P. 1994. 'Diaspora', *Paragraph* 17 (3): 207–12.

Hall, S. 1992. 'The question of cultural identity', in S. Hall, D. Held and T. McGrew (eds) *Modernity and its Futures*. Cambridge and Milton Keynes: Polity and Open University Press, pp. 273–325.

Handler, R. 1988. *Nationalism and the Politics of Culture in Quebec.* Madison: University of Wisconsin Press.

Lawrence, E. 1982a. 'Just plain common sense: the "roots" of racism', in Centre for Contemporary Cultural Studies (ed.) *The Empire Strikes Back: Race and Racism in 70s Britain*. London: Hutchinson, pp. 46–94.

—— 1982b. 'In the abundance of water the fool is thirsty: sociology and black "pathology"', in Centre for Contemporary Cultural Studies (ed.) *The Empire Strikes Back: Race and Racism in 70s Britain*. London: Hutchinson, pp. 95–142.

MacDonald, J.S. and L.D. MacDonald. 1972. *The Invisible Immigrants.* London: Runnymede Trust.

Marin, U. 1975. *Italiani in Gran Bretagna*. Rome: Centro di Studi Emigrazione.

Palmer, R. 1991 [1977]. 'The Italians: patterns of migration to London', in J.L. Watson (ed.) *Between Two Cultures: Migrants and Minorities in Britain*. Oxford: Basil Blackwell, pp. 242–68.

Sodano, T. 1995. 'Italians in Britain and their self-image', paper presentation at a conference on New Perspectives in the History of Italians in Great Britain, London, Institute of Romance Studies, 19 May 1995.

Sponza, L. 1988. *Italian Immigrants in Nineteenth-Century Britain: Realities and Images*. Leicester: Leicester University Press.

Tassello, G. and L. Favelo 1976. 'Rapporto di sintesi sulle caratteristiche, il sistema relogioso, il sistema sociale personale, della seconda generazione Italiana in Gran Bretagna'. Roma: CSER (unpublished).

PART III 'BEING ...'

Part III examines the experience of modernity, now fully 'at large' in a global world, of individuals in industrial, capitalist society who have seen their identity become increasingly dependent upon modern forms of industrial, public sector and voluntary sector work. The restless global dynamics which underpin modern livelihoods have had major consequences for individuals and local communities, such as deskilling, unemployment, de-industrialisation and poverty. In short, modernity has brought anomie, a heightened sense of personal loss, and a fear that one is no longer in control of one's destiny in as much as work and the systems of status and the income which sustained individual self-worth and community have disappeared.

The chapters in this section pursue a central issue of this contemporary dilemma: precisely what connections exist between work and residence which have so great an impact on social identity? It is tempting to speculate that it has been the durability of the twentieth-century bureaucratisation of work and its associated work ethic which have conditioned the modern psyche to accept that half of one's adult life will be spent unemployed and to accept that one's community will decline. Compared to the immediacy and profoundly charged expression of identity among colonised and 'Third World' peoples in Part I, or with the dynamism and connectedness of the cultural diaspora discussed in Part II, the experience of being modern would seem to be one of ambivalence and heightened angst. While clearly not the only possibility which modernity holds for us, the seemingly ever present experience of disorder and loss of purpose are everywhere with us, whether directly through the threat posed by the loss of work-related social status or the declining quality of life in our communities, or indirectly through increased stress, anxiety and illness.

8 'AN AFRICAN RAILWAYMAN IS A RAILWAYMAN' ... OR THE SUBJECT OF THE SUBJECT OF THE SUBJECT

Ralph Grillo

This chapter re-examines material originally collected in Uganda in 1964–65. Fieldwork in Europe (Grillo, 1985), as well as reflections on later research in Africa and elsewhere, led to the realisation that my earlier handling of the East African data had glossed over certain key problems. One of these was centrally concerned with 'identity' which was central to the work of A.L. Epstein whose pioneering research and writing about urban and industrial Africa inspired my own work in social anthropology as well as that of numerous others, including other contributors to this volume.

The initial problem with which this chapter is concerned was signalled in the title of my 1973 monograph *African Railwaymen*. Briefly, a striking feature of the situation of those I studied, but which in the end I took for granted, was the extent to which they were 'committed to industrial employment and [had] in many ways absorbed the values of industrial society' (Grillo 1973: 1), with the result that they were in some sense 'railwaymen'. Committed to what and why? Identifying with what and why? The terms require discussion, and it will be seen that to say 'African railwaymen' is to oversimplify, even misrepresent what is at stake, and that is how the problem begins to change. The end result is a different set of questions to those with which I started, some of which cannot be resolved here.

For those familiar with his work, the title of *African Railwaymen* (also, incidentally, inspired by the magnificent frontispiece of Epstein's *Politics in an Urban African Community*) will recall a remark of Gluckman's (1961: 68), from which part of the title of the present chapter is derived: 'The African newly arrived from his rural home to work in a mine, is first of all a miner (and possibly resembles miners everywhere).' Gluckman has been wrongly criticised for implying a discontinuity between rural and urban in Africa in the colonial period which the work of Epstein and of Mitchell, on whose ethnography he relied heavily, did not support. He was, rather, offering a methodological injunction: the study of Africans in urban and industrial contexts must treat centrally of those contexts. They should not be seen as 'tribesmen in town'. It was also an identity statement. First, from the observer's perspective, Africans on the Copperbelt, say, were identified with their sociological situation as industrial workers engaged in a certain type of work (mining), in a particular economic context (contemporary capitalism), within the framework of the then colonial state. (There is also in Gluckman's remark, and perhaps in Epstein's photo, a hint of romanticism about the traditional industrial working class.) Second, the statement also implies something about the miners' conception of themselves. It imputes an identification on their part, and that is the line explored in this chapter.

'Identification' I take to mean accepting the conception of oneself as a particular kind of social person. One might identify with any (conceivably all, at any rate situationally) of what are usually described as the statuses and roles comprising one's social repertoire. Although the discussion of identification cannot adequately be conducted in terms of role analysis because of the problems it poses for notions of individuality and subjectivity, at least it provides a starting point. Especially interesting are the statuses and roles to which ego is *strongly* attached: those which generally, or in important situations, occupy a central place in the repertoire; identities which define the self as a whole.

The agenda for this type of inquiry is different from that which dominated thinking about identity in British anthropology during the 1980s and early 1990s. There the emphasis was on the nature of the 'person', and how conceptions of 'person', 'identity', 'self' and so on, differ in non-Western compared with what Strathern calls 'Euro-American' societies (Strathern 1992, see also Strathern 1988). Such studies have been primarily concerned with underlying philosophies, and with the difficulty (if not impossibility) of cross-cultural comparison employing 'analytical' categories (for example, 'the individual') embedded in another ('Western') discourse. This is clearly an important agenda, but not one I am able to follow. I have no information on how, if at all, my informants articulated any concept of 'self', and hence the emphasis here is, rather, on *identification* as a social and political process, and on the circumstances which lead to identification with one role or status rather than another.

Discussion of identification in this sense has, in British social anthropology, been largely confined to two kinds of identity: gender and ethnicity. (In fact, so strong is the association with the latter that, casually, 'identity' has come to signal 'ethnicity'.) Reasons for the relative neglect of other kinds of identification include the way in which fieldwork sites and problems have been selected, and (related to that) the way in which some types of identification have seemed analytically less important, or exciting, than others. The neglect also reflects what is undoubtedly the relative salience of gender and ethnicity in the contemporary world as against other forms of identification, including, for example, occupation and class.

There is, of course, a huge literature on ethnic and related forms of identification to which Epstein himself made a significant contribution (notably 1958 and 1978.) One interesting recent addition is Bowman's essay on ethnicity in the former Yugoslavia (1994). There has been a limited but telling intervention by anthropologists in accounts of the Yugoslav debacle. Like their counterparts in Sri Lanka a decade earlier, they were deeply shaken by the nature of the violence that occurred between otherwise friendly (and neighbourly) people. Bowman tries to understand this in two ways. First, he shows how political leaders of almost all persuasions played the ethnic card in the late 1980s and early 1990s, but, second, asks, why was their rhetoric so compelling, and why, above all, did it have such an horrific outcome? Adopting a Lacanian perspective, he argues that:

The nationalist rhetorics which have led to war in former Yugoslavia function ... by prompting persons of a widely diverse range of social and historical backgrounds *to recognize their essential identities as national rather than as based on gender, occupation, class or place of residence* ... this process ... succeeds because it echoes – in the social domain – processes of identity-formation individuals negotiate in their earliest encounters with social reality. (1994: 167, my emphasis)

Anthropologists, as he recognises, will be sceptical of such psychoanalytic explanations, but clearly the question he asks is a fundamental one. The point here, however, is the fact that Bowman expresses what is the standard anthropological position on identification: there are no essences, only constructions. Second, he signals that in the former

Yugoslavia other forms of identification (occupation, class, place of residence) were possible, and indeed were historically taken up: dominant identities, what he calls 'essential identities', were conceivably (and actually) based on something other than ethnicity. What we have to determine is how and why a particular form of identification becomes conceivable. This means locating identification within the economic, political and industrial framework: another methodological injunction of the Manchester School. In this instance it also involves re-engaging with debates which have long since seemed closed and which superficially appear now of no more than historical interest. That they are much more than that will be apparent to those familiar with so-called 'Newly Industrialising Countries'.

AFRICAN RAILWAYMAN, 1964–65

Let me begin with an example of 'Jackson' (see Grillo 1973: 135ff.), an Accidents Clerk Grade B VII in the Control Office of the Kampala Depot of the former East African Railways and Harbours, the EARH (the significance of the technical jargon will become apparent). Early in fieldwork I met Jackson and his workmates and got on with him and them in an informal way. I then made the unfortunate decision to conduct a more formal interview, notebook in hand. It began well, and Jackson described his career in the railways: how after training at the Railway Training School he had been posted as a Pier Clerk Grade B VIII to Port Bell, then transferred to Kampala, to the Parcels Office and eventually the Control Office. He was now, he said, on Grade B V. Unfortunately I knew this to be untrue because his promotion to Grade B VII had just been listed in the railway newspaper *Sikio*. When I mentioned this he broke off the interview saying it was a personal matter.

Despite this we continued to meet. One Saturday afternoon we went together to the bar at Nsambya market where we found the Station Master, the Goods Agent and the Industrial Relations Officer, I was invited to join them and we sat down. The Industrial Relations Officer bought a round for all except Jackson, for whom I bought a drink. The discussion, which excluded Jackson, soon got round to promotion, and the Industrial Relations Officer claimed he was shortly going to Nairobi to a Superscale post. He was now Group A, Segment

I. Shortly afterwards Jackson made signs to leave and we went to his home. There he complained that he had felt 'extremely uncomfortable' in the bar. All those men had been of high grade and he was just Grade B VII. Naively I tried to console him by pointing out how much better off he was than other Africans. He retorted: 'If you say that you are my enemy Number One.' He became increasingly maudlin. He wanted to get abroad for further studies so that when he returned he would be a big man, and people like the Industrial Relations Officer would respect him and he could drink with them. He ended that he was 'useless', and 'better dead'. There is more about Jackson (his keen if temporary interest in extra-mural classes, his attempts to give up drink to buy a car, his stream of applications for higher posts in the EARH and in other services), but the incidents related above are sufficient to illustrate a point I will develop shortly: Jackson's identification with the categories of the railway system.

The background against which this example must be set is as follows. Fieldwork concerned employees of the EARH based at the Kampala Depot and living on the railway-owned Nsambya housing estate in the years immediately following the period in which the East African territories gained independence. The economy was (is) mainly agricultural with some 15 per cent only of African adult males in waged employment, concentrated in a few mainly urban areas, principally Kampala and Jinja. The economic returns to such employees far outstripped those available to peasant farmers. Average wages were about four times the earnings of cash crop cultivators, and the gap was widening. Partly because of this, and partly because the potential labour force had been increasing rapidly through the 1950s and early 1960s as a result of population growth and the expansion of education, the demand for jobs greatly exceeded the supply, which had in any case remained static for a long period. Thus those in steady employment were in a privileged position, and railwaymen were among the privileged of the privileged. With take-home pay some 60 per cent above the average Kampala wage it was not misleading to describe them, at any rate loosely, as a 'labour aristocracy'.

The labour force was, of course, largely migrant. Some 70 per cent of Kampala employees came from outside the immediate region. Historically, such migrants had been short term, entering the labour market for periods of a year or two, in great majority males who were either unmarried, or who had left their families at home. By the mid-

1960s, however, people were staying in employment, often with the same firm, for much longer, and increasingly families, and independent women, were residing in town. This tendency was particularly marked among railwaymen. They averaged 13 years' service with the EARH, 90 per cent were married, and 75 per cent of married men had wives with them. This did not, however, mean severance of ties with rural areas, and most maintained a wide range of social and economic links with their places of origin where they retained homes to which they planned eventually to return.

The EARH itself was a supra-national corporation, based in Nairobi, with some 42,000 employees of all races. The network was divided into districts each with a number of depots, and was run by four main departments which maintained establishments in each District under a District Officer. Departments were divided into sections, for example, at Kampala the Mechanical Engineering Department had a Locomotive Shed, a Carriage and Wagon Examiners and an Office, each with a Section Head (such as Shedmaster). Sections were comprised of sub-sections under supervisors or charge-hands. All employees were assigned a post designated by a title or occupation, grade, department or section, and depot or district (for example, Running Shift Foreman, Grade B VII, Loco Shed, Kampala).

In *African Railwaymen* I claimed that EARH employees had so internalised the norms and values of the industry as to use them as a basis for relationships in their everyday lives. I will discuss this claim, focusing on the congeries of statuses implied in the designation of a post: departmental section, occupation and grade. Let me begin negatively. In April 1966 the recently appointed African General Manager made the following statement:

We on the EARH are one big team; there should be no jealousies amongst us ... Let us think of ourselves not as members of the Engineering Department ... but as members of the EARH in which each of us ... has but one object in view – a better traffic performance. (*Sikio* no. 149, 1 April 1966: 3)

In fact, apart from a certain pride in working for an important enterprise with jobs generally well paid, and much in demand (in 1967, for example, there were over 50,000 applications for 180 places at the Railway Training School in Nairobi), there was little evidence of corporate dedication. Nor, despite attempts to treat them like houses in a public school, did departments generate much corporate ethos.

Undoubtedly interdepartmental rivalries existed, and one department certainly blamed another should there be a mishap in the complex process of assembling and dispatching a train. Usually, however, the closest identification was with specific work unit (section or sub-section) especially where occupation and grade defined a relatively homogeneous group. Running Staff, for example (that is, locomotive drivers, firemen and immediate supervisors), were a group who interacted intensively at and often outside work, and between whom there were obligations of friendship and solidarity which sometimes cut across racial boundaries (see Grillo 1973: 72). Occupational identification – with the post held by an individual (for example, the Station Master at Kampala); with the specialised occupational group formed by those holding similarly designated posts (for example, station masters); and with the wider occupational category within which these may be subsumed (for example, officers) – was also considerable. Take 'Alexander', a Grade B VIII supervisor, or Superintendent as he was designated, of the Carriage Cleaning Sub-section, in charge of some 20 unskilled Group C workers, mostly from Ankole in southwest Uganda, known as 'Alexander's men'. 'Mr' Alexander, as he was usually known, a Luo from western Kenya, would each morning process through the estate in immaculate white suit, sparkling white shirt and solar topee, sedately exchanging greetings with those he passed. Unfortunately the connotations of his job did not quite accord with this image, and among other Luo he was known as *Jachieth*, the 'shitman'. Similarly, locomotive drivers and other skilled workers were staff whose jobs involving shift work and overtime often enabled them to take home considerably fatter pay packets than 'clerks' on the same grade. Relationships between the two groups were frequently hostile, with drivers claiming that the 'clerks hate us because we are illiterate and earn large salaries'. In return they would assert that 'clerk's work is ladies' work. All they want is to sit in an office and wear a white shirt and tie.'

Another source of identity, and in some ways the most important, was grade. In 1965 the grading system consisted of four groups, Superscale, A, B and C, each divided into grades (Group B, for example, ran from XI to I, with an Executive Division of three grades) which determined basic, though not take-home, pay. Unskilled, semi-skilled and apprentice jobs were in Group C; skilled jobs were in the upper reaches of Group C and the lower grades of Group B. Clerical jobs were mostly Group B, and administrative posts in Group A or Superscale. Differentials were considerable: in 1964–65 the minimum wage in Group C was £78 per annum, while those in Superscale Grade I received £3600. In this period there was rapid Africanisation of middle range and higher grades which had previously been reserved for Asians and Europeans. Grade also determined housing entitlement. The EARH provided free housing for its employees usually located on estates like that at Nsambya. There were seven house classes ranging from barrack blocks divided into single rooms known as 'Landies', up to colonial-style bungalows in their own grounds. Nsambya consisted of houses in classes 7 to 3 located in different parts of the estate. In fact the word 'grade' was often applied colloquially only to Group B staff and above, as when someone said 'I have no grade, I am just a Group C man' (note the word 'just', Swahili *tu*). But grade, in the technical EARH sense, together with occupation and to an extent section, were taken to define the person. Or rather, they provided the framework through which the person had the expectation of being defined. Jackson, for example, clearly felt that his existing grade did not reflect his true status. Neither did 'Alan', a Group C Stores Assistant in the Loco Shed who once applied for the post of Shedmaster: 'I am at least Grade VII, and could do work up to Grade III.' However, it is equally clear that both he and Jackson accepted the system even if they rejected the place assigned to them in it.

From this it will be apparent that 'African railwaymen' is misleading if it suggests a close identification with the corporation as a whole. They were not 'organisation men'. However, they did identify with what was involved organisationally in being an EARH employee, crucially with the post, implying occupation, grade and work section, each generating a social category or variety of linked categories, in terms of which self and others could be situated. Out of such elements were composed the occupational and grade stereotypes which individuals and groups had of themselves and others, and at this point the system of grade and occupation (as that term is used here) which has a specifically railway frame of reference linked with the system of social differentiation emerging in the wider society.

Eventually I will discuss how and why this type of industrial identity occurs. There is, however, another form of identification which must be mentioned, for which the term used in migrant labour studies of the 1950s and 1960s was 'commitment'. This was defined by the editors of one influential volume as:

both the short-run objective performance of modern kinds of economic activity and the long-run and deep-seated acceptance of the attitudes and beliefs appropriate to a modernized economy. (Moore and Feldman 1960: v)

The concept was 'thus concerned with overt actions and with norms' (1960: 1). Much of the African migrant labour literature of the 1950s was in fact concerned with 'overt actions' rather than 'norms', even when discussing such normative-sounding concepts as 'detribalisation'. The central problem was labour stability (seen as the product and indexical measure of commitment), and there was a keen interest in labour turnover, as a crucial index of stability. It will be argued below that through much of the colonial period commitment was actually discouraged, by the 1960s the prevailing view in academic, political, administrative and industrial circles was one which encouraged stability (commitment in performance) in the expectation of, or hope for, something called 'modernisation'.

In 1960, Elkan and Fallers (1960: 254) had suggested that in Kampala's labour force commitment to performance was unrelated to normative commitment. The EARH and other data argued otherwise. The railway labour force was not just 'stable'; most of its members had a normative commitment to, and identification with, the labour market and to work in employment in the cash economy. Compared with workers studied in the 1950s (for example, Richards 1954) railwaymen took it as 'natural' that this was what one did if one could. The Kampala data for the mid-1960s thus parallel Parkin's finding (1979) that by the mid-1970s on the Kenya Coast 'work' (Swahili *kazi*) was defined as employment, rather than subsistence activity. To be without 'work' (*kazi*) meant to lack employment, an undesirable state, and as popular songs of the day illustrated, possession of a job was highly valued for itself, as well as for the economic return it provided. There existed, therefore, a normative commitment to employment and to the labour market which increasingly defined the person, at least the male person. It could be argued, and many have, that this was a state of affairs that the colonists had been hoping to achieve in East Africa since the early days, when for example Churchill wrote after his Kenya trip of 1907: 'I am clearly of the opinion that no man has a right to be idle ... He is bound to go forward and take an honest share in the general work of the world. And I do not except the African native' (cited in Hill 1961: 298).

African railwaymen, then, had two kinds of identification: with the social categories associated with their place of employment, and with the role of employee in a labour market. These things structured their lives, and my informants accepted that structure and acted the parts assigned to them in it. Often it was as pertinent to describe someone by reference to the resultant categories as it would have been to say that they were a Luo, a Ganda or a Kikuyu (this is illustrated extensively in Grillo 1973 and 1974). This did not necessarily mean, however, that they accepted their individual or collective place within the structure. This is precisely what individuals like Jackson or Alan complained about, and the history of trade unions in the EARH was in large measure a struggle, interconnected with the struggle for national independence, for equality for Africans, as a race, within the existing system (Grillo 1974). That these workers also, at the same time, accepted an identification as Luo, Ganda or Kikuyu, and that ethnic identify was in some sense 'primary', does not alter the fact of the importance of their industrial identification, though undoubtedly it makes analysis of that identification more complex.

IDENTITY, ALIENATION AND IDEOLOGICAL SUBJECTION

To many people identification with the labour market and with the industry might seem obvious, even 'natural', not in need of explanation. It is therefore worth discussing why, when encountered in the field, it seemed worthy of note.

The first reason is that my informants were migrants, usually though not always first-generation entrants to the labour market. The existing literature, with certain notable Central African exceptions, had stressed the novelty of their situation. In 1963, Guy Hunter had written of the gap between traditional and industrial environments in these terms:

the worker has never worn boots, used a shovel, seen stairs ... attitudes towards authority ... and towards members of other tribes frequently conflict with the status and ranking systems of industrial organisation. (Hunter 1963: para. 15)

A labour expert who had seen my draft research proposal which had talked of 'class' warned against expecting to find such distinctions applicable to people like the Luo. The speed of adaptation to a technical environment, which might have amazed Hunter, I did not find at all surprising. What did astonish me was the close identification with the work process and the roles associated with it. This was perhaps because I expected the opposite, a rejection of that process.

The reason for this was that like others of my generation I had been significantly influenced by Marx – not *Capital* (vol. III, or even vol. I), but the early *Economic and Philosophical Manuscripts of 1844*, and the discussion of alienation. Two aspects of that discussion are relevant here: the idea that in capitalism 'the worker is related to the product of his labour as to an alien object' (Marx 1963: 122); and the insistence that 'alienation appears not merely in the result but in the process of production, within productive activity itself' (1963: 124).

What constitutes the alienation of labour? First, that the work is external to the worker, that it is not part of his nature; and that, consequently, he does not fulfil himself in his work but denies himself, has a feeling of misery rather than well-being, does not develop freely his mental and physical energies but is physically exhausted and mentally debased. The worker, therefore, feels himself at home only during his leisure time, whereas at work he feels homeless. It is not the satisfaction of a need, but only a means for satisfying other needs. Its alien character is clearly shown by the fact that as soon as there is no physical compulsion it is avoided like the plague. (Marx 1963: 124–5)

Work 'is not part of [man's] nature'. Thus central to the argument is, as McLellan says, the idea 'that man had forfeited to someone or something what was essential to his nature – principally to be in control of his own activities' (1971: xl).

Given that orientation, it may be appreciated with what relish I snatched at the scraps of evidence which suggested consciousness of this. For example, the conversation in which Alan revealed his ambition to be Shedmaster occurred during a lunch break. At one point he looked at the clock and found he should be returning to duty. He refused to leave, saying he wanted to 'control his own work', and go where he pleased in his own time. Such comments were, however, very rare, and I found no one to compare with Arthur Seaton, the 'hero' of Sillitoe's *Saturday Night and Sunday Morning*, a book which I can report was read at the time as a literary comment on Marx. Saturday night was the time when 'piled-up passions ... exploded, and the

effect of a week's monotonous graft in the factory was swilled out of
your system in a burst of goodwill' (1958: 1–2), and 'all the rest is
propaganda'. (The phrase was used in the film, but I cannot find it in
the novel.) It could probably be argued that in some objective sense
railwaymen were alienated, but there was little consciousness of this.
On the contrary it was accepted that work and its organization defined
the self in the ways I have described. In order to explore this state of
affairs I will turn first to the writings of someone whose ideas are, in
certain important respects, quite fundamentally opposed to those of
Marx, at any rate the early Marx, and through those ideas discuss the
relationship between identification and ideology.

In the course of a lengthy discussion, which has to be understood
in the context of his other work, and of Marxist writing in general,
Louis Althusser in a well-known phrase proposed that what is
represented in ideology (I would say what he, Althusser, wished to
call ideological) is 'not the system of the real relations which govern
the existence of individuals, but the imaginary relations of those
individuals to the real relations in which they live' (1971: 165). That
sentiment has generated a considerable exegetical literature, and I
comment on the contrast imaginary/real later. For the moment let us
consider 'function'.

'All ideology has the function (which defines it) of "constituting"
concrete individuals as subjects' (Althusser 1971: 171). It thus 'hails
or interpellates concrete individuals as concrete subjects' (p. 173). As
Althusser himself noted (p. 182) the notion of 'subject' is ambiguous.
On the one hand, ideology (say, that of Western capitalist society) makes
of someone a person, or rather an individual ('free, ethical etc.',
p. 171). That is, it creates their subjectivity. At the same time, partly
because that subjectivity is for Althusser illusory, ideology subjects the
individual to what Althusser calls the 'Subject' (capital 'S'), for
example, God.

There is a major difficulty with Althusser's formulation because
sometimes he is discussing what he terms 'ideology in general', that
is, a general feature of all social systems, and sometimes ideology in
particular types of society. In fact, his discussion is hardly ever
contextualised sufficiently to allow us to know, though it often seems
to me that with Althusser, as with other French Marxists of that era,
there was in the background an unspoken context: France. Thus the
argument about subjectivity gives the appearance of having wider

application than it does, and in certain respects he was discussing a special historical case, that of the 'bourgeois' notion of the free individual, of which he disapproved (Thompson 1978: 280).

This indeed may be seen as the product of a certain type of society, a point noted by Mauss in 1938, himself building on certain remarks of Durkheim (for example, 1964: 194ff.). Mauss summarises his own reflections in this way:

From a mere masquerade to the mask, from a role to a person, to a name, to an individual, from the last to a being with a metaphysical and ethical value, from a moral consciousness to a sacred being, from the latter to a fundamental form of thought and action – that is the route we have covered. (Brewster's translation, 1979: 90)

This is not an issue that can be pursued here in respect of data on African railwaymen where I am concerned only with their identification as social persons: what Mauss called *personne* rather than what he called *personnage*. Person in this sense must, of course, be an externally, that is, socially, created phenomenon. But how might an African railwayman's conception of himself as a 'Grade B VIII Clerk', for example, be described, in Althusser's term, as an 'imaginary' one?

This concept has a wider connotation than it might seem. First, it is contrasted with what does not 'correspond to reality' (Althusser 1971: 162). This must be understood as follows:

If it is true that the representation of the real conditions of existence of the individuals occupying the posts of agents of production, exploitation, repression, ideologization, and scientific practice, does in the last analysis arise from the relations of production, and relations deriving from the relations of production, we can say the following: all ideology represents in its necessarily imaginary distortion not the existing relations of production ... but above all the (imaginary) relationship of individuals to the relations of production. (1971: 164–5)

To understand this, we have to see that 'imaginary' implies 'image' which in French has roughly the same range of connotations as the Latin *imago*: it may mean a picture, or a reflection, as in a mirror. The audience, mostly children, who attend performances of *Guignol*, the famous Punch and Judy show of Lyons, are invited to display *images* (picture-cards) of the *personnages* (characters) when they appear on stage. What, then, Althusser meant was that the sense that someone has of themselves as a social person (but beyond that, their subjectivity) is externally derived as an image or *imago*, a term which Mauss reminds us originally referred to a death mask (1973: 352). This image is internalised so that what it says becomes an integral and unthought part of one's being, and thus one becomes in two senses a 'subject'. A similar point was made earlier by Volosinov: 'Personality is itself generated through language ... in the ideological themes of language ... Inner personality is an expressed or inwardly impelled word' (1973: 153). This subjection through ideology is necessary

if the reproduction of relations of production is to be assured ... every day, in the 'consciousness', i.e. in the attitudes of individual-subjects occupying the posts which the socio-technical division of labour assigns to them. (Althusser 1971: 182)

Thus the subjects 'work by themselves' (p. 181).

IDENTIFICATION AND THE INDUSTRIAL SYSTEM

Let me return to the railwaymen data in the light of this discussion. At a superficial level some of Althusser's ideas make good sense in that context. When an African railwayman defined himself as a social person by reference to a labour market which formed part of a colonial or post-colonial economic order, we must agree that an aspect of his identity can only be externally derived, and is perhaps attributable to the exigencies of that order. The system required a labour force, and many institutions (taxes, education, religion), some of which might well be described in Althusser's phrase as 'ideological state apparatuses', worked towards that end. It is, of course, easy enough to state in general that this must be so, much more difficult to show precisely what happened and how. I am reminded of Rex and Tomlinson's comment on race relations in Britain:

British people confronted with immigrants from what used to be the empire cannot but be expected to react to them in terms of the roles which immigrants used to fill. This is not a matter to be established by some naively defined attitude test. It is a matter of history and of logic. (1979: 91)

The trouble is that history and logic do not always point in the same direction. The problem might become clearer if we look more closely at the two aspects of railwaymen's identity: their internalisation of identities derived from the organisation of the work process, and their commitment to employment.

It has been argued that there was in the colonial period considerable doubt about the value of encouraging a stable labour force. Weeks' study of wage policies illustrated the differences that existed between the urban (industrial) and rural (farm/plantation) sectors. Discussing a 1955 report on African wages which stressed the need for stabilisation, and hence improvement in pay and conditions, Weeks pointed out that on plantations all that was required was a regular supply of unskilled labour, which another report suggested could be achieved through a variety of essentially coercive measures. In this case it was sufficient that the potential labourer be available as a commodity on the labour market. Overt action, not a normative or ideological change, was all that was required. In industry, by contrast,

while coercive measures may reduce turnover, they are unlikely to provide an atmosphere in which workers will increase efficiency, maintain work discipline, and acquire skills. (Weeks 1971: 371)

To say that, however, touches on the conditions necessary for what Marxists usually call the 'reproduction of labour power'. Apropos of this Althusser (1971: 131) says that the 'available labour power must be "competent", i.e. suitable to be set to work in the complex system of the process of production'. This reproduction of skills is 'achieved more and more outside production: by the capitalist education system, and by other instances and institutions' (1971: 132). Hence, of course, 'ideological state apparatuses'. Be that as it may, and it is such passages which convince me of Althusser's essential Francocentricity, it is clear that in Althusser's view ideology does much more than create skills. And yet, strictly speaking, is anything more than 'competence', the possession of skills of a technical kind – and perhaps overt obedience – necessary to accomplish the set task ever essential? Consider Arthur Seaton again. It is clear that at one level he has a purely instrumental attitude to work. But he is competent. After the weekend he is there at the work bench, doing the necessary to get paid again on Friday, and apparently doing it well. There is no suggestion that his rebelliousness (lack of normative commitment? refusal of ideological subjection?) makes him incompetent, though it used to be said never buy a car built on a Monday.

There are two points to note here. First, Althusser's account of ideology, particularly ideology in capitalism, gives the impression of a homogeneous force which works with totalitarian efficiency. The parallel with Durkheim's (1964) concept of the *conscience collective* in this and other ways is striking, as Strawbridge notes (1982). Second, the kind of identification found among railwaymen would seem, strictly from the viewpoint of the reproduction of labour power, or the working of the colonial economy, or more simply of the railway system, an unnecessary elaboration, a redundancy, an over-identification, perhaps even a sort of mimesis. Whether it is or not we may see in a moment. I would like to consider a number of not so much alternative as additional explanations for the sort of identification at issue.

The first concerns the place of African railwaymen in the social economy: their structural situation in the colonial labour system. I said earlier that African railwaymen might be described as 'labour aristocrats'. Is that significant? 'Labour aristocracy' is used by social historians of nineteenth-century Britain to refer to workers whose level and regularity of earnings, among other criteria, marked them off as an upper stratum of the working class (Hobsbawm 1964: 273). Although the term is imprecise, reflecting the fluidity of the underlying situation it describes, it is not necessarily so flexible that it can be extracted entirely from its historical context of nineteenth-century stratification and political attitudes. In the African case, therefore, the term is used loosely to describe workers who are definitely a cut above others by the relevant criteria.

For Hobsbawm, the distinctiveness of the labour aristocracy lay in the high level and regularity of earnings, certainly a feature of African railwaymen (or Zambian miners.) For railwaymen, grade and occupation might be said to connote that distinctiveness. Identification with these (though not obviously with work unit, at any rate all work units) thus signalled membership of a workforce which was apart from others. This is not entirely convincing since grade, especially, denoted a way of ordering difference which was internal to the railway industry and not widely known outside it. Among railwaymen it was a local, contextually confined, marker of differentiation. As such it represented a particularly acute form of the status differentiation becoming increasingly prevalent in the wider society.

One way of testing some of these ideas would be to explore the hypothesis that in other, less well-paid, less differentiated industries we might find a lower level of commitment and identification. Unfortunately, I do not know of research, at least in East Africa, which would enable us to do that. There is, however, a different argument relating to what might be described as the political economy of the workplace, which might suggest that certain forms of identification are likely to appear in particular types of organisation. Consider, for example, the so-called 'industrial man' hypothesis:

men's environment, as expressed in the institutional patterns they adopt or have introduced to them shapes their experience, and through this their perceptions, attitudes and values, in standardized ways which are manifest from country to country, despite the countervailing randomizing influence of traditional cultural patterns. (Inkeles 1960: 2)

In other words, an African railwayman is a railwayman and almost certainly like all railwaymen everywhere. It is the logic of the industrial organisation that counts.

This proposition has been widely criticised, and is no longer acceptable, at least in its extreme form (Peil 1972), though it is interesting to consider whether certain types of industry or job are more influential than others in shaping experience and attitudes (see, for example, Weber's discussion of those occupations, 'intellectual work, artistic performance, and work involving high technical performance', 1964: 214, which, he said, were evaluated as a 'calling'). An intriguing question on the other side is whether some 'local' cultures offer stronger or weaker 'countervailing influences' to industrial logic.

A variant of the argument is found in Epstein's distinction between 'unitary' and 'atomistic' structures (Epstein 1964: 93–4). Mining society in Zambia is '"unitary" in the sense that so much of what goes on in the mine is channelled through the mine bureaucracy'. In contrast with the 'atomistic' Township is the close connection between work and residence. The mine compound is comparable to a 'company town', and both on the Zambian copper mines and the East African railways we find a community of work and residence which, certainly in the railway case, is associated with a close identification with roles derived from the organisation of the work process. Further afield, Brook and Finn (1978: 133ff.) in an interesting discussion of British community studies drew attention to a paper by Lockwood (1975) in which he makes a contrast similar to Epstein's. It is an historical one between 'traditional' working-class communities such as Ashton (Dennis, et al.

1956), and the post-war housing estates of the so-called 'privatised' worker. This might suggest that the close identification I am discussing is a feature of certain types of industrial organisation, especially those traditional industries of the nineteenth century (mines, railways, docks) where there was frequently a combination of work and residence of a kind which these industries often require. They might be called 'industries of the barracks'. Certainly in Africa and often elsewhere these are industries frequently associated with strong trade unions, though not always and certainly not exclusively, and this might seem a logical counterpart to the close identification I have described.

In a 'post-industrial'/'postmodern' world such industries have all but vanished, and such identification now seems almost 'quaint'. It is 'atomistic' structures which now, apparently, prevail. 'The breaking up of the grand narratives', says Lyotard, referring to one of the defining characteristics of the postmodern condition,

leads to what some authors analyze in terms of the dissolution of the social bond and the disintegration of social aggregates into a mass of individual atoms thrown into the absurdity of Brownian motion. (1986: 15)

Certainly in the economies of the 'North' there have been major changes in the form of the occupational base, and what many observers have seen as a progressive disintegration of the classic forms of social and political organisation associated with modernity. In many respects it is the displacement of 'class' from centre stage which has appeared to be the most important shift in the transition from modern to postmodern society. In the place of the 'barracks' there are the multiply riven, media-driven, anarchic, post-industrial wastelands found in many parts of Britain, France and the United States.

What we are discussing are, of course, industrial cultures, part of which comprise systems of identification, and the conditions under which those cultures take a particular shape. The thrust of the argument is that an explanation running directly from the economic order (or more abstractly the 'mode of production'), through ideology, to identity is an insensitive one which overlooks many of the intermediate ways in which economy and society structure lived experience. At the same time, however, I am reluctant to leave it at that because this in turn ignores certain issues critical for any discussion of identification in the East African context of 1964–65.

COLONIAL SUBJECTS

During the 1960s, the French West Indian writer Franz Fanon had a considerable influence on thinking about black identity in Africa. Drawing on some of his ideas, in particular the book so evocatively entitled *Black Skin, White Masks* (Fanon 1967) the South African anthropologist Bernard Magubane published in 1971 a ferocious attack on Central African urban anthropology, arguing that Mitchell, Epstein and others had taken the colonial system for granted in their analysis of social change. In particular their account of stratification misinterpreted the way in which, they claimed, Africans evaluated themselves by reference to their adoption of European lifestyles. Moreover:

In associating worthiness with a European identity, Epstein, Mitchell, and others have contributed to that political and cultural subordination of Africans to the standards of Europe and to the prejudices of the colonial power that was the essence of colonialism. (Magubane 1971: 429)

I share Philip Mayer's doubt (1971) whether that criticism could be sustained by anyone who had really read *Politics in an Urban African Community* (Epstein 1958). At times Magubane seemed to suggest (see his comments on Epstein 1961) that Mitchell and Epstein not merely misinterpreted African urban behaviour, but that their ethnography was seriously at fault. If this is what he meant then he was wrong. And to assert, as Magubane did, that 'colonialism and imperialism had robbed Africans of their independence and their land; the sociology of colonialism robbed them of their culture and identity' (p. 429) was patently absurd. He was, however, correct to stress, as did Epstein (1964, 1967), the colonial context and the effects of colonialism, and he touched on a point of considerable interest when asking what he himself felt was the crucial question: 'At what level of socio-psychological experience is it that "Europeanization" stratifies the urban African proletariat?' (p. 429). His reply, '"Europeanization" is confined to the outermost layer of African social–psychological reality' (p. 430), poses a number of empirical, methodological and theoretical problems. I will make three comments.

First, the 'superficiality of "Europeanization"'. It is difficult to disentangle that, but if an African railwayman's identification with the role of Running Shift Foreman or Accidents Clerk may be treated as an instance of 'Europeanization' (and that is not necessarily appropriate) then it would seem neither sociologically nor psychologically superficial. I would, however, accept that it is only part of the story (my informants were much else besides railwaymen), and add that that was how it seemed in 1964–65. Second, 'reality'. Running through Magubane's article, as through other similar writings, is a vision of Africa, and Africans, before the fall, so to speak, which is reminiscent of Marx's vision of pre-capitalist, un-alienated Man, at one in his world (see Grillo 1993). For Magubane, as for Fanon, Europeanisation is a mask which disguises the continuing underlying reality of Africanness, though this reality is one which is very different from Althusser's. Third, Magubane's discussion does raise in an acute way the following question: when we are analysing a culture, whose culture are we analysing? I mean by that produced by whom, for whom? At this point there would seem to be a convergence of the views of Magubane and of Althusser, at least so far as, say, African urban and industrial culture is concerned. Both would interpret that culture as a dominated culture, one which is produced externally and which has a function in respect of the reproduction of labour power. I have already suggested some reasons for supposing that this might be unsatisfactory, at the very least an over-simplification. There are others.

The Althusser/Magubane perspective obliges us to treat human beings as inert subjects moulded by dominant systems. On the contrary, it seems to me that it is possible to argue that in the situations I have in mind what emerges is a 'counter-culture', so to speak, which draws on, even 'recuperates' the values of the dominant system to create something of its own. This recuperation may sometimes take the form of a close identification with the labour process in a way which overrides alienation. (See, for example, the passage in Solzhenitsyn's *One Day in the Life of Ivan Denisovich* where the hero becomes so engrossed in the forced labour task of building a wall that he sees only his wall. It is his own handiwork which he is reluctant to leave when his shift ends.)

In a roundabout way this brings me to a final point concerning the relation between identity, ideology and subjectivity. We might generally agree that identification must be considered as what is conventionally called a social fact, and person a socially constituted phenomenon. In this respect Althusser was saying nothing new (cf. Strawbridge 1982), though like Durkheim he tended to present ideology as a homogeneous and totalitarian force which works with terrifying efficiency to produce its 'effects'. Leaving aside that, and the consequent reductionism that it entails, the major difficulty I have with Althusser/Magubane concerns the implications of their views for our conception of subjectivity.

The problem is generic to certain kinds of structuralism. John Weightman (1982), for example, remarks of Barthes: 'He was the chief proponent of the view that the "author" does not exist, but is simply a nodal point where socially and historically determined lines of force intersect.' For Althusser likewise there is no subject, or subjectivity, other than in and through ideology. This, of course, is an integral part of his interpretation of Marxism. That there are political objections to that interpretation has been abundantly shown by E.P. Thompson, and anyone doubting Thompson should read Althusser's critique of 'humanist' versions of Marxism (for example, 1969). Crucial to that critique is the so-called 'rupture' between early and late Marx, an interpretation which was such as to lead Pêcheux, a devotee of Althusser, to berate one unfortunate writer because he had 'advanced no further than the Marxism of *The 1844 Manuscripts*, the *Theses on Feuerbach* and *The German Ideology*' (Pêcheux 1982: 140). As an unreconstructed bourgeois humanist who still derives much insight from the *Philosophical Manuscripts* I find that distressing.

When I said that the problem is generic to certain kinds of structuralism, I should perhaps have said all kinds, including the structural–functionalism formerly characteristic of British anthropology. When Strawbridge writes: 'Subjects are construed as effects rather than essences' (1982: 134) she is deliberately referring to both Althusser and Durkheim. One of the devices used by post–war British social anthropology to get round this one was the concept of 'actor'. One result of writing this chapter has been to make me look more closely and critically at that concept and the conception of subjectivity implied by it, and by what I now see as an allied term, 'author' (the actor/author 'couple' in fact). What emerges is that in the tradition to which we refer loosely as the 'actor-oriented' approach there was extraordinarily little explicit theorising of the central concept, and on the whole that kind of anthropology was characterised by a naive view of the 'subject'.

Now what there is to say, what the 'black box', as it was one time called, might contain, I do not know. Most anthropologists by their silence at least implicitly agree with the sentiment of 1 Timothy, ch. 6, v. 7: 'For we brought nothing into this world and it is certain we can carry nothing out' (or perhaps the British comedian, Tony Hancock's vision of his epitaph: 'He came, and he went, and in between, nothing'). It may be, to bring in both the Bible and Shakespeare, that in the end we have to agree with Lear who at the height of the storm on the heath cries out: 'Is man no more than this? Thou art the thing itself; unaccommodated man is no more but such a poor, bare, forked animal as thou art' (Act III, Scene 3, 105–11).

But even that bleak vision I find more comforting than that of the 'unaccommodated *trajet*'.

REFERENCES

Althusser, L. 1969. *For Marx*. London: Allen Lane.

Althusser, L. 1971. *Lenin and Philosophy and Other Essays*. New York and London: Monthly Review Press.

Bowman, G. 1994. 'Xenophobia, fantasy and the nation: the logic of ethnic violence in former Yugoslavia', in V.A. Goddard, J.R. Llobera and C. Shore (eds) *The Anthropology of Europe: Identities and Boundaries in Conflict*. Oxford: Berg, pp. 143–72.

Brook, E. and D. Finn. 1978. 'Working-class images of society and community studies', in Centre for Contemporary Cultural Studies (ed.) *On Ideology*. London: Hutchinson, pp. 125–43.

Dennis, D., F. Henriques and C. Slaughter. 1956. *Coal is Our Life*. London: Eyre.

Durkheim, E. 1964. *The Division of Labour in Society*. New York: Free Press of Glencoe.

EARH. 1964–66. *Sikio: the Staff Newspaper of the EARH*. Published in Nairobi.

Elkan, W. and L.A. Fallers. 1960. 'The mobility of labour', in W.E. Moore and A.S. Feldman (eds) *Labor Commitment and Social Change in Developing Areas*. New York: Social Science Research Council, pp. 238–57.

Epstein, A.L. 1958. *Politics in an Urban African Community*. Manchester: Manchester University Press.

—— 1961. 'The network and urban social organization', *Rhodes-Livingstone Journal* 29: 29–62.

—— 1964. 'Urban communities in Africa', in M. Gluckman and E. Devons (eds) *Closed Systems and Open Minds*. London: Oliver and Boyd, pp. 83–102.

—— 1967. 'Urbanisation and social change in Africa', *Current Anthropology* 8 (4): 275–84.

—— 1978. *Ethos and Identity*. London: Tavistock.

Fanon, F. 1967. *Black Skin, White Masks*. New York: Grove Press.

Gluckman, M. 1961. 'Anthropological problems arising from the African industrial revolution', in A.W. Southall (ed.) *Social Change in Modern Africa*. London: Oxford University Press, pp. 67–82.

Grillo, R.D. 1973. *African Railwaymen: Solidarity and Opposition in an African Labour Force*. Cambridge: Cambridge University Press.

—— 1974. *Race, Class and Militancy: an African Trade Union, 1939–1965*. New York: Chandler Publishing Co.

—— 1985. *Ideologies and Institutions in Urban France: The Representation of Immigrants*. Cambridge: Cambridge University Press.

—— 1993. 'The construct of "Africa" in African socialism', in C. Hann (ed.) *Socialism: Ideals, Ideologies and Local Practice*. London: Routledge, pp. 59–76.

Hill, M.F. 1961. *Permanent Way: vol. 1: The Story of the Kenya and Uganda Railway*, 2nd edn. Nairobi: EARH.

Hobsbawm, E.J. 1964. *Labouring Men*. London: Weidenfeld.

Hunter, G. 1963. *Tropical Africa Project: Supplement on Manpower and Training*. London: Oxford University Press.

Inkeles, A. 1960. 'Industrial man: the relation of status to experience, perception and value', *American Journal of Sociology* 66 (1): 1–31.

Lockwood, D. 1975. 'Sources of variation in working class images of society', in M. Bulmer (ed.) *Working-Class Images of Society*. London: Routledge and Kegan Paul, pp. 16–31.

Lyotard, J.-F. 1986. *The Postmodern Condition: A Report on Knowledge*. Manchester: Manchester University Press.

Magubane, B. 1971. 'A critical look at indices used in the study of social change', *Current Anthropology* 12 (4–5): 419–31.

Marx, K. 1963. *Karl Marx: Early Writings*, trans. and ed. T.B. Bottomore. London: C.A. Watts.

Mauss, M. 1973. *Sociologie et anthropologie*. Paris: Presses Universitaires de France.

—— 1979. *Sociology and Psychology*, trans. Ben Brewster. London: Routledge and Kegan Paul.

Mayer, P. 1971. 'Comment on B. Magubane "A critical look at indices used in the study of social change"', *Current Anthropology* 12 (4–5): 433–4.

McLellan, D. 1971. *Karl Marx: Early Texts*. trans. and ed. David McLellan. Oxford: Blackwell.

Moore, W.E. and A.S. Feldman. 1960. *Labor Commitment and Social Change in Developing Areas*. New York: Social Science Research Council.

Parkin, D.J. 1979. 'The categorization of work: cases from coastal Kenya', in S. Wallman (ed.) *Social Anthropology of Work*. London: Academic Press, pp. 317–35.

Pêcheux, M. 1982. *Language, Semantics and Ideology*. London: Macmillan.

Peil, M. 1972. *The Ghanaian Factory Worker*. Cambridge: Cambridge University Press.

Rex, J. and S. Tomlinson. 1979. *Colonial Immigrants in a British City*. London: Routledge and Kegan Paul.

Richards, A.I. 1954. *Economic Development and Tribal Change*. Cambridge: Heffer.

Sillitoe, A. 1958. *Saturday Night and Sunday Morning*. London: W.H. Allen.

Solzhenitsyn, A. 1963. *One Day in the Life of Ivan Denisovich*. London: Gollancz.

Strathern, M. 1988. *The Gender of the Gift*. Berkeley: University of California Press.

—— 1992. *Reproducing the Future: Essays on Anthropology, Kinship and the New Reproductive Technologies*. Manchester: Manchester University Press.

Strawbridge, S. 1982. 'Althusser's theory of ideology and Durkheim's account of religion: an examination of some striking parallels', *Sociological Review* 30: 125–40.

Thompson, E.P. 1978. *The Poverty of Theory and Other Essays*. London: Merlin Press.

Volosinov, V.N. 1973. *Marxism and the Philosophy of Language*. New York: Seminar Press.

Weber, M. 1964. *The Theory of Social and Economic Organization*. edited with an Introduction by Talcott Parsons. New York: The Free Press.

Weeks, J.F. 1971. 'Wage policy and the colonial legacy: a comparative study', *Journal of Modern African Studies* 9 (3): 361–87.

Weightman, J. 1982. 'High priest of modernism', *Observer*, 24 October: 34.

9 CELEBRATING DIVERSE IDENTITIES, PERSON, WORK AND PLACE IN SOUTH WALES[1]

Leonard Mars

None of us has just a single identity; as members of society each of us carries simultaneously a range of identities just as each of us occupies a number of statuses and plays a variety of roles. (Epstein 1978: 100)

The stranger is thus being discussed here, not in the sense often touched upon in the past, as the wanderer who comes today and goes tomorrow but rather as the person who comes today and stays tomorrow. He is, so to speak, the *potential* wanderer: although he has not moved on, he has not quite overcome the freedom of coming and going. He is fixed within a particular spatial group, or within a group whose boundaries are similar to spatial boundaries. But his position in this group is determined, essentially, by the fact that he has not belonged to it from the beginning, that he imports qualities into it, which do not and cannot stem from the group itself. (Simmel 1964: 402, emphasis in original)

The anthropological study of social identity has a long history though not explicitly under the rubric of identity. For example, Evans-Pritchard's *The Nuer* (1940) focused on the ways in which an individual was a member of a named group in one context but of a different group in another context. Membership of these groups was always defined in opposition to similarly structured other groups. Thus a Nuer would say that we are X not Y but as X we may fuse with Y to become Z in opposition to groups A and B who have merged to become C. Identity became salient, and contested, at boundaries and borders both geographic and cultural.

Bill Epstein's *Ethos and Identity* (1978) was, perhaps, one of the first anthropology books to feature the term 'identity' explicitly in its title.

As the quotation at the head of this chapter indicates, he drew attention to the diversity of identities simultaneously held by a member of society. This observation is in line with that of Evans-Pritchard for the Nuer. This chapter, in which I describe and analyse the retirement ceremony of a Scottish, Jewish medical practitioner who had completed 50 years of service in a South Wales valley, will examine the diverse identities of the man and of the locality in which he practised his profession. First I shall examine the general question of social identity, second the issue of Welsh identity, and third that of valley identity.

METHODOLOGY

The study of identity by social scientists has employed a variety of methods – questionnaires, interviews and participant observation. These methods yield different data as Epstein (1978: 111) observes in his analysis of ethnicity in America. He points out that researchers who interview samples of respondents obtain access to what he terms 'public' culture whereas those who employ participant observation (few American sociologists did so in Epstein's commentary) gain admission to what he calls 'intimate' culture. Public culture can be readily quantified by asking questions about the practice of certain customs which attach to a given ethnic identity. A diminution in the practice or observance of a custom is construed, perhaps erroneously cautions Epstein, as a weakening from generation to generation of cultural or ethnic identity. The preoccupation with statistical quantification excludes more elusive behaviour that is not in the public domain but which is manifest in more intimate contexts 'in the ongoing life of the home, in the company of friends, and at ethnic gatherings' (1978: 111). Epstein argues that large areas of 'public' culture may have been abandoned yet significant values and attitudes persist in the intimate culture of the group. These values and attitudes are imbued with meaning and emotional feeling and 'are transmitted to and experienced by the young' (1977: 112). To delve into the subtle and complex problems of ethnic identity, Epstein advocates the

need to develop methods and approaches more fine-grained than those adopted hitherto which take full account of the interplay of the external and the internal, the objective and the subjective, and the sociological and psychological elements which are always present in the formation of ethnic identity. (1978: 112)

To gain access to the intimate culture of the group I employ the method of situational analysis pioneered by Max Gluckman in 1940 to indicate the structural characteristics as well as the cultural values of the society. Using this method the ethnographer observes and describes a ceremony – such as the opening of a bridge (Gluckman 1958), the performance of a dance (Mitchell 1956) or the burial of a local notable (Loudon 1961) – and then considers, after the description of the local scene, the wider relations between the different social groups. After I attended the ceremony described below, I conducted formal interviews with the organisers of the event and informal interviews with the celebrant and his wife.

In an earlier article I examined the retirement ceremony of a Jewish medical practitioner who had worked for over 50 years in a South Wales valley and focused on his retirement ceremony as a *rite de passage* which marked the formal incorporation of the doctor as a stranger into a local community (Mars 1994). I argued primarily that the ceremony incorporated him as a neighbour, as a local and as a friend now divested of his professional status by the termination of his service to the locality. The ceremony, however, was multi-valent and I suggested secondarily in the conclusion that the retirement also celebrated the changing though distinctive local identity of the valley over the period of time that the doctor had worked there. In this chapter I develop the secondary argument about local, Welsh identity. One point of clarification is necessary. Though this ceremony was held in public, in a converted cinema, and was attended by 300 persons, it falls within the domain of 'intimate' culture because the guests were invited by the celebrant personally or came as a result of an open invitation to valley dwellers on a first come basis. The public in fact consisted of intimate associates, local dignitaries and veteran patients. This was a social gathering of the local and the loyal suffused with emotion.

IDENTITY IN GENERAL

An identity crisis is something peculiarly characteristic of the modern industrial and post-industrial world. 'Who am I?' and 'What am I?'

are the questions most frequently posed by persons seeking to identify and locate themselves in society. Contemporary questions about social identity have shifted from an emphasis on that of the collectivity – 'Who are we?' or 'What are we?' which is the question asked of nineteenth- and twentieth-century nationalists – to stress the predicament of the individual, for example, 'Who am I?'

In 'tribal' or 'primitive' societies this crisis did not arise either for individuals or the group: 'We [are] the people' is what tribesmen said of themselves, thereby bestowing the title of human solely upon themselves and denying humanity to others. Indeed, in many cases they did not have a distinctive name for themselves, just simply 'people'. The names which they are known by have been allocated to them by outsiders – missionaries, traders, colonial administrators, perhaps even anthropologists.

With the rise of the nation-state national identity has been allocated by the state in the form of identity cards or passports which declare one to be a citizen of such a state but which might also record a secondary identity in terms of ethnicity, for example, Uzbek, Tartar or Jew in the former USSR; or in Israel the second identity might be religious, for example, Muslim, Jew, Christian.

All identities emerge though social interaction and the interplay of two processes which define one's identity, one definition derives from the individual and consists of how she/he sees her- himself; for example, 'I am an Englishman' or 'I am a Welsh woman' or 'I am a Jew'. However, the process of self-definition is a necessary but insufficient criterion to sustain that identity vis-a-vis others. A relevant example comes from John Dollard's classic study of Alabama in the 1930s, *Caste and Class in Southerntown*, in which he cites the case of a black man who entered a 'whites only' compartment on a train and was forcibly ejected despite his plaintive plea, 'Boss, I'se resigned from de colored race' (1957: 60). In the context of a Jim Crow South, the black man's assertion carried insufficient weight because racial identity was and is subject not only to self-definition but also to the acceptance or rejection of others. Indeed, it often happens that an identity rejected by a person or group is categorically imposed upon them. A classic case is that of the Jew who converts to Christianity, but who is still defined as a Jew by non-Jews. In this manner the identity of some Western Jews is 'inauthentic' and imposed by the force of social stereotyping or anti-semitism. It is a situation in which you do not have to be Jewish to be a Jew. The difficulty of dealing with stereotypes and stigmatised identities is shared by Jews and other 'minorities' though the precise response may differ.

WELSH IDENTITY

Welsh identity, like many national identities, is a slippery concept: it is both distinctive and nebulous. Welshness is particularly manifest and salient at its boundaries and when contrasted with other identities. As Bowie observes,

The English are an essential ingredient in Welsh identity, not in making the people what they are, but providing a symbol of what they are not. It is in opposition to Englishness that Welshness is defined. (1993: 190)

We should not jump to the conclusion that Welshness is a negative entity – that which is not English – an empty vessel to be filled with cultural bric-a-brac. There are positive elements in Welsh identity which are based on a cluster of geographic, historic and linguistic components (Balsom 1985: 2). The territory of Wales is brought into sharp relief by its border with England, the nation whose conquest, domination and near assimilation of its Celtic neighbour over several centuries is symbolised in the Act of Union (in fact annexation) of 1536 which imposed English institutions – legal, political, religious and educational – on the Welsh. Successful efforts in east and south Wales were made to suppress and eliminate the Welsh language. The English were the rulers of Wales and were seen as the archetypal Other who symbolised and possessed power. Emmett writing about northwest Wales, the heartland of Welsh language, draws a sharp distinction between what she calls '*ruling England* – a concept which includes all foreign capital and power that influences the local economy – and ... the Welsh community' (1982: 171).

With the passage of time the impact of English cultural, economic and political domination has resulted in the emergence of diverse forms of Welsh identity. Consequently, although outsiders may classify the Welsh as homogeneous, the Welsh perceive themselves as diverse groups expressing a variety of identities. The principal cognitive boundary is the primary division between Welsh-born Welsh-speakers and Welsh-born English-speakers. Native Welsh-speakers in north and west Wales stake a claim to authentic Welshness, a stance that is resented and rejected by south Walians who would be excluded by their inability to speak Welsh (Bowie 1993: 184). Balsom divides Wales into three: the Welsh-speaking Welsh are referred to as *Y Fro Gymraeg* (1985: 6). Those who identify themselves as Welsh but who do not speak the language he refers to as 'Welsh Wales'. The third area/group who neither speak Welsh nor identify as Welsh he calls 'British Wales'. Balsom's data is based on a sample survey and was intended to test the relationship between types of Welsh self-identification and voting behaviour in general elections. As he himself acknowledges, 'The technical limitations of survey analysis allow only a broad regional approach, rather than one related to individual localities' (Balsom 1985: 3). My material relates to one valley in Welsh Wales, which I shall call Coal Valley, and allows a somewhat detailed exploration of aspects of the 'intimate' culture of the locality as a means of grasping the complexity of Welsh identity.

Coal Valley is one of a series of mining valleys which run parallel to one another on a north–south axis in the south Wales coalfield which stretches 60 miles from east to west. This is the area of Balsom's Welsh Wales which has a generic Valley Welsh identity but which also has strong, individual, local valley identities. On the whole this is an English-speaking area but as one moves westward of Swansea more Welsh is spoken. However, there are pockets of Welsh-speakers in individual valleys and recently some Welsh-speaking schools have been established. The 'Welshness' of these valleys has tended to be neglected or minimised in earlier analyses which have stressed the mining and class identities of the people and the place. The emphasis on the dominant working-class, socialist identity so pervaded the literature that a recent writer on a neighbouring valley voiced his 'surprise' on finding the 'feeling of Welshness' so strong (Roberts 1994: 80). Since the closure of the last of Coal Valley's three collieries in 1983, along with that of nearly the entire coalfield, the Welshness of the population may have become more obvious and salient.

Coal Valley has a structure which it shares with similar mining valleys in south Wales giving it a segmental quality akin to that of the Nuer. These valleys may be physically distinct but they combine together, or did so in the past when the mines were operating, as a unit linked by the coal industry, the trade union movement and socialism. Activities such as choral singing, rugby, and miners' libraries, were found in each valley and gave local distinctiveness within a shared culture. Local institutions also provided a focus for local feeling voiced in part through competition and rivalry, for example in rugby. Within each valley one found diversity which resulted from the recruitment of labour for the mining industry. Immigrants came to work in the pits from other areas of Wales, England, Scotland and Ireland and from as far afield as Spain, Italy and Tsarist Russia. Members of various professions also immigrated to serve the local population. Over time strong attachments to individual valleys developed, but adherence to valley identity did not necessarily preclude a person having other identities or allegiances. The development of a strong local Coal Valley identity took on salience in particular situations but, on a day-to-day basis within the valley it was not strictly speaking exclusive of other identities. In short, Coal Valley tolerated a variety of different identities on condition that incomers demonstrated commitment, for example through residence and work, as the following ethnography of the retirement ceremony shows.

On Saturday night, 23 March 1991, the Coal Valley Welfare Committee welcomed 300 guests to the retirement presentation for Dr Lionel Strachan. I had been invited as a friend of the doctor though I was not from that valley nor a family member. Our friendship stemmed from the time I had taught him modern Hebrew during the hours when my children and his grandchildren attended religion classes on Sunday mornings at the Swansea synagogue where we both were members.

The community centre, a converted cinema, was filled to capacity with family, friends, patients and distinguished guests including the local Member of Parliament, the MP for the adjacent constituency and the mayor. The front row of seats was occupied by the retiring doctor and his immediate family, the next three rows by specially invited people whose names were affixed to the seats, and the remaining places by guests whose chairs were unnamed. This innocent seating arrangement concealed behind the scenes political manoeuvring which only became apparent afterwards when the organisers were subsequently interviewed.

The ceremony consisted of a series of performances by various groups and individuals that represented the valley and who were linked to Dr Strachan as patient and neighbour. This ceremony was the culmination of several similar but smaller events; for example, the local rugby club which he had served in a medical capacity, had received him a few weeks earlier and had given him a presentation, so too had the St John Ambulance Brigade in which Dr Strachan acted as Associate Serving Officer, and a local old folks' home. This occasion was the ceremony of ceremonies, the definitive incorporation of the doctor as he ceased to be a local general practitioner and became simply a local.

The programme and its content reflected the composition of the valley. Speakers, singers, politicians and colleagues paid their respects to the retiring doctor. There was no precedent for this particular event though retirement presentations are common in offices and factories. This occasion represented a *bricolage* and, though formal, had elements of spontaneity and intimacy. No rehearsals had occurred and the event was a one off. The ceremony was video-recorded by a local photographer/video maker. I shall now briefly describe the various parts of the ceremony in the sequence in which they occurred.

The proceedings was chaired or commèred[2] by a patient, Mrs Cooper, who stood on the stage and commenced by welcoming the guests, specifically mentioning the two Members of Parliament. She described the occasion as a sad-happy event since they were losing their doctor but they hoped that he would remain as a neighbour. She referred with precision to the length of his service – 50 years, 2 months, 3 weeks and 5 days. After these opening remarks the commère introduced the mayor who made a presentation on behalf of the local council and who hastily left the hall with the apology that he was obliged to attend another function.

The commère then presented the Coal Valley Male Voice Choir, neatly attired in dark blazers, white shirts, ties and slacks. About 50 in number, they were mainly middle-aged or old men. Their programme comprised a medley of eight songs chosen in some cases for their aptness for this particular retirement and in others for their rousing, rallying tempo. They began with the Negro spiritual 'Where Shall I Be?' and continued with 'Some Enchanted Evening', Andrew Lloyd Webber's 'Any Dream Will Do', 'Amazing Grace' with a solo voice, 'The Rose', 'Softly as I Leave You', 'Hava Nagilah', a Hebrew song, and concluded with 'The Battle Hymn of the Republic' in which the audience joined enthusiastically.

The seriousness of the choir was followed by a comedienne, a patient of Dr Strachan and a semi-professional entertainer. She commenced her act by praising the doctor but remarked that he did, alas, suffer from a major defect, namely that after 50 years' residence in the valley he still retained his broad Scottish accent and did not speak like a valley person. (Dr Strachan was born and brought up in the Gorbals, Glasgow, and graduated from that city's university.) She adopted the persona and accent of a Professor Bronwen Rees-Jones from Cardiff, 'a real Welsh lady through and through'. She declared that she would give a lecture on 'How to talk tidy and speak more like us', that is she would discuss 'the Art of Wenglish', or Welsh-English as it was spoken in the valley and particularly in that locale, since 'foreigners begin at Cardiff', immediately corrected to 'Porthcawl and Bridgend'. She gave examples of Wenglish that included repeated usage of the word 'tidy', for example, 'he's got a tidy bit in the bank'. Various double-entendres including the well-known one of 'being in bed under the doctor' were well received. She urged her audience to be considerate when giving advice to foreigners who visited the valley. Thus, those who sought directions should not be told 'it's a tidy step' but 'it's a long way'. What were foreigners to make of the phrase, 'Don't give it to me now, give it to me again', or even more confusing, 'Don't give it to me now, give it to me now next'? She concluded her act by urging her audience to 'be kind to foreigners'.

The commère, who was Chairman of the Valley Welfare Council, recited a poem entitled 'To Dr Strachan' that she had composed in his honour. She indicated to a knowing audience that she was not only his patient but also a seamstress and tailoress who had worked for him in that capacity over the years. The poem commenced with the doctor's arrival in the area during the war and wondered how long he would stay since there had been a turnover of doctors in the valley; it continued by noting the disappearance of the collieries and ended by remarking on Dr Strachan's enduring and continued presence.

Humour gave way to song when the comedienne teamed up with another female patient to sing karaoke duets from the musical *Chess*, one of which was 'I Know Him So Well', another was 'You are the Wind Beneath my Wings' containing the line 'Did you ever know you are my hero?'

The next item was a tape recording. The doctor's granddaughter, a young woman of 20, and a novice broadcaster for a local radio station, had recorded an interview a few weeks earlier with the well-known Welsh comedy actor, Windsor Davies, who had been starring in a Christmas pantomime at a Cardiff theatre. Windsor had met Lionel a few years previously when both had been awarded a prize by the

Coal Valley Council. Windsor Davies recalled the occasion, regretted that he could not attend the retirement in person and joked that he wanted a sick note from the doctor so that he could evade a Saturday matinee performance in order to attend the Wales–England rugby match. His message to Lionel was 'good luck and God bless you Dr Strachan', ending with the hope that they would get together again for a drink or two.

Another duet from two female singers performed the song 'I Dreamed a Dream' from the musical *Les Misérables*.

The Townswomen's Choir then mounted the platform and sang six songs. This choir, smaller than the male voice choir, was composed mainly of older women dressed in pink blouses and long black skirts. They commenced with 'Oklahoma', the eponymous song of that musical, and then performed 'Eli Jenkins' Prayer' from *Under Milk Wood*; next came 'The Colours of My Life', followed by the Jewish lullaby 'Schlaf Mein Kind' sung in Yiddish and English. The leader of the choir prefaced this last piece with the information that Dr Strachan himself had taught them the song for a performance at an Eisteddfod 15 years earlier. The next song was introduced by a statement which pointedly declared that they were a Welsh Choir and would sing a song in Welsh (unlike the Male Voice Choir) composed by Daniel Prothero. They concluded their repertoire with a rousing, lusty rendition of the 'Gypsy Wedding Ring'.

The first half of the celebrations, the musical and comic programme ended and the next half commenced. Dr Strachan's wife, Patricia, was presented with a large bouquet of flowers on behalf of the patients by Mrs Elaine Jones, who noted that behind every doctor there must be someone at the end of the telephone. This presentation was followed by the longest speech of the evening delivered by Councillor Kate Bittle. She recalled Dr Strachan's involvement with the valley and described him as 'our beloved doctor' and spoke of the days when there were three collieries in the valley (now there are none); in those days men earned less than £3 per week, accidents were common and the doctor would go underground to treat sick and injured men. Medical facilities were poor; patients had to travel to hospitals in Cardiff for treatment until shortly after the end of the Second World War when 'Neartown' acquired a hospital.

Councillor Bittle pointed out that miners had run their own Medical Aid scheme before the advent of the National Health Service (NHS) whereby they paid local doctors to treat their members. Miners could be treated in the local surgery which had a dispensary so that there was no need to go outside the valley for treatment. 'Now we have to go to Neartown and queue.' With such sparse medical facilities the family doctor became extremely important. She referred to the political legacy of the Thatcher era which had increased unemployment in the valley and observed, with some satisfaction as she addressed Dr Strachan directly, 'Maggie Thatcher decided you should retire but in the end Thatcher went before you' (a reference to the latter's ousting as Prime Minister and Leader of the Conservative Party which had occurred a few months earlier). She noted that Lionel and Patricia had spent their golden wedding anniversary in Jerusalem last year, and remarked that 'we selfishly hated you going on holiday, we never felt safe without you'.

Councillor Bittle then presented Dr Strachan with the proceeds of a public collection that had raised £1300. She remarked how collectors had gone from house to house. She herself had personally collected and could tell many stories but would relate only one: she was refused by one woman who had said, 'Sorry but I changed my doctor last week.' From the money, £300 had been spent on a video recorder and the £1000 balance was contained in a cardboard tube wrapped in paper decorated with white heather and tied with a tartan ribbon. She remarked that it was given with love and appreciation and concluded her speech with the words, 'Well done our good and faithful servant.'[3]

The next speaker was Dr Strachan's medical partner, Dr Patel, an Indian, who described his friendship and quasi-kinship with Lionel. He recalled how he had first encountered his future partner in Porthcawl in a newsagent's shop when each was sporting their professional emblem, a stethoscope hanging out of their pockets. They had not exchanged a word but nevertheless noticed each other; a few days later Dr Patel replied to an advertisement for a medical partner and arrived in the valley for an interview. In pouring rain he mounted the formidable steps that led to Lionel's house, knocked on his door and to their mutual amazement they recognised each other from their earlier, silent encounter. Dr Strachan accepted him into the practice, the first Indian doctor in the valley.

Dr Patel spoke warmly of the kindness of both Lionel and his wife, Patricia, 'it was like with my own people', 'he [Lionel] looked after my children like his grandchildren'; 'they are my relations'. He noted that they had been in partnership for 16 years and declared that he would 'miss someone I took for granted'.

In a moving and emotional speech Dr Strachan concluded the ceremony. He began by nervously dropping his notes which elicited sympathetic support from the audience. He paid tribute to his wife whom he described as 'a modern Florence Nightingale without a lamp but with a portable telephone'. He informed the audience about his schooldays in Glasgow where he had been taught geography by Dr Andrews'[4] father and how he had learned that Wales had four large cities, Cardiff, Swansea, Merthyr and Newport and produced much coal. He did not know much about Wales on his arrival but since then his two daughters had been born in Cardiff and his two granddaughters in Swansea. At this point he again dropped his notes. He recalled that his first visit to the valley in December 1940 had been marked by torrential rain but simultaneously blessed with a triple rainbow which he considered a good omen. However, he never did find a crock of gold at the end of it. He spoke of the 'acceptance, appreciation and honour' that he had received, including his appointment as an adjudicator in first aid at the local Eisteddfod. He devoted a considerable part of his address to the changes in medical practice during his career; when he had arrived in the valley there was no penicillin, no antibiotics; he and his patients had used goose grease as an ointment to treat chest infections; asthma had been rife; now there was more emphasis on the prevention of disease; life expectancy had increased; several diseases had been eradicated. He concluded by declaring that he had loved every minute of his 50 years in the valley.

The audience warmly applauded him and sang 'For He's a Jolly Good Fellow', followed by three cheers. Members of the audience approached him and the women kissed him and the men shook his hand. At the buffet supper after the reception one of the guests, herself a great-grandmother, informed me that Dr Strachan had treated six generations of her family.

COMMENTARY AND ANALYSIS

What can be learned about the social identity of Coal Valley and its inhabitants from an examination of this ceremony? Beyond the valley, what can be adduced about Wales and its position in the UK? There is the usual tension here between the particularity of 'Wales' as a place and social entity, and the generalising, theoretical concerns of the disciplines' of sociology and anthropology. If we emphasise academic arguments, then Wales becomes a chance locale in which to conduct our sociological and anthropological craft; the principal concern tends to shift away from the particularity of Wales and/or Welshness. As a sociological–anthropologist I too share a concern with overarching structural issues, though I feel uneasy about the relegation of place, people and culture. The focus on social–structural features in British anthropology and sociology has downgraded the status of culture in our research, while American cultural anthropology has tended to focus on the nitty gritty of cultural specificity to the neglect of social structure.

One response to the failure to combine cultural specificity with sociological generality is that of Anthony Cohen, editor of *Belonging*, subtitled *Identity and Social Organisation in British Rural Cultures*. Note his emphasis on the rural[5] whereas I am concerned with an industrial (or formerly industrial) valley; nevertheless the general issue is the same, namely to tease out the sense of local distinctiveness from the broad canvas of British society. Cohen in fact does argue that his concern with peripheral cultures need not be restricted to geographical peripherality but can include marginal areas, by which he presumably means those which are economically and socially marginal (1982: 6). Coal Valley is, in Cohen's sense, a marginal area.

The retirement ceremony represented a tribute to a man, a general practitioner, who had chosen to spend the whole of his professional life in a remote and economically marginal part of Britain. The audience was fully aware that he had not been obliged to live and work amongst them because it had proved difficult both to recruit and to retain doctors. This message was transmitted both to Dr Strachan and to the audience in the praise poem composed by the commère. The audience were acknowledging his loyalty, dedication and commitment to their valley and to them. He had joined, identified with and remained among them for 50 years, in short his commitment meant that he belonged there. He had almost become one of them, by putting down roots he had become a fixture. What was the nature of the community that he had joined? The commère's hope that Lionel would remain a neighbour intimated that as a professional person who had entered the valley as a stranger his contractual obligations to the them were concluded and, like others before him, like his fellow Scot Dr Andrews, he might depart after retirement. Her hopeful plea represented an appeal to Dr Strachan in terms of moral rather than contractual claims up on him. It constituted an entreaty based on what Cohen terms 'equalitarianism', namely 'the muting of social differentiation' rather than on the hierarchical doctor–patient relationship (1982: 17). Dr Strachan's continued presence was accepted, if he so chose, not on the basis of his profession but as 'one of us'.

The major feature of the valley and the *raison d'être* for its settlement was, or had been, the coal industry. Repeated mention was made of the three collieries, none of which were in operation. Dr Strachan knew about Welsh coal from his Scottish schooldays; Councillor Bittle lamented the demise of the three pits and the consequent unemployment; mining was arduous, dangerous and poorly paid but it had supported the valley community; the miners had organised themselves so that they had local health care before the NHS was formed. Although it was not publicly stated, there was no need to since the audience knew full well, Dr Strachan had actively participated in the Medical Health Council, unlike some local doctors, and he had actively supported the subsequent development of the NHS. Though not a miner himself, he had shared their danger and risked his own life underground when accidents had occurred; he had also given expert witness in court for miners seeking compensation for work accidents and industrial diseases. Mrs Cooper in her poem likened the doctor to an institution that had endured longer than the collieries or the Workmen's Hall. They had gone but he had remained. He was so much a fixture that they had taken him for granted but now he too had retired: 'All good things have to end. Without Lionel, we've all lost a friend.'

Although the coal mines were no longer worked they remained central to popular culture and were part of a collective folk memory; there were still physical reminders of their operation such as the pit head and its winding gear. Dr Strachan was recalled in the same breath as these collieries, he had outlasted them, he too was part of the collective memory, he was a living almost mythical figure who had treated generations of patients.

In terms of social class, ethnicity and religion Dr Strachan was an outsider to a predominantly working class, Welsh, Nonconformist industrial valley. However, these aspects of his identity become less significant over time as local people perceived his commitment to the locality through his work and general behaviour. Dr Strachan and his wife manifested their loyalty to the valley over many decades residence, in part by raising their family there. And, like other families in the valley, they have seen their children migrate to pursue a career. At an individual level, local people recognise and celebrate difference in part through the bestowing of nicknames, for example, 'Stefan the Pole', 'Jack Twice' (whose name was John John), or 'Davies Llanstephan'. At least partly for this reason, Lionel and his wife did not feel the need to suppress their Jewishness (they originally joined Cardiff's Cathedral Road synagogue, later moving to the Swansea Hebrew Congregation). The participants in the ceremony acknowledged and paid tribute to Dr Strachan's Jewishness by singing Hebrew and Yiddish songs in his honour and by recalling his golden wedding anniversary in Jerusalem. Not only was he Jewish but he was a Scottish Jew, obvious from his accent so affectionately and innocently satirised in the comedy sketch.

The jocular reference to his Scottish accent simultaneously played on those elements that both linked Lionel to and separated him from indigenous valley dwellers (Radcliffe-Brown 1952). While this use of humour affectionately placed Lionel in the category of 'foreigner', the ability to gently tease him was also an index of acceptance in a collectivity that permitted and acknowledged individuality and diversity of all valley dwellers. That Lionel was not English may have been to his advantage since Celtic solidarity consisted partially in an oppositional identity to the English. It is possible that his Scottishness may have compensated for his Jewishness in the early days of his career in the valley, alternatively there may have been relatively few times when his Jewishness was relevant in local social situations.

Initially there was some concern about Dr Andrews' recruitment of a Jewish physician to his practice. The evidence for that concern is limited but indicative: Lionel informed me that an old, female patient approached him after the farewell ceremony and confided, 50 years later, that she had bluntly asked Dr Andrews why he had brought a Jew into the practice. He had replied in reassuring tones, 'There, there my dear, no need to worry, remember he's a Scot and different from the others.'

The anecdote is quite revealing. In 1941 some valley dwellers found a Scottish identity more acceptable than a Jewish or English identity. However, it also indicates that with the passage of time a stranger may, by virtue of his/her demonstrated commitment to local people, gain acceptance while retaining his/her individual difference(s). Furthermore, the anecdote indicates a willingness to confess, in private and after a 50-year relationship, one's prejudice and acknowledge its unjustified basis. The confession was, on the one hand a poignant acceptance of the doctor as a person and friend and, on the other hand reflected a marked degree of ambivalence with regard to his perceived difference from the woman towards his Jewishness and non-local status.

Lionel's social position as a doctor clearly elevated him in terms of social class, yet the retirement ceremony explicitly downplayed status difference. The ceremony manifested features of both hierarchy and equalitarianism. Thus, political leaders were introduced by name and assigned specific seats. At the same time, Lionel's personal and physical characteristics were singled out in the praise poem where specific mention was made of the need to alter his clothes because of his short, squat stature. This reference brought out his ordinary, man-of-the-people qualities. Windsor Davies, himself a famous Welsh and national figure, also played down his status by jocularly requesting a sick note to attend the international rugby match, a gesture which indicated an identification with the doctor and as a local.

Lionel's fumbling, the dropping of his notes and losing his place in his speech helped reinforce his social standing in the community; such behaviour was regarded with charity and empathy, a further sign if one were needed that he was an ordinary person, unaccustomed to public speaking and overcome by the occasion. This behaviour was characteristic of the man because, unlike many doctors of the pre-NHS epoch, Lionel had not sought to elevate himself above his patients, he had not flaunted his status but remained a man of the people. He did not distance himself from his patients but rather maintained an egalitarian manner. This was no pose for it *was* his character, formed in the deprivation of the Gorbals settled mainly by Russian-Jewish and Irish-Catholic immigrants, and informed by the same socialist principles which attracted him to the valley. He told me that when he started to practice he had been given two pieces of advice by experienced GPs: 'Make the patient feel important' and 'Remember it's the patient you don't see who dies on you', and so he made a point of seeing all of his patients and keeping in touch with them.

The extent to which Dr Strachan belonged to and participated in the community contrasted sharply with his junior partner, Dr Patel, and his former senior partner, Dr Andrews. Although Dr Patel had spent 16 years in the practice, he had yet to gain the acceptance accorded to his senior partner. I tentatively suggest several reasons for the different presentations of self offered by the three medical doctors employed in the practice. The reasons relate to the different styles in which each doctor presented his professional authority, which in turn are linked to their ethnic and psychological backgrounds.

Dr Strachan's predecessor, Dr Andrews, resided in the valley and behaved as Lord of the Manor, holding banquets at his home where his wife convened embroidery classes for the wives of the local professionals and gentry. He commenced his practice in the days before the NHS when medical doctors were remote and powerful figures to working–class patients. He knew his place and they knew theirs, and the gulf between them was wide.

Dr Strachan presented himself as a man of the people, in a modest, unassuming manner, which he carried with him from his Glasgow, Jewish ghetto background. He minimised social distance and made himself available; his appearance was unthreatening, his suits not too fashionable with a homespun quality, bought off the peg and altered by the local seamstress.

Dr Patel, Indian and Catholic, adopted yet another professional strategy. The first Indian doctor to practise in the valley, he nevertheless chose to live outside the valley, literally distancing himself from his patients; he also dressed in impeccably tailored suits. Intentionally or not the remark that Dr Lionel's patients did not feel safe when he was away in Jerusalem represented a slight rebuke to Dr Patel.

In terms of 'foreignness', Dr Strachan's Scottish and Jewish identities were perhaps easier for locals to bridge than Dr Patel's Indianness and Catholicism. Dr Strachan's downplaying of his professional role eased incorporation into local society, whereas Dr Patel's emphasis of his medical position tended to stress formality in his self-presentation. Social interaction based on five decades of equality and service contributed to a measure of solidarity with the local community resulting, in the public arena at least, in the relegation of differences of class, ethnicity and religion to a secondary position. Dr Strachan was not seen as a member of the English ruling class,[6] he was not remote from people, quite the opposite since he enjoyed frequent and daily interaction with them. Rather he was perceived as a servant whose work and presence benefited the community (recall Councillor Bittle's acknowledgement, 'Well done *our* good and faithful servant').

The ceremony can be considered as a rite of incorporation, the ultimate accolade (Fortes 1962: 56). We would expect that the various parties participating in this rite possess different perceptions. On a strictly personal level, Dr Strachan's medical career is ending, and with it his professional role and working life. His wife and family undoubtedly also have a somewhat different view, retirement might reasonably be expected to create time for leisure and family. Within the local community doubts have been expressed about his departure: will his successor adequately fill Dr Strachan's shoes? Will the nature of the practice change? To what extent has an era of personal service and loyalty to locality ended with the doctor's retirement?

The most overt of political statements was made by a local Labour councillor, Mrs Bittle, one of the two main organisers of the ceremony. A veteran of the valley, she compressed a considerable amount of history into her speech. She made the link between Dr Strachan, local history, coal mining and social and medical welfare. A major theme of her address was the poverty of the wartime period when the doctor arrived and the hardship suffered by the miners and their families in those days. Coupled with this narrative of suffering was a proud recollection of the steps taken by the mining community to tackle its problems, an account that stressed sturdy independence and mutual interdependence manifest in the creation and operation of a local medical scheme that anticipated and in some respects was superior to the NHS since residents had no need to leave the valley to seek medical assistance.

In this respect the valley had recently seen regress rather than progress. Her quip about Margaret Thatcher's demise linked Dr Strachan's compulsory redundancy, brought about by recent legislation that compelled doctors over the age of 70 to retire, to the rise of unemployment in the valley as a result of the policies of Margaret Thatcher's government. The doctor too, was portrayed as a victim, like the miners, of a malign central government that did not care about a Welsh mining valley. Just as he had identified with them by his commitment to the valley, so he had suffered their fate, an enforced end to his working life.

I have tried to show in this chapter how an examination of a particular and very special occasion can illuminate our understanding of a South Wales industrial valley. The discussion has shown how a stranger in terms of class, ethnicity and religion has been incorporated into the local community by virtue of a lifetime of dedicated service. The various elements of his identity that distanced him from the indigenous, Welsh population have, in the context of the doctor's retirement ceremony, been set aside because of his proven allegiance to the place. These elements were not, indeed are not, irrelevant since they are noted and, to a degree, celebrated, but at this time they are insignificant.

As Simmel points out, the stranger is in a relationship with a group into which he was not born but to which he has become attached, in this case as an occupant of a specific professional role. In the absence of an 'organic connection' to the locality, it is the professional role (with its orientation outside the community), which he imports into his social relations with local people. Easily able to pack up and move on, medical doctors inject a degree of 'objectivity' and formality to their social relations with patients which are characteristically somewhat ambivalent, 'he is near and far *at the same time*' (Simmel 1964: 407, emphasis in the original). Simmel argues that the tension between nearness and distance causes the stranger to be conceived of not as an individual person but as 'a stranger of a particular type' (1964: 407). In other words, Simmel is suggesting that a stranger is not seen as a person but as a member of a category. His nearness is only a nearness in *general* terms and so too is his distance.

My material highlights and qualifies the value of Simmel's concept of the stranger as one who is perceived in categorical rather than in individual terms, for long-term residence may give rise to qualitatively different, non-formal social interaction. At the same time, we need to pay attention not only to possible long-term changes in status and identity, but also to the significance of social context in which certain aspects of individual/group identity may be played down or stressed. It is true that early in his career Dr Strachan was seen by locals in categorical terms as a Jew and as a doctor, and that his medical partner, perhaps for public relations reasons, talked up his Scottish identity. However, as time elapsed and as Dr Strachan and his family became more integrated into the local community through his medical work, so his Jewish and Scottish identity became elements of an overall professional identity shaped fundamentally by his role as a doctor. Moreover, his Jewishness, which distinguished him from others, was tapped and put into the service of local Welsh valley culture. Thus Dr

Strachan taught Yiddish and Hebrew songs for performance at the local Eisteddfod. In my opinion his acceptance as an individual was facilitated by the character of coal valley itself and by his personal conduct.

The valley's history from the nineteenth century was based on a coal industry which had attracted immigrants from Wales and Europe; at different stages it had also seen its own sons and daughters emigrate. Hence though Coal Valley was a close-knit community it was not, strictly speaking, an insular or parochial place. It inhabitants had experienced national political, religious and social ideas and practices and had accommodated a diversity of people. Dr Strachan too, as I have shown, immersed himself in the locality in a variety of ways and not just as a professional. Sure of his own identity as a Jew, a Scot, a medical practitioner and a socialist, over time he became immersed in social relationships with the entire community as a result of which local people came to perceive him as an individual – that is, a person, a neighbour, a father and so on – sharing common attributes with the community *and* as a social person manifesting specific formal, objective characteristics relating to his profession, his ethnicity, and so on.

It should not surprise us that different aspects of his identity became salient in different social contexts, and that involvement in different activities and contexts undoubtedly meant different things to different people: the ceremony discussed above was simultaneously a retirement ceremony and a means by which to mark and celebrate the identity of the locality and of its people; the culmination of a personal career that touched many people, and an ambivalent leave-taking for an individual who was never really a local.

The analysis has also demonstrated how the celebration of local difference, especially Welsh identity and the sub–identity of valley, is acknowledged in a spontaneous performance which involved poetry, singing, humour and speeches carrying a political message to a knowing audience.

What we see in the ceremony is a representation and celebration of local identity. Localism is a representation of group identity. On this particular occasion, it also constitutes a restatement of a shared though threatened group identity. The citizens of the valley were in fact expressing opposition to their own communal extinction. By asserting themselves through a ritualised leave-taking and through recalling their history they are saying 'we are here and we would like to stay here' (Nadel–Klein 1991: 514).

Dr Strachan's retirement provided an occasion to redefine community, in part by retelling the valley's history, particularly significant for the older generation who organised and attended the ceremony. That past was characterised by hardship, suffering, communal organisation. The occasion celebrated the valley's accomplishment by honouring the accomplishments of man who was closely tied up with its history and who, in this context, stood in as its symbol.

The ceremony was a collective event that included Lionel's social network of family, friends and residents of the valley. While formally marking his retirement, the ceremony celebrated the different components of his identity at the same time as it remarked upon the celebrants' own sense of shared history, of belonging together. Since van Gennep's classic research (1960) it has become a truism to look at how a person's status changes through the lifecycle. The emphasis in anthropological studies has been on ceremonies relating to birth, adolescence, marriage and death, but as Myerhoff observes little has been written 'on the adult life cycle in our society' (1982: 127). This chapter, to a modest degree, addresses that gap in the literature though further research on ceremonies of retirement clearly remains to be done.

Though retirement may often go unremarked, Coal Valley took the opportunity to observe the occasion and to commemorate a lifetime of service to a community that itself had experienced traumatic change. Lionel's retirement became a collective event whereby group values, the history of the locality and the identity of Coal Valley were celebrated and affirmed by focusing on one person. In some respects Lionel was an atypical representative on whom to focus since he was a stranger – a Scot, a Jew, and a medical doctor. When he first entered Coal Valley there was some ambivalence, even hostility expressed towards him. The Scottish and Jewish identities into which Lionel had been born were not unconnected with his arrival in the valley as a doctor. He acquired an occupational identity at an early stage of the adult lifecycle which became his most significant identity in the valley, and which retirement subsequently divested him of. Long-term, professional service coupled with a lifetime of residence served to incorporate him into Coal Valley society. Residence involved an engagement in local life such as going down the mines, judging Eisteddfod activities, attending rugby matches, sending his children to local schools and participating in church and chapel services for the *rites de passage* of his patients. Living in the community, and being available at all hours of the day and night to provide medical care, meant that his Scottish-Jewish identity was sublimated to or became secondary to his professional role.

Over 50 years he had become a local, part of 'Welsh Wales', as attested to by his abiding commitment and attachment to the valley. As Cohen notes, 'Very often, to remain in these communities is itself an expression of commitment' (1982: 6). His Welsh identity was not acquired at the cost of excluding or disavowing his ethnic and religious identity, rather it had been added to them. Lionel was a Scot, a Jew and a socialist in Coal Valley simultaneously, and the ceremony clearly also bestowed a local identity upon him; as such his life and retirement became an appropriate symbol of and occasion to embody the valley's complex and diverse history and identity.

NOTES

1. An earlier version of this chapter was given at the European Association of Social Anthropologists' Conference, Prague, 28–31 August 1992; an abbreviated version has been published (Mars 1994). I have changed the names and disguised the location of the valley. Dr Lionel Strachan died in February 1992.
2. *Oxford English Dictionary* (2nd edition) vol. III (1989: 533) defines commère as a female announcer.
3. An adaptation of the phrase from the Gospel of St Matthew 25: 21.
4. Dr Andrews recruited Lionel to Coal Valley as his medical partner in 1941.
5. Nevertheless, despite his sub-title, one of the studies in his volume deals with a Welsh industrial town, Blaenau Ffestiniog, examined by Isabel Emmett.
6. Contrast with Emmett's discussion of class and of the role of professionals in a North Wales industrial town (Emmett 1982: 173ff.).

REFERENCES

Balsom, D. 1985. 'The three Wales model', in J. Osmond (ed.) *The National Question Again: Welsh Political Identity in the 1980s*. Llandysul: Gomer, pp. 1–17.

Bowie, F. 1993. 'Wales from within: conflicting interpretations of Welsh identity', in S. Macdonald (ed.) *Inside European Identities*. Oxford: Berg, pp. 167–93.

Cohen, A. (ed.). 1982. *Belonging: Identity and Organisation in British Rural Cultures*. Manchester: Manchester University Press.

Day, G. and D. Thomas (eds). 1994. *Contemporary Wales: An Annual Review of Economic and Social Research*, vol. 17. Cardiff: University of Wales Press.

Dollard, J. 1957 [1937]. *Caste and Class in Southerntown*. New York: Doubleday.

Emmett, I. 1982. 'Fe godwn ni eto: stasis and change in a Welsh industrial town', in A. Cohen (ed.) *Belonging: Identity and Organisation in British Rural Cultures*. Manchester: Manchester University Press, pp. 165–97.

Epstein, A.L. 1978. *Ethos and Identity*. London: Tavistock.

Evans-Pritchard, E.E. 1940. *The Nuer*. Oxford: Oxford University Press.

Fortes, M. 1962. 'Ritual and office in tribal society', in M. Gluckman (ed.) *Essays on the Ritual of Social Relations*. Manchester: Manchester University Press, pp. 53–88.

Gluckman, M. 1958 [1942]. *Analysis of a Social Situation in Modern Zululand*. Rhodes-Livingstone Paper No. 28. Manchester: Manchester University Press.

Loudon, J.B. 1961. 'Kinship and crisis in South Wales', *British Journal of Sociology* 12: 333–50.

Mars, L. 1994. 'The incorporation of a stranger: analysis of a social situation in a Welsh valley', *The Jewish Journal of Sociology* 36 (1): 19–26.

Mitchell, J.C. 1956. *The Kalela Dance*, Rhodes-Livingstone Paper No. 27. Manchester: Manchester University Press.

Myerhoff, B. 1982. 'Rites of passage: process and paradox', in V.W. Turner (ed.) *Celebration: Studies in Festivity and Ritual*. Washington, DC: Smithsonian Institution Press, pp. 109–35.

Nadel-Klein, J. 1991. 'Reweaving the fringe: localism, tradition, and representation in British ethnography', *American Anthropologist* 93: 500–17.

Osmond, J. (ed). 1985. *The National Question Again: Welsh Political Identity in the 1980s*. Llandysul: Gomer.

Radcliffe-Brown, A.R. 1952. 'On joking relationships', in *Structure and Function in Primitive Society*. London: Cohen and West, pp. 90–104.

Roberts, B. 1994. 'Welsh identity in a former mining valley: social images and imagined communities', in G. Day and D. Thomas *Contemporary Wales: An Annual Review of Economic and Social Research*, vol. 17. Cardiff: University of Wales Press, pp. 77–95.

Simmel, G. 1964 [1908]. 'The Stranger', in K.W. Wolff (ed.) *The Sociology of Georg Simmel*. New York: The Free Press, pp. 402–8.

Turner, V.W. (ed.) 1982. *Celebration: Studies in Festivity and Ritual.* Washington, DC: Smithsonian Institution Press.

van Gennep, A. 1960 [1909]. *The Rites of Passage*. London: Routledge.

10 THE ORGANISATION OF DEVELOPMENT AS AN ILLNESS: ABOUT THE METASTASIS OF GOOD INTENTIONS

Philip Quarles van Ufford

Since the world drives to a delirious state of things, we must drive to a delirious point of view. (J. Baudrillard 1990)

Having read somewhat erratically in the various branches of the social sciences for some time now, I have the feeling that a serendipitous pattern can be discerned in terms of major changes in the premises of our understanding of human culture – changes which are taking place simultaneously, but whose interrelationships are not clearly understood. Our perceptions of – to come directly to the issue which I shall address – the rationality of the development effort are being transformed fundamentally, yet we may only be partially able to grasp its manifestations.

The theme which I shall address in this chapter is the following: how can we understand the paradox that meticulously applied development policies almost automatically lead to systematic failure? What is it that goes wrong? How can the dynamics of this paradox be explained? Why is the rationality assumed in various models of public administration and the policy process only valid to some extent? Why, and at what point, does the effort to increase a development policy's rationality turn sour with regard to its 'effectiveness', 'impact' or any other symbol of administrative rationality one might wish to apply?

The concepts and metaphors relating to illness and metastasis are helpful to gain a better understanding of the complex dynamics of the development policy process. Conventional theories of public administration seem to assume too linear a model of rational behaviour, a problem I shall return to. What causes the milk of human kindness to turn sour? Why do systematic applications of good intentions lead to their 'metastasis' and to a serious outbreak of disease which may literally harm those who are exposed to it, administrators as well as so-called beneficiaries?

In this chapter I shall put forward three interrelated theses concerning development policy practices. First, the practice of implementing development policy occurs in a kind of 'natural' contradiction to the that of formulating policy and defining intentions. Second, the various actors and institutions involved in the overall development policy process share one specific 'defensive' point of view: they speak and officially act as if the contradiction between intentions, implementation and outcomes can be overcome by good management. Or, even worse, as if such contradictions can be ignored. In the short run the image of manageable development may be upheld, but in the longer term unintended and potentially dangerous consequences result from such a position.

All this, however, leads to my third thesis, namely that such contradictions result in increasing disorder, turbulence, dismay, and in the gradual erosion of the vitality of development institutions. Good intentions turn sour, actors come to find themselves under increasing stress, and an empty exploitation of practical understandings, skills and commitments sets in.

I shall refer to organisation and chaos theory, and to Jean Baudrillard, the 'deliriously' perceptive lonely wolf of French social science. What I learn from these sources corroborates some of the suggestions made by A.L. Epstein (1992) in his discussion of the shortcomings of an anthropology which stresses the cognitive at the expense of emotive dimensions of human life. However, I shall apply Bill Epstein's criticism of conventional anthropology in a different way by arguing against the biases of cognitive metaphors in the analysis of development policy practice.

Following Epstein's argument, we may indeed have to reassess certain anthropological notions which are manifest in popular 'constructivist' metaphors developed since the early 1980s. It is highly instructive to look at the catalogues of major social science publishers where it becomes evident from book titles that, following a decade of postmodern analysis, social scientists have preferred to understand human society as if it were the product of the minds of (social) engineers. There is an enormous proliferation of book titles associated with calculation, designing and planning which employ metaphors about the 'construction', 'invention', and 'making' of this or that social phenomena. The idea that culture, organisations and policies are being rationally planned, on the drawing tables of human engineers as it were, has become dominant since the early 1980s. However, the notion that organisations may not so much be designed as born, and that this birth may be accompanied by a lot of pain and suffering, is not widely understood. On the contrary, the preference for intellectual, macho metaphors is also evident in the popularity of metaphors derived from politics (the negotiation of meaning and so on) and of war (battlefields, arenas, target groups). It is indeed quite clear that the dimensions of planning, politicking and fighting in human interaction have been overemphasised at the expense of other dimensions.

Yet, as mentioned above, I have the feeling that there *is* more at stake than so far mentioned. While conventional notions of the manageability of development have been under attack for some time, strangely enough these deconstructive efforts have not provided alternative political and/or cultural policy options. In the study of development policy since the early 1980s we have lost sight of the need to rephrase the ethical, moral, and indeed metaphysical questions of what constitutes development – about what is right and what is wrong, and what can best be done about it (Bauman 1993).

POLICY ANALYSIS: LINES, CIRCLES AND TURBULENCE

Baudrillard (1990) has suggested that we are now facing a post-metaphorical phase in which the notion of meaningful reference has been lost. As he sees it, words and action move around in increasingly erratic and even dangerous ways. The notions of order and purpose have been lost in our state of hyper-modernity. What has happened?

In an overview of organisation theory, Broekstra (1992) distinguishes three phases through which our scientific approach to organisational phenomenon has been moving. The first two phases can be characterised by the prevalent metaphors of each: organisations have been perceived as *machines*, and as *organisms*. These two metaphors resemble one another in the sense that they share notions of order and assume the manageability of social change. Organisations can be effective, the two images tell us, although this effectiveness differs. Conceived of as machines, organisations are designed to change their environment. They are 'tools', 'things' which are constructed to achieve a goal or fulfil some need. Organisational rationality and process can be studied by examining the 'costs' of achieving specified goals.

The relationship between an organisation and its environment is conceived differently if one makes use of the metaphor of organism. When conceived of as organisms, organisations are primarily seen to be confronted with changing environments. The basic questions are not related to either the question of effectiveness or the organisation's capacity to change the environment. Conceived of as organisms, organisations must primarily adapt to external transformation and consequently change their internal functioning in order not to perish. The key notion is 'survival', with all sorts of struggles and battles which must be fought in order to be successful. The concept of manageability in a way is turned inside out when compared to the machine metaphor, in that survival takes precedence over substantive rationality. But in both cases the promises of the manageability of social change prevail: one can 'conquer' and change the environment when adequate machinery is available; or, when the organisation is sufficiently flexible to adapt to the external transformations it will be able to survive.

The assumption of manageability and the promise of effectiveness through 'rational' engineering or adaptation, however, are left behind in the third phase which is characterised by a new mode of looking at the relationships between an organisation and its environments. One can no longer take for granted any rationality of goals and means or of survival. While we are uncertain about the transformation of the environments in which organisations operate, the organisations themselves are unpredictable and change in erratic ways which cannot be fully explained as a response to external changes. The transformations within the organisations as well as in their environment occur at the same time without being conditioned by one another. They just seem to happen. Now the images of manageability engendered by many a reassuring metaphor – brains, systems, bodies, machines and so on (see Morgan 1986) – are no longer appealing. Notions of order and disorder as interrelated phenomena are emerging. Organisation and the eclipse of any sort of discernible order now seem to occur at the same time and may even be interrelated processes. In this formulation order, be it internal or external, cannot be taken for granted nor can it provide a baseline for analysis.

In their introduction to chaos theory, Briggs and Peat (1990: 47–9) elegantly elaborate and contextualise the three notions mentioned above: the rationality of the engineer designing machines; the rationality of organisms trying to survive; and organisations and their environments transforming in erratic ways at the same time. They suggest that we should think of these three stages as alternative theories of organisations in that the metaphors may be of value in certain contexts and *not* in others.

Briggs and Peat describe what happens to the water of a small gently flowing stream guided by the force of gravity. When increased pressure is applied and more water starts to flow all of a sudden the lines of the stream may turn into circles, with increasing amounts of water not only flowing faster downhill but also remaining in place. When the speed of the water is increased it starts going in more directions. Next to the lines we can see an increasing number of circles. The water, moving faster and faster, also remains in place. Gravity, as well as the lines of force generated by the circles, increasingly directs the flow of the water.

When the pressure on the stream is further increased as a result of even more water entering it, the two-dimensional order of the circle is also broken and the water may go up and down, to and fro, rushing in all sorts of directions at the same time, even upstream. Vortices appear, and the stream becomes unpredictable and dangerous. No order is discernible any more.

The key concepts for the three stages in which the water flows are: *lines*, *circles* and *turbulence*. There is some similarity to the three stages which were distinguished above:

(a) organisations are guided by the forces of goals and means;
(b) organisations adapt themselves to changed circumstances and so change in order to survive; and
(c) organisations and their environments consist of erratic and unpredictable movements, which result in the two preceding kinds of order being dissipated.

There is some value in looking at the relevance of these different conceptualisations for an understanding of policy processes.

(a) A great number of theories exist which adopt the point of view of one set of actors as their focus. In this view each organisation is based upon a particular set of hopes, intentions, perhaps even interests to be achieved through central planning, decentralisation or participation. Any handbook of comparative public administration tells about this approach. In this category we may place so called 'emic' theories, popular for a while among some anthropologists because they promised an understanding of political process from 'the' participants' (note the inclusive plural) point of view, as opposed to an ethnocentric modern conceptualisation.

Other actors are defined in terms of a 'context', they are seen as 'constraints' or tools, they become 'thing-like' and neatly classified – or so it seems – rather predictably as 'the' problem of underdevelopment.

Observe, however, that these theories are all voluntaristic in the sense that each takes the world view of one particular group of actors as a baseline for theorising and constructing a particular rationality. In developmental sociology this was the period when the mood of anger or imperial benevolence in the post-colonial phase prevailed and the agenda of the development enterprise was constituted.

(b) Following upon earlier developmental 'moods of doing', whether of anger or benevolence in early development studies, much work has emerged since the late 1970s in which academics dissociated themselves from practice altogether and took pride in being able to distance themselves from and 'grin' at the developers. We saw the emergence of a metaphoric mood, referred to above: all of a sudden everything was constructed, invented or negotiated, including organisations (if we look at the tradition of 'bureaucratic politics' in political science) as well as traditions, tribes, villages, indigenous or modern knowledge, to mention only a few discussed in anthropology. The first phase organisational theory which we might call 'reflected doing' was replaced by a dissociation from practice. Increasingly, deconstruction was seen to be constructive, and a facile imprisonment in the increasingly isolated and politically irrelevant corridors of universities was regarded as a precondition for and symbol of serious academic work.

In a way development theory and practice, and the deconstructive irony to which these gave rise, must be seen as birds of a feather. The postmodern critiques depended mostly on the practices carried out by others whose minds were still clouded by the now unfashionable and thus 'unscientific' ideologies associated with actually doing something. There was some sort of hidden assumption that deconstructive analyses were a precondition for better policy making, better construction work, better inventions or negotiations in the policy process. But before this hidden assumption could be made explicit and debated, scholars and practitioners had run back to their separate places, perhaps in the belief that some sort of 'invisible hand' would finish the good work for them.

The emergence and increasing popularity of the postmodern mood and studies added to the pressures exerted on those still involved in development policy and practice. Increased insecurity, loss of purpose, feelings of irrelevance, in short all sorts of 'turbulence' began to occur as a result.

(c) My use of chaos theory becomes clear, I hope, by applying some of its heuristic consequences to the fascinating ethnographic study of policy analysis, and especially to development policy 'movements'. This is a field in which the interconnectedness of order and chaos can be discerned most clearly, with optimistic notions of purposeful manageability going hand in hand with a formidable series of so-called failures and dangerous turbulence. As I see it, we are faced with a situation in which different sets of actors swimming in the stream of development are confronting various, often conflicting and erratic forces of gravitation and survival at the same time. Not a few have drowned, with the more powerful surviving because they have been able to take a 'firm grip' on the shoulders of some weaker others in the organisational water. As Mintzberg (1989: 351) has perceptively observed concerning the ways in which management and chaos are interrelated:

Thus professional management, by putting the systems ahead of the people, has had the effect of bleeding out of organisations, slowly and gradually, their capacity to do mental work as it must be done ... workers ... managers and analysts ... have been dehumanised by the whole effort.

In what follows, I present some case material which I hope corroborates my point of view that 'lines', 'circles' and 'turbulence' emerge and condition one another in the complex setting of development policy practice. After presenting some extended cases I indicate that we may have to assess the ethical and moral implications of all this if we wish to retain anthropology as worthwhile discipline, practically and theoretically.

LINES AND CIRCLES: FROM GOALS TO SURVIVAL

In the story of the stream, lines are expressive of promises and gentleness. The water is only guided by the forces of gravity when there is a little pressure. This may help us understand why the attractions of proclaimed rationality inherent in early theories of the development process were so great. Nothing much was happening. And thus dreams of the amount of water the riverbed was capable of carrying could still be fostered. The dreams consisted of clear definitions of the problem of development and of the belief that what counted was sufficient political support and will power, that is, sufficient means to transmit more of the life-giving water. Indeed, far away more and more people could be heard, so it was said, requesting more water as their needs were so great. An irrigation project was started, and more and more water started to flow. This led subsequently to more and more schemes, requiring an infrastructure for the division of the water.

CASE 1: PROMISES VERSUS OUTCOMES AS REPRESENTED WITHIN A DUTCH NGO

In the mid-1980s a serious conflict erupted between two agency directors. Although much was said about their personal incompatibility, and indeed some of this may have been true, the conflict was expressive of much wider issues. This became clear when the one responsible for a team engaged in advising, monitoring and evaluating tasks was fired, ostensibly because some of his staff sometimes produced critical reports of agency programmes. Moreover, the section reporting to the fired director was engaged in writing a major policy paper concerned, amongst other things, with the delegation of decision-making power over funding to Third World organisations. The advocacy of this policy had implications for the work of many colleagues in regional departments. Quite understandably, this led to tensions and conflicts between members of staff. The relationship between the two directors was, therefore, burdened by far more than personal considerations.

The outcome was not only that one director was fired, but also that the section involved in monitoring and evaluation was dismantled. Some staff left, while others received new positions in the regional departments. Subsequently this led to a lengthy discussion between members of the board, who represented different constituencies of the development organisation and Dutch society. Faced with the dilemmas of survival and knowledge, the NGO placed the highest priority on its identity as a *Dutch* NGO and on information gathering and analysis, and its staff played only a secondary part.

One of the topics in the discussion concerned the issue that, for staff members engaged in the funding decisions in regional departments, it would be rather hard to be more than only barely informed about the way in which programmes were carried out.[1] As some individuals stated during the meeting, the organised ignorance that would result from dismantling the monitoring section and firing its director would make it very hard for the organisation to learn from its failures or its successes.

During the board discussion the issue of constructed ignorance was quite clear and uncontested. While for some the answer that this was too great a price to pay was self-evident, for others it was not. The latter defended their decision on several grounds. First, the issue was not that the organisation, which continued to make important funding decisions, would not pay a heavy price. It would. Rather, they argued that the alternative would result in continued in-fighting, a deepening of conflicts which had been going on for quite some time and which had to be ended in one way or another. In a way, the quest for better feedback over policy-making was conflicting with the very survival of the organisation itself. What would the consequences be if it became widely known that the agency was fraught with deep internal conflicts? Might it not in the longer run lead to a loss of public support and thus endanger its sources of funding?

The decision to close ranks was upheld by the majority. However, one member cynically remarked that the board appeared to be willing to reject the central concepts of the organisation's official policy, namely social justice and compassion. One answer to this was: 'Yes this is true. These words no longer refer to the people for whom we are, in the end, doing this for. But how could we be honestly pursue these goals when it would be at the expense of our own people and organisation?' As another board member who represented one of the major Dutch churches put it:

Yes, my role on the board is to help keep alive the ideals of social justice in the world as a whole. But I can do this best by trying to keep these notions alive among the staff members for whom I have direct responsibility. If this conflicts with wider responsibilities, this is my choice.

At this point, the water within the organisation increasingly started to flow in circles. The force of gravity was not as effective as it had been, for instance when the 'promises of learning from experience' had led to the setting up of a special department within the NGO. Disturbances within the organisation which resulted from the setting up of two lines of movement towards the stated goals resulted in a new order, a circle emerged as a new force resulting in quite a new movement of the water. But the organisation restored some sort of order in its internal relations and at the ideological level. Stability was achieved by attaching more importance to survival than to the earlier belief in a linear set of goals and means and the belief in a 'rational' organisation of development practice. Yet officially the discourse of lines and goals was maintained. Survival made it imperative – or so it seemed at the time – to separate official discourse from the reality of policy and practice. A 'machine' had become a living and adapting 'organism'. The operational dimensions of the organisation were starting to become increasingly segmented from the expressive. Speech and action began to take a different and closed course. Perhaps the sudden emergence of various circles in the water was seen to be an effective prevention against the alternative of the dykes breaking down, and lands being dangerously flooded by good intentions? It appears that the new circular order was not planned at all but was instead the inevitable outcome of a period in which internal pressures had increased and linear thinking had come up against clear limitations.

CASE 2: THE INDONESIAN PLANNING BUREAU, BAPPENAS – COPING WITH INTERNAL CONTRADICTIONS AND DONOR REQUESTS

In terms of bilateral development cooperation, the Indonesian and Dutch governments had prioritised area development schemes since the late 1970s. These are rather complicated undertakings in which a great number of different tasks have been carried out in an integrated way involving: large-scale wet engineering operations, such as land reclamation, drainage, irrigation; other large-scale schemes such as land settlement and housing; and in some cases land reform. Added to these large infrastructural schemes, the area development programmes have also included agricultural extension and small-scale economic programmes, some of which were aimed at poor peasants, women and so on.

Having visited and studied the dynamics of regional development schemes in various parts of Indonesia for many years, in 1991 a colleague, W. Wolters, and I received an interesting invitation from the Dutch Ministry of Development Cooperation to organise a seminar in Indonesia in which the histories of two of the larger schemes of area development, which had been going on for seven to nine years in south Sumatra and south Sulawesi, would be reviewed. The schemes were to be stopped soon and it was argued that a systematic review by the various actors and agencies involved in their planning and execution would be beneficial. Our counterpart in the organisation of the seminar was Bappenas, the national planning agency in Indonesia, directly involved in the supervision of development programmes as well as in international negotiations concerning development aid. Despite intensive work, the outcome of the seminar regarding 'lessons learned' was a total failure and never took place. Nevertheless, the four weeks in which we travelled around and discussed various options and ways of dealing with all sorts of sensibilities and conflicting responsibilities at national and regional levels of the Indonesian administration was most instructive.

When I returned to Indonesia four months later on a different assignment, after hot blood had cooled, I revisited some of the senior officials at Bappenas to discuss what had happened. The failure of our seminar aimed at learning from past experiences had come to fascinate me.

After one discussion in which a 'friendly openness' with one senior executive had been achieved, I immediately rushed back to my hotel to write down the discussion verbatim as well as I could, part of which I reproduce here for two reasons:

(a) discussion indicated the extent to which flexibility in constructing and evaluating past experiences of area development depended upon political calculations concerned with future negotiations; and

(b)   discussion also indicated that the entire idea of 'development practice', of distinguishing between the normative and political dimensions, had been lost. In short, under extreme work pressure and responsibility, the highly skilled senior civil servants of Bappenas, the 'cream' of Indonesia's administration, had become prisoners of mental and administrative 'circles' or closed worlds which they had constructed in order to undertake their work. In a way, borrowing a metaphor from Morgan (1986), the official had entered a 'psychic prison' in which the normative had almost totally encapsulated the notion of practice.

M: You know, the situation is not very difficult. When you, the Dutch decide to spend money on area development, you must make up your mind first. Do you give priority to the technical dimensions? Well then it is OK. That will imply that you don't need to see me. As you know, my colleague at Bappenas has the responsibility of negotiating with you on behalf of the Ministry of Public Works. But if you decide that the aspects of agricultural extension, land reform, etc. are more important, well than that is OK too, then you deal with me and the Ministry of the Interior takes responsibility and delegates it to the regional authorities.[2]

Q: You are right, that is how the programmes will be planned. But, you know, in the two area development programmes which we have studied, the project staff had to deal with different ministries at the same time, and the responsibilities were not as clear cut as we all would have wished. Various problems resulted from this situation.

M: But that is not of much importance and can be solved easily. Let me explain the situation to you again. [And M. walked to the blackboard and started to draw the official lines of authority within the Indonesian administration, indicating that when the Dutch made up their mind first, there need not be a problem.]

Q: Yes, I understand your explanation, it is quite clear. This is how things should be. What you say is of the utmost importance for planning. It enables you to delegate responsibility and allocate funds. If you don't plan like this, everything will be a mess. And you cannot do that.

M: That is right. When we do our planning we cannot take into account the concrete experiences in the field. We don't have the time for it. It may well be that the seminar 'Lessons learned' should not have been planned together with Bappenas in the first place. Our planning framework may be at too high a level. Why don't you organise the seminar in the Netherlands, then we would all be willing to come and discuss the experiences?

The discussion indicates again the constitution of ever smaller circles of thought and action in the movement of the policy process. First, increasing segmentation within the national planning bureau, expressive of the dual structure of the governmental administration – direct as well as indirect rule – had made it impossible for M. to sit at the same table with his colleague. Both men were of the opinion that we could only come through one door at a time and accept the consequences.

Second, it became clear that for both individuals two notions of development practice existed and were in conflict with one another, namely practices within the small arena of international negotiation with foreign donors, and practices in the field as constructed in our reports.

Third, the official language of development administration stressing coordination, feedback, learning and an integrated area approach could only be upheld if its consequences could be sufficiently segmented from the dynamics of the various small circles. Words, symbols, thought and planning were important, but it was vital not to relate these notions directly and in any encompassing way to the various circles of practice which were involved. My own belief that one should learn from past experiences turned out to be rather naïve, a naïveté which I could foster because of my distanced position at the university far from the rushing streams and circles of development policy practice. This naïveté might, indeed, be quite dangerous for the various actors involved, as it could lead to more disturbances and perhaps chaos later on.

Fourth, what appears to be absent is a special circle, an *agora* or marketplace in which debate and learning is possible without direct consequences for subsequent actions. A special circle for public discourse, far removed from the small circles of daily practice is needed to which the various actors could come, discuss and learn. As M. suggested, 'Why don't you organise it in the Netherlands, then we would all be able to come?'

FROM CIRCLE TO TURBULENCE: EMERGING CHAOS

As the pressure on the stream of development practice continues to increase, Briggs and Peat suggest that all sorts of erratic and unpredictable movements may suddenly occur. The forces of attraction within the circle are broken, centripetal forces begin to dissipate. How does this come about? What might constitute a force capable of breaking the circle's survival?

When the emergence of circular movements in development policy was discussed, I suggested that a segmentation came about between the practices of the implementing actors in the agency and the officially proclaimed rationality of the agency's discourse. That implies that the language of 'rational' administrative behaviour continued to be used officially in relations with others in the outside world upon whom the agency depended. Part of the stream thus still continues to flow downstream following the lines of substantive rationality. Official policy papers and public speeches do not change very much. Their impact on the actual operations of staff members becomes minimal indeed. However, as the pressure increases, circles emerge next to some of the remaining lines.

With the notion of 'psychic prison', the encapsulation of individuals within increasingly small worlds, we suggested that actors might altogether lose sight of the incongruity of their situation. For them the contradictions between the discourse of goals and means and what is actually being achieved may no longer be visible. The exigencies of survival make it imperative for the top leadership of development agencies *not* to confront their official language with the dynamics of the emerging circles. We find these attitudes mostly at the highest levels of development organisations. There the first priority has come to be the maintenance of some sort of internal order, since this keeps others at bay. The images of effectiveness must be nurtured and upheld as the organisation depends on the increased speed of the water.

Yet the tight circle also becomes increasingly vulnerable, osmosis a deadly danger.[3] There are various ways in which the tightening circle may break down and unpredictable movements start to occur. The first consists of a process of internal organisational involution. The requirements of unity start to destroy the personnel within the organisation; the circle becomes smaller and smaller.

The second way in which breakdown may occur comes from increased outside pressures. Mostly the two go hand in hand.

CASE 3: HEAVY PRESSURES AND UNPREDICTABLE MOVEMENTS, THE EMERGENCE OF CHAOS

Recently Dutch development agencies have been confronted with major changes in their operating context, namely greatly increased public scepticism about the impact of established traditions of development aid. At the same time, a new Minister of Development Cooperation confronted the situation of increased uncertainty head on by sharpening the requirements of the policy process and increasing political demands on agency administration. In addition, and in line with the new political fashion in the West, development agencies were required to show *results*. This was a major transformation and threat to the agencies. In a way, this new demand for results which are in line with official goals created an impossible no-win situation. As argued above, the official language of development with its promises and goals was not supposed to interfere with the actual practices of 'implementation'. On the contrary, any effort to make 'lines' and 'circles' fit into one pattern would result in great *turbulence*, conflict and contradiction, and possibly in the decline of the agency (as some board members had argued). But now politicians, in an almost Anglo-Saxon manner of Thatcherite or 'consumer choice' politics, began to make such demands.

Further, funding agencies turned into accountability machines as well. Staff had to spend increasing amounts of time keeping financial sponsors happy. Internal control also became much tighter leading to greater difficulties in their dealings with Third World development agencies who had to adapt to increasingly precise procedures. The amount of uncertainty, anger and frustration increased considerably within agencies. Ironically, the official accounting of development performance became increasingly hollow in so far as official notions of effectiveness were undermining the very development practices required for effectiveness. Beautiful images of the exalted goals of official development discourse and deep internal turbulence were clearly interdependent. Together these changes put a much heavier burden on the various agencies than they had previously confronted.

UNPREDICTABLE MOVEMENTS

Since 1989 three of the older, larger, well established Dutch development organisations have 'all of a sudden' undergone a period of serious internal crisis. All personnel with the exception of those at the highest level were officially dismissed; staff received a letter which informed them that they could, if they so wished, reapply. Hundreds received such a letter. Most were re-hired, happy to be once again bound by the disciplining fears of a mortgage, their minds were almost totally fixed on their tasks. This reorganisation was a most unexpected event which took nearly everyone by surprise and resulted in a great amount of fear and insecurity.

In particular, dozens of senior staff resigned or are actively seeking another job. When one NGO staff member sent a short statement to a newspaper outlining some of his personal views on broader issues of the development problematic, he was immediately fired.

While most NGOs had earlier dismantled their monitoring and evaluation units, these were hurriedly reinstated at the end of the 1980s. Moreover, the growing scepticism about the effectiveness of the agencies suddenly resulted in a large-scale research operation in six countries. However, once public discussions about the results of the study subsided, most of the NGOs quickly dismantled their autonomous monitoring and evaluation units, putting them firmly under the control of directors. Once again, too much was at stake.

Amongst staff there is a serious morale crisis, as internal consultant reports written during the process of reorganisation clearly indicate. Such a situation is shocking indeed.

It is not an exaggeration to state that the agencies are in a period of turbulent crisis which, as I see it, is deepening. In a way the circle is already broken, not by any sort of 'big bang' but by increasingly unrelated movements which have begun to occur. One of the main reasons for the turbulence and dangerous movement of the water now emerging is the notion that one integrated machine-like whole can be reinstated. In short, a re-emerging notion of manageability is greatly increasing pressure on development agencies. This becomes clear when we see the efforts by agency directors and boards to close ranks, which indeed has had many unintended and adverse effects: cynicism and despair not only among their own staff but also in counterpart organisations in the Third World who are paying a high price for their efforts to make development policy 'effective' again. Metastasis has set in. I still believe that some surgery is possible.[4] Others believe, however, that carcinogenic cells have already spread too far in the 'system'.

CONCLUDING REMARKS: DEVELOPMENT POLICY PRACTICES – PROMISES, STRUGGLES AND EMPTIED HEARTS

I have argued that in the course of time the nature of development organisations changes. These changes are conditioned by increased pressures resulting from an increase in scale. The organisations thus must cope with increasingly complex environments and undergo internal transformations as well. One might say that development organisations can be studied over time in three varying ways:

(a)   Initially, as espousing a *substantive coherence* between goals, means and outcomes, the definition of development problems and the role of the organisation (at this point still untainted). At this first stage the unifying attraction of coherence is powerful because policy practices are just starting. The first rain is starting to fall. 'Dreams' may still shine since nothing much has happened yet. Problems of development are there to be solved.

(b)   Second, as *expressing a loss of unity and effectiveness*. At this stage conflicts between the different fields of development practice begin to manifest themselves. The stream of policy movements changes as pressures increase. It is now a *multi-centred whole*, with an increasing number of closed circles containing small groups of actors engaged in a struggle for survival.

(c)   Finally, as *expressive of anxiety and fear*.

Promises of development are most appealing if they are untainted by the constraints required for implementation. The need to publicly account for results and to indicate good performance and effectiveness comes after this phase and at that time when the various actors involved in increasingly complex policy practices no longer constitute a unified 'systemic' whole. On the contrary, struggles between various interest groups become more intense. Thus it is impossible for development agencies to produce results in line with official promises and goals, in part because there is no longer a centre capable of steering the process. Various relatively closed circles of actors have arisen whose interrelations have become increasingly problematic. The notion of manageable development becomes increasingly uncertain. Now all actors begin to panic as public support starts to erode.

At present, life has become increasingly dangerous in the erratically moving river. The relatively closed circles of development agents may turn into dangerous vortices. Promises are empty, concrete practices of implementation lose their meaning. All of a sudden everything seems to be in a mess, and any kind of order seems to have been lost.

Development organisations in the Netherlands have been confronted with a series of decisive crises in the last few years. The increasingly turbulent river of development policy and practice has led to a series of sometimes fatal accidents. The turbulence has become more intensive as one tries to apply old remedies issuing from the ideology of manageable development. When the general public or politicians start making demands which deny the multi-centrality of practices, they only deepen the accountability trap in which development agencies have found themselves in of late. The core of this crisis is cultural, perhaps even quasi-religious. We are not only confronted by the need to reformulate key issues of development and to reassess our notions of manageability but also to seek legitimate answers to the question: are the efforts worthwhile? We have lost sight of these questions and a new order will only arise if we leave conventional answers behind us. Development is more than a form of 'applied enlightenment'.

NOTES

1. A fact recently confirmed by a study of Dutch NGOs which showed that the average amount of time a Third World project was directly visited by project officers was seven minutes per year.
2. The Indonesian civil service is dual in the sense that there are some ministries which centrally plan and operate their activities in the various regions.
3. The increased tightness and vulnerability becomes clear if one looks at the images produced by public relation firms. The content

of the messages concerning development are increasingly simple, digestible within three seconds. The involuted language starts to resemble the notions of metastasis of communication analysed by Baudrillard.

4. In a recent article I have made use of some of the insights of the principal-agent model which has been defined in 'institutional economics'. It is a model which defines 'zones of uncertainty' between the different sorts of actors and organisations involved in a particular sector of policy practices. It is a fundamental break with linear planning and 'rational' models of policy (Quarles 1992).

REFERENCES

Baudrillard, J. 1990. *La Pensée du mal*. Paris: Galilée.

Bauman, Z. 1993. *Postmodern Ethics*. Oxford: Blackwell.

Briggs, J. and D. Peat. 1990. *Turbulent Mirror: An Illustrated Guide to Chaos Theory and the Science of Wholeness*. New York: Harper and Row.

Broekstra, G. 1992. 'Chaossystemen als metafoor voor zelfvernieuwing in organisaties', in C. Van Dijkum and D. de Tombe, *Gamma chaos; onzekerheid en orde in de menswetenschappen*. Bloemendaal: Aramith Uitgevers, pp. 113–26.

Epstein, A.L. 1992. *In the Midst of Life: Affect and Ideation in the World of the Tolai*. Berkeley: University of California Press.

Mintzberg, H. 1989. *Inside Our Strange World of Organisations*. New York: The Free Press.

Morgan, G. 1986. *Images of Organisation*. Beverly Hills, CA: Sage.

Quarles van Ufford, P. 1992. 'Armoedebestrijding als bedrijfstak; constraints en dilemma's in georganiseerde compassie', paper presented at a conference on NGOs, Institute of Social Studies, The Hague.

—— 1996. 'Reality exists: acknowledging the boundaries of active and reflexive anthropological bodies of knowledge', in A. van Harskamp (ed.) *Conflicts in Social Science: Dutch Experiences*. London: Routledge.

INDEX

294

Index complied by Auriol Griffith-Jones

DATE DUE

Demco, Inc. 38-293